THE COLONIAL LEGACY
Loyalist Historians

THE
COLONIAL LEGACY

VOLUME I

Loyalist Historians

Edited by
LAWRENCE H. LEDER
Lehigh University

HARPER TORCHBOOKS
Harper & Row, Publishers
New York, Evanston, San Francisco, London

THE COLONIAL LEGACY, Volume I

First TORCHBOOK edition published 1971.

LIBRARY OF CONGRESS CATALOG NUMBER: 70–131624–9

STANDARD BOOK NUMBER: 06–131624–9

Designed by C. Linda Dingler

CONTENTS

CONTENTS

THE COLONIAL LEGACY
Loyalist Historians

1.

The Loyalist Historians: An Introduction

Lawrence H. Leder

Historical literature has a refractive quality: it mirrors both the time *about* which it was written and the time *in* which it was written. Indeed, the understanding a history offers of the author's time may be greater than the understanding it offers of the chronological segment he selected as his topic. (Sometimes, of course, the two coincide.) As much as historians immerse themselves in and empathize with the past time about which they are writing, they never escape from their own generation and its problems, and their work reflects this dualism. This is true of those historians who wrote at the time of the American Revolution, and especially of those whom we label loyalists.

American loyalists have suffered the fate of those who lose the contest—history has relegated them to brief paragraphs at best, or to footnotes at worst. By refusing to repudiate their monarch, loyalists condemned themselves to exile during the revolution and to historical oblivion afterward. As anachronisms opposing America's progress toward a seemingly great destiny, they have appeared irrelevant to those seeking to explain that progress and to elucidate that destiny. Whenever Americans have questioned their dream, however, loyalists momentarily become reputable subjects for historical inquiry.

Loyalists as a phenomenon have been studied by Lorenzo Sabine in his *Biographical Sketches of Loyalists* (Boston, 1864), published in the midst of the Civil War's most serious challenge to American unity; by Claude Van Tyne in his *Loyalists in the American Revolution* (New York, 1902), written when America was sharply divided between urban and rural values; and by Lawrence Henry Gipson in his *Jared Ingersoll* (New Haven, 1920), produced after the balloon of American idealism had burst. The appearance in a new edition of Professor Gipson's work (New Haven, 1971), fifty years after its first issuance, coupled with the recent publication of William Nelson's *American Tory* (Oxford, 1961), Wallace Brown's *The King's Friends* (Providence, R.I., 1965), and Paul H. Smith's *Loyalists and Redcoats* (Chapel Hill, 1964) reflects perhaps another questioning of the nature of our national destiny and of the concept of progress.

Concern about the phenomenon of loyalism has been heightened at this time by the recently begun cooperative program, under the direction of Professor Robert A. East, to collate information on the loyalists from the United States, Canada, and Great Britain. This program will undoubtedly stimulate a far greater research effort than has been previously undertaken and may offer a better understanding of the American Revolution as its bicentennial approaches.

Twentieth-century scholars have argued vociferously and voluminously about the meaning of the American Revolution. Charles M. Andrews and the imperial school concluded that the revolution upset a beneficent and liberal system. Sir Lewis Namier and his disciples insisted on a continuity between the Old Empire and the New Nation by emphasizing the mildness of revolutionary change. Socio-economic historians underlined the duality of the revolution as Americans fought both British rulers and local aristocrats. Neoconservatives such as Robert E. Brown emphasized the revolution's attempt to preserve the status quo of democratic society. Finally neo-Whigs have suggested that the revolutionary struggle led Americans to accept their differences from Europeans as elements of pride rather than marks of inferiority.

Each of these interpretations, so abruptly summarized here, offers useful insights into the revolution. The debate has not ended, and it will not do so for generations to come, if ever. However, historians, by focusing on the phenomenon of loyalism, may add still another dimension to our understanding of the American character as shaped by the revolution. The loyalists, after all, were the obverse of that movement, and the movement itself cannot be fully understood by examining merely one side.

Moreover, loyalists were not all cast in one mold. Some were fanatical devotees of monarchy, others were sycophantic placeholders, but most fell somewhere between and probably took the view that "kings are not always wise; sometimes they are just there." Loyalists had shared with other Americans a dual reverence. They revered America *and* England, with provincial self-consciousness and imperial pride. When the moment of truth arrived, when Americans had to choose between local and imperial connections, those who chose the latter did so for a variety of reasons.

The diversity of loyalist attitudes is reflected in the histories that they wrote during and after the revolution. Some emphasized theoretical explanations of events, while others simply described the events as they saw them happen. Some dwelt on the revolution itself, while others cut short their histories before the traumatic moment. Yet they all wrote to offer explanations of what had happened, to justify their own decisions. Faced with the destruction of the British Empire, they needed to convince themselves and the world around them that they had taken the proper path. In offering their varied individual explanations, however, they also offered a multidimensional view of the revolution.

The loyalists possessed a unique vantage point, but their histories also reflected certain eighteenth-century preconceptions which they shared with the patriot historians. These included a fatalistic faith in the ability of posterity to read the historical record and to judge it dispassionately. (Sir Henry Clinton reportedly saved every scrap of paper so that future generations would have the evidence with which to draw his true portrait, for he had no hope that his own generation would understand him.) They also believed firmly in the pedantic value of history; the American Revolution clearly offered a major lesson for the entire world.

Among those who viewed the revolution as a study of the consequences of improper management of an empire was George Chalmers, the Maryland loyalist. He tried to vindicate the viewpoint of the exiles in his *Political Annals* by challenging the whole pattern of British colonial policy, not just in the 1760s and 1770s, but from the founding of the colonies in the seventeenth century. Britain's failure to impose its authority on the colonies—and more particularly, Parliament's failure to play its proper role in colonial affairs—seemed to Chalmers to create all of the empire's difficulties. Americans, never pressed by Parliament's authority, developed over the years fallacious assumptions about rights and immunities. When Parliament finally challenged these colonial assumptions after 1763, the Americans insisted that Great Britain had changed the rules of the empire. This Chalmers flatly denied. For him, Parliament's power over the colonies had never changed, but British policy had vacillated unwisely.

Chalmers continued this approach to imperial problems in his *Introduction to the History of the Revolt*. He dwelt on the problem of American loyalty, which he claimed had always been left to chance. He denied vigorously that the colonists at any time operated under natural law but insisted that English law continuously governed them and cited numerous instances when the colonists flaunted the law and specific occasions when the Board of Trade warned of the ill consequences. Part of the problem of colonial loyalty lay in the nature of the rights the colonists claimed. Again, Chalmers emphasized that the rights of colonists were strictly bounded by those they could claim as Englishmen, and that these always depended upon obedience to British laws and submission to British government. To Chalmers, reason was the·sole guide, not emotion; he admitted that both colonists and British administrators had neglected to use reason for some time. The colonists had a clear-cut right to live under law as dependents of the British Empire; the British had an obvious obligation to govern the empire reasonably. Neither side fulfilled its commitment, according to Chalmers, and so the tragedy of the revolution destroyed the promise of the empire.

Chalmers had migrated to Maryland shortly before the revolution; thus his shock at the turn of events was more understandable than that of Joseph Galloway, a native Marylander who migrated to Pennsylvania. Yet both men found that the revolution contradicted reason, and both consequently found themselves spending their remaining days as exiles in England.

While Chalmers viewed the revolution with some detachment and could seek its antecedents in the pattern of Anglo-colonial policy and attitudes, Galloway could find nothing but conspiracy by a few individuals as the root cause of the debacle. His own plan of union, refined through a number of stages, seemed to him to offer a viable answer to those concerned with the preservation of both colonial liberty *and* the Anglo-American connection. He could only conclude that the majority of Americans had never had a chance to consider any plan of union because of trickery by a small minority who seized control in a moment of stress.

Galloway too dealt with the question of American loyalty, and he argued that inherent in the American character, as a consequence of its Calvinist background, was a republicanism that produced hostility to the Crown. This republicanism quickly drifted into radicalism, and that astonished Galloway, because he found British treatment of the colonies consistently benevolent. Indeed, American claims to rights independent of government also shocked Galloway, for he could not visualize any rights save those emerging from one's relationship with others as expressed through representative institutions. For him the most beneficent of representative institutions was Parliament which, together with the Crown and the Church, was the fount of all justice. This view convinced him of the urgency and value of his own plan of union; by formalizing the connection between the colonies and Great Britain he would formalize and preserve the rights of Americans as Englishmen. The failure of his fellow colonists to understand and accept this simple fact baffled Galloway.

Another Marylander, Jonathan Boucher, took a much more philosophical approach toward the causes of the revolution. Like Chalmers, he had recently emigrated to the colony, but his analysis of the situation presented an extreme aspect of the loyalist spectrum. Boucher constantly condemned British policies as errors of judgment, but he condemned American reactions to those errors as violations of moral duty. Sir Robert Filmer (rather than John Locke) offered an analysis of society and government which seemed amenable to Boucher, for he was a religious traditionalist for whom the American Revolution represented an abrupt break with the past. Filmer's doctrine, called *patriarchalism*, held that government was divinely ordained to rule men in the same way that fathers were ordained to rule families.

The challenge to traditional ways which Boucher saw in the revolution especially disturbed him, since Americans had rebelled over such trivial matters as the Townshend duties. They forgot that obedience made society and government possible. No people could resist a lawful government, for that would reject the will of God. And while not all government actions were lawful, only passive obedience provided a feasible answer. Ultimately the people might resist with force, but then they must accept the civil penalties involved.

From his extremely conservative viewpoint, Boucher shared certain attitudes with Chalmers and Galloway. He too understood the weakness of American social and political institutions, their inability to withstand the pressure upon the imperial bonds exerted by a minority of Calvinist republicans in the 1770s. He viewed the revolution as a transatlantic contest between Whig and Tory, as a historical movement which expanded beyond the Anglo-American world to incorporate the French Revolution and its upheavals on the continent. As a traditionalist, Boucher resisted all challenges to well-established order; indeed, the colonists' inability to develop and maintain such an order foreshadowed the inevitable revolution.

Not all of those who controverted the American rebellion in their historical writings dealt with the colonies in general; some concentrated on particular colonies. Israel Mauduit discussed several facets of the revolution in Massachusetts. He had never visited the colonies, though he became intimately involved in the affairs of Massachusetts in the early 1760s when he served in the Massachusetts agency in London. Although he assisted that colony in its dealings with British officials, he never questioned one principle—the supremacy of Parliament. When Massachusetts led the colonial opposition to parliamentary policy in the mid-1770s, Mauduit quickly sniffed rebellion in the air.

Mauduit emphasized the pragmatic nature of representative institutions in Massachusetts, denying the elevated status claimed for them by Americans. They were practical solutions to existing problems, not the consequences of natural rights. He similarly denounced the sacrosanct principle of "no taxation without representation," which had a hollow ring because of the very limited franchise practices in seventeenth-century Massachusetts. Mauduit

especially attacked the idea that the Massachusetts charter offered
shelter to the rights of Americans. It simply guaranteed, he insisted, that that colony's people, when in another part of the
empire, would receive the same treatment as an Englishman; it
did not convey any special authority or power to a colonial legislature. Indeed, such a body was always limited by the requirement
that its statutes conform to British law.

As a historian, Mauduit did not have the stature of Chalmers or
Galloway, nor did he share Boucher's philosophical orientation.
Yet he clarified several aspects of the loyalist position in his historical pamphlets. The popularity of his works in England amply
demonstrated the extent to which the British understood and
accepted the loyalist view of colonial events, and showed the depth
of British misunderstanding of the position of the rebellious
colonists. It made easier the imposition of restrictive measures—the
Coercive or Intolerable Acts—when the times required greater
understanding and sympathy. As a propagandist-historian,
Mauduit helped doom moderate efforts like Galloway's, which
could get a hearing on neither side of the Atlantic.

A more penetrating account by a loyalist of the affairs of a
particular colony was Alexander Hewat's study of South Carolina.
Completely within the eighteenth-century school of rationalistic
history, Hewat shared the passion for tradition, the hope for the
pedantic value of history, and the abhorrence of unreason that
marked most loyalist historians. Like Chalmers, Hewat felt that
the British record in North America was spotty, that mistakes had
been made over the years (particularly in the proprietary periods
of South Carolina's and Georgia's history), but that most of these
had been corrected or were being corrected at the time of the
revolution.

Hewat pointed to what he called the forces of destruction in
society and to the factors which had permitted them free reign in
early South Carolina and Georgia. Religious dissension, Indian

problems, and slavery were among these; their mishandling by the proprietors gave rise to controversies which threatened the well-being of the colonies. Only after the institution of royal government did South Carolina and Georgia come into their own and take advantage of the opportunities presented by their environment. Thus Hewat equated royal government with peace, progress, and harmonious relations.

In treating the emergence of Anglo-American hostilities, Hewat considered the causes endemic in colonial society. The colonies had been founded by religious dissenters who had always opposed monarchy. The work of the Reverend George Whitefield in the South had played upon this underlying antipathy and gave rise to republicanism. When combined with the gradual weakening over the generations of Anglo-American affections, this republicanism led naturally to agitation and finally to conflict.

Although much of British policy seemed wise and fair to Hewat, he agreed that the British failed to understand the American colonists and the conditions under which they lived. The colonists' indebtedness and British restrictions on trade and taxation without formal colonial consultation gave rise to a misconception among Americans that the British intended to enslave them. Such misconceptions encouraged a spirit of independence, which Hewat felt many Americans had secretly harbored for some time. He, like Galloway, argued for a common colonial council which would have aborted the argument over Parliament's authority. However, Parliament's insistence upon its power, while it failed to buttress royal officials in the colonies, led to an inevitable collapse of royal control in America. Ever true to his rationalism, Hewat remained optimistic that the connection between England and its colonies, in one form or another, could some day be restored.

Not all loyalist historians followed Chalmers, Galloway, Boucher, and Hewat into exile in England. Robert Proud remained in Pennsylvania throughout the war and afterward continued his career as a schoolteacher until he retired to complete his *History of Pennsylvania*. Throughout the revolution and the years thereafter he remained an anglophile, constantly denying the glory of the American Revolution and constantly bemoaning the destruction of the British Empire.

To Proud, the revolution repudiated the virtues of peace, order, and harmony—the very virtues which patriot historians argued had been promoted by the revolution. Proud's anglophile attitude was reinforced by his Quakerism and its concomitant pacifism. Although he preferred tranquility to tumult, America of the 1770s offered him only the latter. To justify himself and to assuage his pacifist temperament, he withdrew during the war from all activity except the writing of his history.

Proud used two previous histories as foils for his own views. He attacked Samuel Smith's study and Richard Jackson's exaltation of Benjamin Franklin's politics. Proud viewed the history of Pennsylvania politics as a decline from pristine purity to total degeneracy; he placed the blame on the society which developed, not on the Quakers themselves. William Penn represented for Proud the epitome of benevolence, exalted views, and political wisdom. Penn's absence from the colony in its early days led to intermittent turbulence and a passionate party spirit. Pennsylvania developed an enviable reputation for liberty, but it attracted thousands who differed from Quaker principles and who stimulated party conflict within the colony.

Proud regretted Pennsylvania's departure from its first principles. He looked upon the revolution as an aberration, a time of novelty and change. As a conservative, he longed for the orderliness that no longer existed and hoped for the reinstitution of a deferential society that was no longer plausible for America. Since according to Proud the revolution destroyed the essentials of a well-ordered society, he retaliated by never once mentioning the movement in his history. Thus he made himself even more anachronistic by his outright rejection of the revolution, his determination that it represented the opposite of everything claimed for it by the Whig historians. Rather than suffer physical exile in England, Robert Proud endured intellectual exile in his adopted Pennsylvania.

Some loyalists made new homes for themselves in Canada. William Smith, Jr., son of the New York loyalist historian, shared his father's exile in Canada and his hostility to the American Revolution. Although only a youngster at the time of his father's departure from New York, young Smith imbibed enough pro-British sentiment, especially during a sojourn in England with his father, to reflect this attitude in his *History of Canada*. His full-blown bias became evident in a variety of ways, despite his efforts to hide it through increasing use of documents rather than historical commentary in discussions of the years after 1759.

Smith's *History* represents the continuation of a tradition in Canadian historiography rooted in the events of the American Revolution. The tradition carried on, though in a more subdued manner, the bias of the loyalists who found themselves displaced citizens. Smith, because of his youth, was luckier than most loyalists, for he acclimated well to the new Canadian environment and easily created a place for himself. Most others did not adjust as readily. Although Chalmers had managed to find an agreeable place for himself in England, Galloway, Boucher, and Hewat could not recreate their lives or careers in England, and Proud remained out of tune with his surroundings, though he never left the familiar locale of Pennsylvania.

The tragedy of the loyalists in general, as reflected in the writings of their historians, lay in their failure to belong anywhere. Outcasts in the nation in which they had grown up and prospered, and outcasts in the society with which they identified themselves, they represented a lost generation. Yet their identification with America was so intense that they could not resist the temptation to explain what had happened, to spread on the printed page the lessons of the past as the loyalists witnessed and understood them, to appeal to posterity for a vindication of their defense of tradition and virtue.

2.

George Chalmers and the *Political Annals*

LAWRENCE HENRY GIPSON

George Chalmers, author of *Political Annals of the Present United Colonies, from their Settlement to Peace of 1763* . . . (London, 1780), left behind him a far greater body of writing on various parts of the eighteenth-century New World British Empire than any other American loyalist. He approached his subject as a lawyer chiefly interested in constitutional questions, and his circumspect use of sources won the respect even of those whose views differed markedly from his own.

When George Bancroft donated to The New-York Historical Society the unpublished part of the *Political Annals,* he and two other distinguished historians of the Society, John Romeyn Brodhead and George Henry Moore, were appointed to edit it for the Society's *Collections.* In a prefatory note the committee said:

Chalmers first distinguished himself by the publication of his *Political Annals* . . . which showed a thorough knowledge of colonial history, colonial law, and colonial policy. . . . His assiduous labor in the literary field, his large and valuable contributions to knowledge, his integrity, his patriotism and public spirit, fully entitled him to the character which was drawn of him by a friend as a "faithful servant of the public who had spent a long and active life in the honorable discharge of public duties and the zealous dissemination of useful knowledge."

Jared Sparks, editing Chalmers's *History of the Revolt,* wrote:

Notwithstanding the tone and object of Chalmers's *Annals*, the work
has ever been quoted by American writers with entire confidence and
respect, and this circumstance speaks clearly in favor of the author's
candor and honesty. . . . The author was a lawyer, and he has discussed the subject before him in the spirit of his profession, adhering
strictly to legal interpretations and distinctions. It is probable that any
American lawyer, taking the same premises, would come to the same
conclusions; and it may be admitted that the premises are correct, since
they are drawn from state papers and legal records of the highest
authority.

Because of its importance, the *Political Annals* demands consideration by the student of American colonial history. Since
Chalmers's interpretation of this history differs in some respects so
radically from what came to be the traditional account, it will be
well to review leading events of his life that help indicate the type
of person he was and what influenced his point of view.

George Chalmers, a Scot, was born on 26 December 1742, in
the little village of Fochabers in Elginshire. Descended through a
cadet branch from James Chalmers, a large seventeenth-century
landowner of Morayshire, he was entitled to display the family
coat of arms, which appears in some of his books. His parents were
of modest circumstances; in fact, his father was the village postmaster. Nevertheless, the boy attended the local parish school and
King's College at the University of Aberdeen, where he was
apparently guided chiefly by the distinguished Dr. Thomas Reid,
professor of philosophy, whose courses included not only logic and
ethics but also mathematics and physics. How long Chalmers
remained at Aberdeen is not clear; nor is it clear how long he
remained at Edinburgh reading law.[1] In 1762 he published his

1. See in this connection *The Public Life of George Chalmers* by Grace
Amelia Cockroft (New York, 1939). This biography is well-balanced, although,
in view of the absence of materials, Chalmers's more personal life could not
be developed.

first pamphlet anonymously under the title *Considerations relating to the Late Order of the Two Banks established at Edinburgh by which they have recalled One-Fourth of their Cash-Accompts.*[2] A year later, at age twenty, he went with an uncle to Maryland.

Chalmers settled in that delightful colonial city, Annapolis, the capital of Maryland; three years later he moved to the new frontier town of Baltimore, where he practiced law. That he was not impecunious while living in Maryland is indicated by his receipt in 1764 of a warrant for over one thousand acres in undeveloped Worcester County on the Eastern Shore; he paid not only for the land but for the fees. Nor was he without friends, despite the death of his uncle soon after they reached the province. Among the most highly respected of his friends was a fellow Scot and Aberdonian, the Reverend David Love, pastor of All Hallows, Anne Arundel County, who for many years enjoyed close relations with Governor Sharpe.[3] During his residence in Baltimore Chalmers developed a considerable practice centered largely around mercantile activities of fellow Scots who exported tobacco and imported British and other goods.[4] He gained a reputation for ability and dependability.

2. See Samuel Halkett and John Laing, *Dictionary of Anonymous and Pseudonymous English Literature,* ed. James Kennedy, W. A. Smith, and A. F. Johnson, 6 vols. (Edinburgh and London, 1926–32), 1:419.

3. See "Letters from the Reverend David Love to Horatio Sharpe, 1774–1779," ed. James High, *Historical Magazine of the Protestant Episcopal Church* 19 (1950): 355–67. Sharpe was governor between 1752 and 1769; after his term of office he settled in the province until he removed to England in 1773.

4. The manuscript division of the New York Public Library has a large number of transcripts relating to loyalists drawn from the Audit Office papers in the British Public Record Office. Volume 35 of these transcripts contains the Chalmers memorial, without date, under the title, "The Memorial of George Chalmers formerly of Baltimore Town in Baltimore County, Maryland, Counsellor at Law but now of Park Street in the City of Westminster." Chalmers lived at Park Street between summer 1784 and spring 1785 before going into lodgings at Berkeley Square. In 1787 he moved to Green Street, Grosvenor Square; in 1805 he made his last move to James Street, Buckingham Gate. See Cockroft, *Public Life,* pp. 45, 177.

When Harford County was created out of the northern part of
Baltimore County, he was appointed in the spring of 1774 "clerk
of indictment and prosecutor of the lord proprietor's pleas."
Chalmers described the post as that of a "Deputy Attorney General
of Maryland." As such he became a part of Maryland's proprietary
establishment.[5]

Doubtless Chalmers's attitude toward the Stamp Act of 1765,
which placed heavy taxes on certain types of legal papers, was critical like that of most American colonial lawyers. It is important to
point out, however, that his opposition to such taxes did not challenge the fundamental right of Parliament to pass such laws. This
was also true of his position on the Townshend legislation of 1767,
which placed import duties on certain commodities entering colonial ports. When, in view of intense opposition to them in
America, Parliament removed all duties except those on tea, the
flame against the British government died down; one colony after
another rescinded its nonimportation acts against British goods.
However, Parliament's passing of the Tea Act in 1773, permitting
the East India Company to import tea directly into the colonies,
reignited the flame. Destruction of the tea in Boston harbor in the
fall of that year and the passing of the Boston Port Act in 1774 led
directly to hostilities and the War for American Independence.

In Baltimore, as in other American towns, the people were
divided in sentiment: there was the loyal group, supporters of the
British government, and the patriots, supporters of colonial rights.
A meeting was held at Baltimore County courthouse on 31 May
1774 to ratify certain resolutions passed six days earlier by the
inhabitants of Annapolis. These supported Boston and favored
creating an American Association that would stop importations
from Great Britain to the colonies until the Boston Port Act was

5. *Maryland Gazette*, 23 June 1775.

repealed—all of which, it was declared, would "preserve North America and her liberties."[6]

Among the resolutions passed at Annapolis was the following: "That it is the opinion of this meeting, that the gentlemen of the law of this province bring no suit for the recovery of any debt, due from any inhabitant of this province to any inhabitant of Great Britain, until the said act be repealed."[7] This resolution was passed by a vote of forty-seven to thirty-one. However, on 27 May, at another meeting of Annapolis inhabitants, the above resolution had been protested by 162 signatures, among them that of Daniel Dulany.[8]

According to William Buchanan, those patriots who planned the 31 May gathering in Baltimore invited to it the committee appointed to organize the Annapolis meeting. The Annapolis committee was to speak to the 25 May resolutions. This the Baltimore loyalist faction, headed by Henry Thompson and John Ashburner, determined to prevent, as well as participation by anyone not an inhabitant of Baltimore. They had decided instead to have Chalmers give the main address, which we must assume would have been directed against the Annapolis resolutions of 25 May. But the Baltimore friends of the British government were too few, and when Thompson and Ashburner attempted to use force against those favoring the Annapolis resolves, they were ejected from the hall. Thompson emerged from the scuffle "bloody and disheveled."[9] Well knowing that he was now a

6. Ibid., 26 May 1774.

7. The resolutions of 25 May are in the *Maryland Gazette* of 2 June 1774; see also William Eddis, *Letters from America . . . from 1769 to 1777, Inclusive* (London, 1792), pp. 159–60. Eddis was at the time surveyor of customs at Annapolis.

8. These resolutions with the signers are printed in the *Maryland Gazette* of 2 June 1774.

9. Ibid.

marked man, Chalmers avoided all meetings, went armed when going out, and slept with pistols beside him.[10]

Chalmers's close friends James Dick and Anthony Stewart, ship-owners and merchants of Annapolis, soon afterward found themselves in serious trouble. Their vessel, the *Peggy Stewart*, arrived in Annapolis in the autumn of 1774, carrying a number of indentured servants and seventeen packages of tea ordered by T. C. Williams and Co., an Annapolis firm that had for years been importing tea.

Four years earlier, in 1770, another of Dick's and Stewart's brigs, *Good Intent*, had arrived from England with a valuable cargo. The colonial nonimportation movement, resulting from the Townshend taxes on imports, created so much opposition to unloading the cargo that the ship had returned to England without breaking the seals of the hatches.

But the *Peggy Stewart* was not so fortunate. Two things counted heavily against the vessel's owners in the eyes of the local committee appointed to enforce nonimportation: the importers had ordered a much larger quantity of tea than ever before; and Stewart, chief owner of the brig, although not personally concerned with the tea, had paid all duties on it. Stewart claimed that he paid in order to permit the servants and other passengers to leave the vessel where for three months they had been confined. But there was such an outcry against him that he felt compelled, perhaps for his own safety, to set fire to the *Peggy Stewart*. With its contents, including the tea, it burned to the water's edge.[11]

10. Chalmers's testimony with respect to loyalist claims. He went on to affirm that he was "determined not to exist a single moment longer than he could live free from personal insult." For this testimony see the New York Public Library transcripts under the title "American Loyalists. Audit Office Manuscripts," 35:5–42.

11. This episode was well described by William Eddis in a letter written on 26 October 1774, which includes Stewart's letter to the Annapolis committee and the affidavit of Richard Jackson, master of the *Peggy Stewart*. See

With the forward sweep of the revolutionary movement in Maryland, Chalmers and his conservative loyalist friends found the ground for maneuver ever more restricted. As a result of the resolutions of the First Continental Congress, the inhabitants of Baltimore set up a Committee of Observation to watch the vessels arriving at their port and report on other developments.[12] On 16 January after the Maryland Convention voted to form a militia, the Baltimore committee resolved that whoever refused when called upon to contribute to the purchase of arms and ammunition for the militia would have his name presented to the committee.[13]

The following day the local committee brought to task a prominent native son of Maryland, the Reverend William Edmiston, pastor of St. Thomas Church in Baltimore, who had been very outspoken against the radical proposals. He was summoned to appear at the courthouse within two hours. In his plight Edmiston sent a note to his friend Chalmers appealing for advice. Chalmers went to the manse to help frame a reply.[14]

Among other damaging statements charged to the pastor were: "that all persons who mustered [into the militia, under the present circumstances] were guilty of treason" and that he "approved publicly the Quebec Act." The reply to the first of these charges was such that only a lawyer could have prepared it. Edmiston frankly admitted that he had spoken the above words, but "in warmth." Then came an explanation framed with language of such obtuseness that doubtless few of the committee members could fathom its meaning:

Eddis, *Letters from America* . . . , pp. 168–88; see also the *Maryland Gazette*, 27 October 1774.

12. *Maryland Journal*, 30 November 1774 and 2 January 1775.

13. William Eddis's letter of 13 March 1775 in Eddis, *Letters from America* . . . , pp. 189–201.

14. Chalmers's memorial, Audit Office papers, bundle 13:60, British Public Record Office.

What I meant had a reference to political opinions which prevail, and was founded conditionally, that is, they who do not apprehend a departure on the side of government from fundamental express stipulations, could not, consistently with their oaths, arm or prepare for war; but I did not, and do not, mean to charge any person with perjury or treason, who really thinks that his rights are or may be invaded, as to justify resistance.

Edmiston then stated that his political sentiments differed from those of most people and that, in order not to spread confusion, he would in the future refrain from expressing them. He also indicated that he had changed his views about the Quebec Act since "it establishes the Roman Catholic religion in the province of Quebec, abolishes the equitable system of English laws and erects a tyranny there to the great danger . . . of the neighbouring British colonies." He ended by voicing his deep love for his country and expressing the hope "that brotherly love will bury in oblivion all animosity between me and my parishioners."[15] The committee, doubtless mystified, accepted the explanation.

Chalmers in 1775 actively promoted an association in Baltimore "among the friends of government for their protection." To that end he and another person, not named, waited upon Governor Eden to ask for arms. But by that time the province's war materials had passed into the hands of the Maryland revolutionary Convention.

This Convention came into existence as a result of a resolution passed by the Baltimore town meeting of 31 May 1774, which was firmly controlled by patriotic inhabitants. The resolution recommended that each county choose a congress of deputies to assemble in Annapolis. The provincial congress met on 22 June and voted for a congress of deputies from all colonies (or Continental Congress) to implement commercial nonintercourse with Great Britain until the Boston Port Act was repealed. The provincial

15. *Maryland Gazette*, 26 January 1775.

congress met again on 21 November to ratify the actions of the First Continental Congress. Upon reassembling in December, the Convention passed resolutions to promote the manufacture of woolen goods, to keep prices within bounds, to provide for a militia, and to raise £10,000 by subscription. Meeting again on 24 April 1775, it selected delegates for the Second Continental Congress. On August 14 it ratified the association projected by the Continental Congress to enforce nonintercourse and resolved, if necessary, to repel force with force.[16]

Political events were limiting Chalmers's activities in Maryland. The law courts were closed to all cases involving British creditors. His law practice, based on the needs of exporters and importers, disappeared, and with it his livelihood. As Chalmers would neither contribute to purchase munitions designed for use against the king's government nor enroll in a militia company to oppose the king's troops by force of arms, he had little choice but to leave the province and return to Great Britain. Chalmers became a refugee and reached England in November 1775 with a deep hostility toward American revolutionaries that was never overcome.

There is much obscurity about George Chalmers's movements for the next five years, which even Miss Cockroft's excellent biography cannot penetrate. Certainly by 1780 he had established himself in London. That he had earlier settled there might be inferred by his anonymous *An Answer from the Electors of Bristol to the Letter of Edmund Burke, Esq. on the Affairs of America,* published in London in 1777.[17] Chalmers's answer to Burke deserves attention.

16. Ibid., 30 June 1774, 1 December 1774, and 15 December 1774; "Journal of the Maryland Convention, 26 July–14 August 1775," *Archives of Maryland,* 11:6–7, 15, 19.

17. Chalmers's collection of his own *Miscellaneous Works* includes this pamphlet of ninety pages. See Cockroft, *Public Life,* p. 45, n.3. See also Halkett and Laing, *Dictionary of Anonymous and Pseudonymous English Literature,* 1:92; and the British Museum, *Catalogue of Printed Books.*

Burke, a member of Commons elected by Bristol, addressed
John Farr and John Harris on the affairs of America, giving them
permission to communicate the letter to his constituents. The
letter, over fifty printed pages, represents a major effort by the
great orator.[18] Burke expressed his "detestation" of the war
against American colonists and his most unqualified disapproba-
tion of all the steps which had led to it and tended to prolong it.
He denounced the parliamentary statute for a partial suspension of
habeas corpus for Americans involved in commerce raiding as
possessing "a much deeper malignity" than the issuance of letters
of marque and reprisal, to which he was also opposed. He was
especially outraged that the act respecting *habeas corpus* should
confine Americans as "pirates." Application by Parliament in 1769
of the law of treason of Henry VIII to the acts of certain Americans equally outraged him.

In answer to Burke's letter, Chalmers turned on Burke's
"American Party" in Parliament, charging that its tactics had
created discontent and distrust of the government by American
colonials—which had led directly to their Declaration of Independence. How much more candid and honorable it would have
been, Chalmers stated, had this party in Parliament at once
adopted "the celebrated policy of a very respectable Dean and
boldly moved for the independence of the colonies!"[19]

Burke charged that all the steps taken by the government had
led to the war then waging. Chalmers agreed, but because he

18. See *The Works of the Right Honourable Edmund Burke*, 12 vols.
(London, 1889), 2:191–245.
19. [George Chalmers], *An Answer from the Electors of Bristol to the
Letters of Edmund Burke, Esq. on the Affairs of America* (London, 1777).
Reference in this pamphlet is made to Dr. Josiah Tucker, Dean of Gloucester,
who in 1774 published his *Four Tracts*, among which was "The True Interest
of Great-Britain set forth in Regard to the Colonies and the Only Means of
Living in Peace and Harmony with them." He argued that all colonies, past
and present, "aspire after Independence, and to set up for themselves as soon
as ever they find that they can subsist, without being beholden to the Mother-

thought the government had been too lenient with the Americans. As an example he cited repeal of the Stamp Act because of colonial opposition. Had the government been firm in supporting the Act, he argued, it would have stopped the fount from which flowed all later evils. Nor was it too late. The war was not hopeless, Chalmers said, "unless we suppose an impossibility, that those in power . . . will act a similar part with the repealers of the Stamp Act." Nor would the colonists be "thrust back to slavery" at the conclusion of the war, as asserted; they would simply be required "to reassume the character of subjects under the mildest government upon earth."

In the same year the young Earl of Abingdon strongly supported the colonists. Feeling that Burke had not gone far enough, he published under his name his *Thoughts on the Letters of Edmund Burke Esq. to the Sheriffs of Bristol, on the Affairs of America.* Chalmers, deeply disturbed that a peer of the realm should defend the Americans, produced an anonymous reply in 1777 in his *Second Thoughts: or Observations upon Lord Abingdon's Thoughts on the Letter of Edmund Burke, Esq., to the Sheriffs of Bristol, by the Author of the Answer to Mr. Burke's Letter.* This reply went much further than his earlier publications in finding Parliament possessed of complete sovereignty. Chalmers heaped scorn upon the views of both Burke and Abingdon who, he asserted, denied the legal omnipotence of that body; neither did he spare such a colonist as Benjamin Franklin. In none of his writings was Chalmers more emphatic in setting forth this constitutional position.

While Chalmers pressed his own claims for financial assistance, as well as those of his fellow Maryland loyalists, upon the British

---

Country." The government should freely extend this recognition of their independence to the American colonies. Tucker, it may be noted, recommended this a year before the outbreak of hostilities.

government, he had the irresistible urge to vindicate the point of view of those who had become exiles. In so doing he examined the development in the American colonies of the revolutionary movement for independence. Closely connected with this growth of New World radicalism, he was persuaded, was a party in England that encouraged it at the expense of the mother country, through the formulation and carrying out of mistaken colonial policy.[20] With tremendous zeal he gathered materials to illuminate with accuracy this unhappy aspect of the history of English colonization. He drew upon his friends and others in America to aid his enterprise, and he went to higher sources of information. William Knox, undersecretary of state for the colonies, with the hearty approval of Lord Germain, his superior, requested the "Digesters of State Papers" in the Office of the King's Remembrancer to permit Chalmers, who was "engaged in writing the History of the British Colonies in North America to make extracts of such papers as he should judge proper for his purpose." Chalmers drew liberally in 1780 upon the vast number of manuscripts in what was then described as "the Old Paper Office."[21]

The same year that the state papers were opened for his use saw

20. Under date of 18 September 1780, Chalmers addressed a very long letter to Lord Mansfield detailing mistakes made in colonial policy and the need to correct them once the revolt had been ended. He pointed out that Robert Hunter while governor of New York (1710–1719) wrote to Secretary of State Henry St. John, Viscount Bolingbroke, that while colonies "were then infants sucking their Mother's breasts yet [were] such as would wean themselves when they come of age." Chalmers stresses that the predictions not only of Hunter but of earlier "sagacious monitors have been fully verified. The seeds of separation sown in the imperfections of provisional establishments, only required time to ripen . . ." (pp. 3–4). This letter is in the John Carter Brown Library at Brown University.

21. Knox to Sir John Ayloffe and Thomas Astle, 4 March 1780, C.O. 5:251, Domestic dispatches, p. 301. For a description of the "Old Paper Office" see C. M. Andrews, *Guide to Materials for American History to 1783, in the Public Record Office of Great Britain*, 2 vols. (Washington, D.C., 1912, 1914), 1:24.

the completion and appearance of his *Political Annals of the Present United Colonies from their Settlement to the Peace of 1763: Compiled chiefly from Records, and authorized often by the Insertion of State-Papers. Book I.* It covered the period from colonization to 1688. Chalmers subsequently completed three additional chapters of the *Annals* that brought them down to 1696. These remained in manuscript for the remainder of his life.

Two years later his *An Introduction to the Revolt of the Colonies: Giving from the State-Papers, a Comprehensive View of their Conduct, from the Successive Settlement of each, to their Declaration of Independence, and of the Policy of Britain during every Reign, Volume I,* was privately printed. (It was not published until after his death, and then in Boston.) The *Annals* chiefly stresses the sovereign power of Parliament, while *The Revolt,* as the title would imply, stresses the desire of the colonies for independence. *The Revolt* was suppressed after being printed, Jared Sparks suggested, because Chalmers desired public office. Unless he refrained from publication of this work his hope for a post would not be realized—so anxious was the government, with the American war drawing to a close, to let bygones be bygones.[22]

Chalmers, influenced by the writings of Adam Smith as well as those of Dean Tucker,[23] was by 1782 no longer convinced that loss of the American colonies would seriously affect the prosperity and power of Great Britain. To bring others to the same point of view he published in that year *An Estimate of the Comparative Strength of Great Britain, during the Present and Four Preceding Reigns, and of the Losses of her Trade from Every War since the*

22. See Preface, p. vii of the 1845 Boston edition of *Political Annals.* This edition included the history of the reign of George II which Chalmers had left in manuscript in 1782 and which Jared Sparks added to the earlier printing. The title of the 1845 edition differs somewhat from that of the 1782 edition.

23. Cockroft, *Public Life,* pp. 62–63.

Revolution. The work, heavy with statistics relating to ships, cargoes, and balances of trade, was well received and went through six editions—as well as reprintings, with the introduction in each new edition of up-to-date tables. In the 1786 edition Chalmers wrote: "And the nation, for years, had been factiously informed, that the independence of the malcontent colonies must prove, at once the destruction of our commerce and the downfall of our power." He asserted—supported by tables of exports and imports—that the opposite had happened: "For by comparing the exports to the *discontented colonies*, before this war began, with the exports to the *United States*, after the admission of their independence it will appear . . . that we now supply them with manufactures to a greater amount, than even in the most prosperous times [when they were colonies]." Further than this, Great Britain had gained and the former colonists had lost "the ship-building, the freights, and the fisheries; of which the colonists had too much partaken."[24]

Closely related to the *Estimate* was Chalmers's *Opinions on Interesting Subjects of Public Law and Commercial Policy arising from American Independence,* issued first in 1784 and in a second edition in 1785. In it he questioned the status of those born British colonists but now citizens of the United States. In contrast to loyalists who fled from the colonies and who therefore remained British subjects, "the revolted Colonists forfeited to the law all that the law had ever conferred," and Parliament by the Treaty of Peace of 1783, recognizing Americans as an independent people,

24. For example, in the 1786 edition of this pamphlet, opposite page 207, is "A Chronological Account of Commerce in this Island, from the Restoration to the Year 1785." (See pp. 147 and 152 of the 1786 edition.) It may be noted that the sixth edition of this pamphlet (Edinburgh, 1812) carried the title, *An Historical View of the Domestic Economy of Great Britain, and Ireland, from the Earliest to the Present Times: With a Comparative Estimate of their Efficient Strength, arising from their Populosity, and Agriculture, their Manufactures, and Trade, in every Age.*

"expressed the assent of the community, to the expulsion of the American citizens from the social compact"; they therefore became foreigners.[25] These works, each appearing under his name, established his standing not only as a political economist but as an interpreter of British law as applied to Americans after the Treaty of Paris of 1783.

Parliament in 1782 did away with the Board of Trade created by William III. Its place was filled in 1784 by a new body of unpaid privy councillors under the title "Committee for the Considerations of all Matters relating to Trade and Foreign Plantations." Two years later it was reorganized and made a permanent body.

The first important task of the committee was to develop a commercial policy for the British West Indies that would be fair both to its planters and to merchants and shippers of the mother country. The big question before the committee was, To what extent should the United States regain its former great role in the economic life of these islands? The man most influential in the new committee was Charles Jenkinson, its president, whose views corresponded closely to those already set forth by Chalmers, especially in his hostility toward the United States.[26] Chalmers appeared before the committee in April 1784 when it considered the West Indies trade. His testimony related largely to commercial

25. John Reeves, appointed to the staff of the Board of Trade in 1787 as a law clerk, took a different point of view from Chalmers in his *Two Tracts Shewing that Americans, born before Independence, are, by the Law of England, not aliens. First, a Discussion, etc. Second, a Reply to the Restatement of Mr. Chalmers's Opinion on the legal efforts resulting from the Acknowledged Independence of the United States* (London, 1816). His position was that a natural-born subject could not lose his rights by any procedure, not even by "the law of the land." For a broad discussion of this interesting subject, see J. Mervyn Jones, *British Nationality Law*, rev. ed. (Oxford, 1956). See especially Part II, "Evolution of British Nationality Law: I. British Subjects at Common Law. Calvin's Case."

26. See Anna Lane Linglebach, "The Inception of the British Board of Trade," *American Historical Review*, 30 (1925): 701–27. In 1786 Jenkinson was raised by the king to the peerage as Baron Hawkesburg.

relations between the islands and Maryland; it also bore upon trade between that state and Great Britain, especially in tobacco. In view of his ability to amass and organize data, it is not surprising that Chalmers should come to the attention of Jenkinson and that after the Board of Trade's reorganization in 1786 he should have been appointed chief clerk with a staff of five assistant clerks (increased to eight by 1812).[27]

With a salary of £500 (later raised to £800), as a bachelor with no family responsibilities, and apparently under little pressure from his superiors since he could pass routine assignments on to his assistants, Chalmers settled down to pursue his intellectual interests both among and outside the collections of official papers of the Board of Trade relating to the British Empire.

It is not practicable to list all of Chalmers's writings published or in manuscript.[28] His writings on political subjects were all characterized by his firm adherence to and defense of what he understood to be the constitution of Great Britain. This defense included support of George III and his chief minister, Lord North, in the course of the War for American Independence. However, after North's resignation in 1782 and the coming to power of the short-lived Rockingham and Shelburne ministries, a coalition formed between Charles James Fox, Edmund Burke, and Lord North—former political enemies—brought in the Duke of Portland ministry in the spring of 1783. This coalition signed the Treaty of Paris with the United States on 3 September. The following year Chalmers seems to have fathered two satirical pamphlets, *The Beauties of Fox, North, and Burke, Selected from their Speeches from the passing of the Quebec Act, in the Year*

27. Ibid., p. 713; and Cockroft, *Public Life,* chapter 3.
28. The student should consult not only the *General Catalogue of Printed Books* in the British Museum, issued 1966, but especially the excellent bibliography in Cockroft, *Public Life,* which includes not only works published under Chalmers's name or anonymously, but also those in manuscript, and gives the locations of the latter.

1774, down to the Present Time . . . and *The Deformities of Fox and Burke, Faithfully Selected from their Speeches . . .,* in which the writer quoted both Fox and Burke in their earlier denunciations of North.[29] While Chalmers's hostility to Burke abated in the course of years, especially after the latter attacked the French Revolution, his hostility to Fox remained.[30]

Chalmers was committed to upholding the British mercantile system, as indicated by his opposition to the old freedom of trade between what was now the United States and the British West Indies. He supported William Pitt's efforts in 1785 to relax the restrictions on Irish trade and shipping—something opposed by British business interests. He may well have felt that this would bind Ireland closer to Great Britain in its interests. In support of the relaxed policy toward Ireland Chalmers issued anonymously in that year three pamphlets: *A Short View of the Proposals Lately made for the Final Adjustment of the Commercial System between Great Britain and Ireland; The Arrangements with Ireland Considered;* and an *Answer to the Reply to the Supposed Treasury Pamphlet,* which Chalmers thought was from the pen of Burke.[31] But Pitt's liberalizing plan was so altered during the proceedings in the House of Commons that the Irish Parliament rejected the amended measure.

Chalmers's enlightened attitude did not extend to the problem of Negro slavery. In 1789 the Society for Effecting the Abolition of the Slave Trade came into existence. William Wilberforce, who

29. See Halkett and Laing, *Dictionary of Anonymous and Pseudonymous English Literature,* 1:183 and 2:34; and Cockroft, *Public Life,* pp. 66, 183–84, for these two anonymous pamphlets together with a third, *Opposition Politics Exemplified* published in 1786.

30. This change of attitude is indicated in Chalmers's *Parliamentary Portraits: or Characters of the British Senate, containing the Political History with Biographical Sketches, of the Leading Members of the Lords and Commons . . . By the author of the Beauties of Fox, North, and Burke, etc.* (London, 1795).

31. Cockroft, *Public Life,* pp. 76n. 74, 78–79.

had entered the House of Commons in 1780, became chief spokesman of the Society in Parliament for many years. William Pitt, as the king's chief minister, was sympathetic to its aims; even before the Society was organized he issued an order in council that authorized the Committee for Trade to collect evidence on the traffic in human beings. This evidence was brought together and organized by the clerical force of the committee under Chalmers's supervision. One might have thought that the evidence presented would have changed the pro-slavery attitude he acquired in Maryland. But this was not the case. Undoubtedly the position of his patron Jenkinson on the slave trade reinforced his views. In fact, Jenkinson, when elevated to the rank of Earl in 1796, chose the title Earl of Liverpool and was invited by the borough of Liverpool to quarter its arms with his own—so grateful was this chief center of the slave trade for Jenkinson's continued support of this inhumane institution.[32]

To what extent Chalmers's views on slavery were influenced by his desire for an additional office is not clear. In 1792 Chalmers became London agent for the Bahamas, a post he had actively sought. This he added to the post he held at the Board of Trade.[33] Until 1804 his services as agent were highly regarded by all parties in the Bahamas, but after that date and until his death in 1825 the governor and council rather consistently opposed him, although strong Assembly support insured his continuance in

32. Elizabeth Donnan, ed., *Documents Illustrative to the History of the Slave Trade in America*, 4 vols. (Washington, D.C., 1930–35), 1:599n.

33. This was not an exceptional case. Charles Delafaye, who became London agent for Jamaica, was a clerk in the office of secretary of state for the southern department, while John Pownall, agent for the Virgin Islands, had served as secretary of the old Board of Trade. See Lillian M. Penson, *The Colonial Agents of the British West Indies . . .* (London, 1929), p. 167; and C. M. Andrews, *Guide to the Materials for American History to 1783, in the Public Record Office of Great Britain*, 2 vols. (Washington, 1912), 1:86–87.

office.[34] Unhappily, in supporting the Assembly on public questions, he placed himself in opposition to growing sentiment within the British Empire against slavery and the slave trade.

Chalmers apparently still felt little pressure from either of his two offices. As a result there came from his pen a steady flow of books and pamphlets up to the time of his death. Some were compilations, such as his useful *A Collection of Treaties between Great Britain and Other Powers* which appeared in 1790 in two volumes. The *Collection* was followed by the hostile *Life of Thomas Pain, the Author of the Rights of Men, with a Defense of his Writings, by Francis Oldys, A.M., of the University of Pennsylvania*, which went into some ten editions as well as many reprintings in both Great Britain and America.[35]

In 1795 the two-volume *Parliamentary Portraits: Or Characters of the British Senate, containing the Political History, with Biographical Sketches, of the Leading Members of the Lords and Commons, to which is prefixed a Review of the Present Administration . . .* (London, 1795) appeared. Attributed by many to Chalmers (as a campaign document in support of Pitt), it nevertheless presents problems, especially in the tribute paid to Wilber-

---

34. Miss Cockroft (*Public Life*) deals admirably with Chalmers as London agent of the Bahamas in chapter 4. Among the manuscripts in the John Carter Brown Library, Brown University, are five volumes of "Papers relating to the Bahama Islands, 1728–1818," which contain a good deal of correspondence rescued by Chalmers.

35. The misspelling of Paine's name and the altering of the word "man" to "men" was doubtless deliberate, as the ascription of the book to Francis Oldys most certainly was. It should be mentioned that Joseph Sabin, while he himself identified Chalmers as the author, at the same time included a note in his *Dictionary* that reads as follows: "This work is usually attributed to Chalmers, but in the year 1864, I sold a long letter, written by Chalmers, in which he indignantly denied the statement." See Joseph Sabin et al., *Bibliotheca Americana: Dictionary of Books relating to America from the Discovery . . .*, 29 vols. (New York, 1868–1936), 3:467. Sabin in 1864 was in the rare book business.

force, whom Chalmers had earlier consistently denounced for his abolitionist activities.[36]

Passing over those of Chalmers's writings unrelated to the British colonies (including his unfortunate espousal of the genuineness of the documents exhibited by the young forger William Henry Ireland as original Shakespeare writings), we come to his efforts to identify the author of the famous "Junius" letters. In 1800 Chalmers published *An Appendix to the Supplemental Apology for the Believers in the Supposititious Shakespeare-Papers; being the Documents for the Opinion that Hugh McAulay Boyd wrote Junius's Letters;* seventeen years later *The Author of Junius Ascertained, from a Concatenation of Circumstances, Amounting to Moral Demonstrations.* Two years later came *A New Edition, with a Postscript, evincing that Boyd wrote Junius, and not Francis.* All one need say is that Chalmers's mistaken identification of "Junius" placed him in good and numerous company.[37]

No account of George Chalmers would be complete without some reference to his vast compilation of documents relating either to Great Britain or to its colonies, with emphasis on the eighteenth century. For example, the Manuscript Division of the New York Public Library possesses twenty-five volumes of documents pertaining to North America collected by Chalmers. The Manuscript Division of the Library of Congress has some nineteen volumes of his documents, most of them relating to the British Empire in the New World outside what became the United States. Other collections of documents are in the Harvard Univer-

36. Miss Cockroft (*Public Life*, pp. 183–84) arrives at the reasonable conclusion that not all the sketches were Chalmers's.

37. See Chalmers, *An Apology for the Believers in the Shakespeare-Papers* (London, 1797), and also his *Supplemental Apology* (London, 1799). Over fifty people have been identified as "Junius." However, the weight of critical opinion today is that Sir Philip Francis was the real author. On this problem see Lawrence Henry Gipson, *The British Empire before the American Revolution*, 15 vols. (New York, 1936–70), 11:205; 12:278; 14:42–43.

sity Library, the John Carter Brown Library at Brown University, and the Library of The New-York Historical Society; four volumes of his correspondence are in the British Museum. Manuscripts collected by Chalmers are also in both the National Library of Scotland, Edinburgh, and the University of Edinburgh Library.[38]

The *Political Annals* was George Chalmers's most important contribution to the history of the British Empire. The plan that he outlined and announced would have extended its scope from the beginning of British colonization of the New World to the year 1763—the year that witnessed the Peace of Paris and the expulsion of France from North America. But in his writing Chalmers never got beyond 1696, the year William and Mary established that important advisory body to the Privy Council, the Lords Commissioners for Trade and Plantations, generally known as the Board of Trade. There the *Annals* abruptly ends. This is especially to be regretted since Chalmers not only had access to but made use of vast resources of official documents. The *Political Annals*, nevertheless, established his reputation as a scholar of high standing in the field of British colonial history. Each of the chapters is replete with footnotes, many of which incorporate complete contemporary documents of importance in illuminating the text. While the history of every English colony in existence before 1696 is given attention, the chief emphasis, logically enough, is placed on the early years of the Virginia and Massachusetts Bay colonies. The reader of the *Political Annals* must remember that the author was striving to present a point of view in consistently emphasizing one thing that Americans disputed—the sovereign authority of the King's High Court of Parliament throughout the empire. Explaining in the preface why he wrote the book, with the War for American Independence of the thirteen colonies still in progress, Chalmers comments:

38. See Cockroft, *Public Life*, pp. 216–23.

Nothing more was originally intended than to offer a general account of the civil transactions of these colonies prior to the present reign; in order to lay before the public something as an introduction to the history of a war, the most singular in many respects to be met with in the annals of recorded time. But, upon a nearer view of the subject, it was perceived that almost every capital fact [with respect to the constitutional relations between England and the colonies] had been controverted; that every principle of public law had been disputed, that a shade had been thrown over the whole; either by the inattention of former writers or the misrepresentation of the present. . . . When ancient privileges were said [by the Americans] to have been invaded, it seemed of the greatest importance to investigate, with precision, what immunities the colonists were originally entitled to possess; when chartered rights were said to have been infringed, it was deemed of use to ascertain what the charters really contained; when it was zealously contended that a different rule of colonial administration had been adopted soon after the peace of 1763, it became necessary to exhibit the genuine spirit of every government, whether of kings, or parliaments, or protectors, antecedent to the present reign [of George III].

Concluding Book I of his *Political Annals,* Chalmers summarized the points that he attempted to make. He went back to the ancient history of colonization as practiced by Greece, Carthage, and Rome, in order to provide perspective for the constitutions of the "ancient dependencies of England." He assessed the nature of Parliament's authority over colonies and outlined broadly the privileges enjoyed by those who emigrated from England to America. His views about Parliament's power in fact do not differ from those of his contemporary, Sir William Blackstone, or from those of the seventeenth-century interpreter of the English constitution, Sir Edward Coke. He did differ sharply with the political principles of James Wilson, a fellow Scot who had settled in Pennsylvania and who, as a member of the Constitutional Convention of 1787, influenced its deliberations. However, he agreed with Wilson's statement in his *Considerations on the Nature and Extent of the Legislative Authority of the British Parliament*

(Philadelphia, 1774) that no line could distinguish the power that Parliament had over the colonies, on the one hand, from the power it did not have, on the other hand. Wilson agreed with Benjamin Franklin in consequence of this premise that there remained no alternative to Americans but to deny that Parliament had *any* authority over them. In contrast, Chalmers agreed with Blackstone who quoted Coke, that Parliament's power was "so transcendent and absolute, that it cannot be confined . . . within any bounds."[39] This gives the *Political Annals* a most distinctive place in the eighteenth-century literature of the Old British Empire. Supposedly concerned with the annals of the colonies only to 1696, Chalmers never lets the reader forget that he is writing during the last stages of the War for American Independence. He insists that Parliament claimed the same powers over provinces in 1696 that it continued to claim after 1763 and up to the Treaty of Paris of 1783.

39. Blackstone, *Commentaries on the laws of England*, 4 vols., 4th ed. (Oxford, 1770), 1:160–62.

3.

George Chalmers and *An Introduction to the History of the Revolt*

John A. Schutz

For most Americans the revolution came as a sharp break with the past. They were amazed by the turbulence around them; they saw small groups of men grab the reins of government and elect new officials. George Chalmers, a Maryland lawyer who had migrated to the colonies from Scotland in 1763, saw the outbreak of violence touch his friends and disrupt his law practice. While he rushed to aid some victims of mob brutality, he was no counter-revolutionary, nor was he willing to risk serious injury. When violence intensified in 1775, he closed his law practice rather than comply with the regulations of the revolutionary junto, and escaped.[1]

After his arrival in England, he joined other Maryland refugees much less fortunate than himself. They soon gathered in London, where Chalmers rented an apartment, got in touch with Scottish friends, and prepared to attack British politicians who had advocated conciliating America. He assailed Edmund Burke, parliamentary spokesman for the Rockingham Whigs, in two pamphlets, but then turned to the problems he and his fellow Tories often pondered: Why did the American rebellion occur

1. Chalmers's testimony before the Loyalist Claims Commission, 21 November 1783, British Public Record Office, Audit Office (P.R.O., A.O.) 12, 35:16–18.

and why am I suffering exile in London? A diligent lawyer, he thoroughly researched these problems by examining official state papers and reading available histories. The evidence he collected was equally hostile to British administrators and colonial leaders; it illustrated the pattern of development from the founding of the colonies until the revolution. Describing what he found, he was often bitter and accusatory, sometimes reflecting in his writing the blows Britain was then taking in the war. The first volume of *An Introduction to the History of the Revolt of the American Colonies* was printed in 1782 but withdrawn before it was released for public sale. Apparently friends, realizing the harm that the history would do to his patronage ambitions, advised Chalmers to confine himself to a partisan assault on Burke, Charles James Fox, and other members of the Whig opposition and an analysis of the political implications of the war. The book was put aside and remained among his papers until 1845, twenty years after his death, when the noted American editor Jared Sparks secured the book and an additional manuscript of the work and published both.[2]

I

When Chalmers left Scotland in 1763, he was nearly twenty-one years old. He and an uncle intended to join other relatives and family friends in Maryland and invest in colonial land. Chalmers also intended to practice law. They had apparently sold their inheritances in Scotland and committed themselves to permanent residence in the colonies.

George was the second son of James Chalmers, postmaster of Fochabers, a small impoverished village in Morayshire. He matriculated at King's College, the University of Aberdeen, where he

2. See the Sparks introduction to Chalmers's *An Introduction to the History of the Revolt of the American Colonies*, 2 vols. (Boston, 1845), 1:iii, xii.

apparently did not take the examinations in order to graduate. His years there, nonetheless, had been rewarding; he developed strong interests in philosophy, history, and antiquarianism which became his hobbies in later life. In Aberdeen and Edinburgh he read law, gained some knowledge of finance, and published an essay on the currency.[3] He became convinced, perhaps through the advice of relatives, that he should not remain in Scotland if he wished to take full advantage of his education. Instead of following other young Scots to London, he went to America.

Sailing with his father's younger brother, George arrived at Annapolis, Maryland, in August 1763 and was soon attracted to the company of some Scottish settlers, particularly to a graduate of Aberdeen, the Reverend Mr. David Love, who became a friend and client.[4] These new friends soon eased the blows of a tragedy, his uncle's premature death during the first year of their residence in Maryland. His uncle's only heir, George invested the inheritance in land. Later he disposed of the land at a substantial profit, and reinvested the money in commerce.

But his principal income came from his law practice, which grew yearly and brought him over £500 sterling in 1774.[5] His briefs were erudite in appearance; his pleas before the local courts were praised as eloquent. He fought hard for his clients and enjoyed verbal combat: "A genuine disputant," he once wrote, "should never admit the truth of any position, however demonstrated, or however certain, since his adversary is sure to build on his admission, as a rocky foundation, whose stability defies attack."[6] These

3. George Chalmers, *Considerations relating to the Late Order of the Two Banks established at Edinburgh* . . . (Edinburgh, 1762).
4. Chalmers's letter to David Love, 25 August 1772, Aukland Papers, Library of Congress.
5. Loyalist Claims Commission, Old Claims, P.R.O., A.O.12, 2:176. Chalmers later scaled this estimate of annual income down to £354 sterling.
6. Chalmers's testimony before Loyalist Claims Commission, 21 November 1783, P.R.O., A.O.12, 35:27; George Chalmers, *Political Annals of the*

encounters in the courtroom gained the respect of the proprietary agents and in 1774 he was chosen clerk of indictment and prosecuting attorney for Harford county.

During the first five years of his residence in Maryland, he lived in Baltimore and soon became the town's leading lawyer. Many of his clients were merchants; some had violated the trade boycotts, first against the Townshend duties and later against the Tea Act. Chalmers was involved in protesting local coercion and in reducing assessments against the merchants. As the bitterness of the revolution mounted, he planned with his Scottish friends to raise and train a corps of loyal guardsmen who would support the proprietary government. When the governor refused this help, because of possible political repercussions, Chalmers offered his services in other ways.[7] Like the governor he was thoroughly frightened by the disorder, particularly when his friends were confined to their homes, tarred and feathered, or unnerved by threats. He decided that "all was lost in Maryland." During these months he had suffered no personal harm, nor had his name been proscribed as an enemy of the people; he had decided, nonetheless, to turn his wealth into sterling and leave for England.

Shortly after his arrival in England, he may have done some private work for the ministry that took him for a time to the continent, but by early 1777 he was back in the capitol and looking for a position in the government. He was well known through his pamphleteering. In May he answered Edmund Burke's famous *Letter to the Sheriffs of Bristol on the Affairs of America* and a few weeks later attacked an essay by Lord Abingdon.[8] In both

---

Present United Colonies, from their Settlement to the Peace of 1763; Compiled chiefly from Records and authorized often by the insertion of State-Papers (London, 1780), p. 172. (Hereafter referred to as *Political Annals.*)

7. Chalmers's testimony before Loyalist Claims Commission, 21 November 1783, P.R.O., A.O.12, 35:10–16.

8. [George Chalmers], *An Answer from the Electors of Bristol to the Letter of Edmund Burke, Esq. on the Affairs of America* (London, 1777);

pamphlets Chalmers insisted that British policy toward the colonies had been too lenient. His Whiggish view of Parliament
allowed no room for a theory of natural rights, vested rights, or
limited government. He thus assailed the Declaration of Independence, for only Parliament could express the will of the British
people and only it had the power to release Americans from their
obligations as British subjects. His refutation of Abingdon's
pamphlet was a bitter diatribe against both the author and the
pro-American party in Parliament. For good measure he even denounced Benjamin Franklin as a "monstrous man" who was "only
less contemptible as a negociator, than as a friend."[9]

The heat of these attacks favorably attracted some members of
the ministry. They showed their regard in August 1777 by award-
ing him a modest pension of one hundred pounds. This initial
success encouraged him to request more money and a position.
While his efforts were unsuccessful, he became active on behalf of
fellow Tories, meeting regularly with them and carrying on an
extensive correspondence with those living outside London. His
growing involvement in these circles brought him wide acquaintances in the government and a new occupation. Sir John Dal-
rymple, who had a high opinion of Chalmers's abilities, suggested
that he write a history of the American colonies. With the Scot's
help and that of Lord George Germain, the secretary for colonies,
he was granted liberal access to the public archives. During the fall
of 1780 he published the first of a projected two-volume study
entitled *Political Annals*, a well-researched and developed history
of the American colonies.[10] The first volume, ending with 1689,

*Second Thoughts; or Observations upon Lord Abingdon's Thoughts on the
Letter of Edmund Burke* . . . (London, 1777).

    9. Chalmers, *Second Thoughts*, pp. 21, 63.

    10. Chalmers left incomplete most of Volume Two, but George Bancroft
procured a manuscript fragment during the sale of Chalmers's library. This
manuscript, which takes the political story of the colonies down to the middle
of William III's reign, was published in the *Collections of The New-York Historical Society for the Year 1868* (New York, 1868), pp. 1–176.

emphasized the constitutional relations of the colonies with England, the fairness of British rule, and the realities of distance in ruling the empire. The impression is unmistakable: England had a right to rule its colonies and had done so, while the colonies had accepted their dependency and had benefited from it.[11]

Though this relationship of England with its colonies was usually beneficial to both, Chalmers was critical of the restrictions the mercantile system imposed on trade; he did not question its legality but questioned the harm it was doing to the natural flow of commerce within the empire. Monopoly privileges undoubtedly brought rewards to certain individuals, but the nation as a whole suffered from the burdens placed on the free movement of trade.[12] These ideas modified time-honored mercantilist practices, contending that free trade in the empire was a greater benefit to all than the creation of monopolies for some. Chalmers stopped short of advocating free trade with foreign nations. He ventured at times, however, to cast doubt on the value of colonies and to question the good that discovering America had brought Europe.

These speculative points raised many new thoughts in Chalmers's mind while he was preparing the second volume of *Political Annals*. He eventually broke off his work and gathered material on the Canary Islands, amassed trade statistics, and discussed colonial policy with Lord Mansfield. In a very long letter he suggested possible lines of reform to be imposed on the colonies when they were finally conquered. These observations probably deflected his mind from the second volume of the *Annals*, for he now began writing a two-volume history of the American revolt. He penned a careful but sharp analysis of the weaknesses of colonial policy in the spirit of a critic of Anglo-American relations

---

11. Chalmers, *Political Annals*, p. 75. Chalmers was blunt in his comments on the foundations of colonial institutions. Of Virginia's he gave this summary: "Such then was the rotten foundation whereon was erected, with so great skill, the superstructure of the Virginian immunities and laws" [p. 17].

12. Ibid., p. 312.

and entitled the essay *An Introduction to the History of the Revolt of the Colonies*. It was too critical of the British government, however, for his ministerial patrons, who apparently warned him of the political consequences. Upon reflection he reluctantly agreed with their appraisal of present politics. Though he withheld from circulation almost the whole printing, he gave some copies to friends.

In later years he made minor revisions on personal copies of the printed history but never finished the announced plan of his study. His manuscript ended with the death of George II in 1760, even though he had collected documents for the remaining period before the revolution. He partially revealed his plans for later publication by altering the title of his study to read: *The History of the Revolt of the United States of America. By George Chalmers, formerly of Maryland.*[13] As other projects intervened, or as politics had to be served, he did not finish his revisions and postponed indefinitely the publication of his work.

Though he had suppressed his bold criticisms of colonial policy, he remained openly hostile to American sympathizers Edmund Burke and Charles James Fox. When Lord North joined them in forming a ministry, Chalmers was also antagonistic to him. These barbs were undoubtedly intended to attract political support, for Chalmers was looking for an administrative post and clearly made his ambitions known to his Scottish friends whenever he met them. He often favored them with data on trade and sometimes even sent them formal reports. These reflected his efforts to improve his bargaining position, increase his knowledge of colonial affairs, and establish himself as an expert on the public record. His reports in 1783 before the commission on loyalist claims cover such complicated subjects as American currency, Rhode Island legal problems, and wartime politics. His books on trade were over-

13. A revised copy of the 1782 edition of *An Introduction to the History of the Revolt* is owned by the Huntington Library. Chalmers's revisions were generally minor, mostly changes in words or phrases.

whelmingly statistical.[14] A year earlier he had published his best-known treatise, *Estimate of the Comparative Strength of Britain, during the Present and Four Preceding Reigns.* Its seven editions over the next thirty years testify to its popularity, but more beneficial for his career was the acceptance of its thesis by George III and the ministry.[15] Chalmers attacked those pessimists who had predicted the decline of Britain because of luxurious living and the loss of the American colonies. He cited statistics for decade after decade of the eighteenth century to show how the kingdom had expanded, prospered, and progressed. He amassed evidence and explanations to impress officials, and most of them apparently accepted his thesis that the loss of the thirteen colonies was a momentary setback for Britain in a general movement of progress.

Chalmers's mastery of commercial matters was recognized again in 1784 when a royal committee investigated colonial policy and the working of the mercantile system. He was invited to testify and to present a written report on Scottish trade with the West Indies. His strong support of mercantilism and rejection of trade concessions to the United States as an independent nation were reflected in the committee's report. But he struck even more effectively against granting special treatment to the West Indies. He opposed subsidies or specific benefits which would develop unusual market conditions. For this reason he later joined the movement to reform Ireland's trade relations with England, writing pamphlets against the exclusion of Ireland from the imperial market.[16]

The many activities in favor of free trade within the empire

14. Loyalist Claims Commission, Old Claims, P.R.O., A.O.12, 1:131–45, 160.
15. George Chalmers, *An Estimate of the Comparative Strength of Great Britain during the Present and Four Preceding Reigns.* (London, 1782). The editions in 1786, 1794, 1802, 1804, and 1810 were published in London, while the last edition in 1812 had an Edinburgh imprint.
16. George Chalmers, *Opinions on Interesting Subjects of Public Law and Commercial Policy arising from American Independence* (London, 1784); *A Short View of the Proposals lately made for the Final Adjustment of the Commercial System between Great Britain and Ireland* (London, 1785).

(and of restricted trade outside it) attracted him to Charles Jenkinson, a leading member of the royal committee on trade. In 1786, when its responsibilities were taken over by the Committee on Trade and a formal governmental agency was created, Jenkinson was named its head. He in turn offered Chalmers the position of chief clerk and the impressive salary of £500, which was most acceptable. This appointment marked a significant change in Chalmers's fortunes. Since he had left Maryland in September 1775 he had lived on his savings, his small pension as a loyalist, and his royalties as a writer.[17] He lived modestly on his income, for he had simple tastes. He was almost a recluse, working unceasingly on his manuscripts and searching tirelessly in the public archives. Rummaging through these records, he copied documents by the thousands for his personal use and surrounded himself with an enormous library, his sole dissipation. He remained unmarried, and in his later years encouraged a nephew from Scotland to live with him and become his heir.

II

For the next thirty-nine years George Chalmers served as chief clerk of the Committee for Trade; during half these years he and Jenkinson (Lord Liverpool) set the pattern of British colonial policy. Chalmers managed the office, drafted official papers, wrote for official signature letters to colonial governors, and handled matters that came before the president of the committee. He resisted modifications of the mercantile laws, particularly those affecting trade with the United States, and opposed reform of the slave trade. He had little sympathy for slaves as human beings and apparently believed that the West Indian planters gave slaves a satisfactory standard of living. The slave trade he regarded as a

17. Grace Amelia Cockroft, *The Public Life of George Chalmers* (New York, 1939), pp. 82–83. In 1783 his annual pension was increased to £300.

nursery of seamen, and whatever aided or promoted mercantilism Chalmers generally favored.

He espoused these ideas in spite of his other official position as colonial agent for the Bahamas. From 1792 until his death in 1825 he looked after the London interests of the Bahaman legislature, helped remove corrupt officials, and aided in the promotion of trade. He usually avoided compromising his first responsibility to the Committee for Trade, but in his later years passed privileged information to the Bahaman legislature and was reprimanded by the president of the committee.[18] His opinion of colonies remained constant: they were maintained for the benefit of the mother country, and its general interest should not be sacrificed for the colonies' particular interests. Chalmers thus vigorously opposed trade concessions for the United States in the West Indies. In his capacity as agent for the Bahamas, he backed a liberalized trade policy that made the free port of Provincetown a flourishing commercial center.

After Lord Liverpool retired as president of the Committee for Trade, Chalmers's power in the committee progressively diminished. Succeeding presidents preferred the services of other clerks, and Chalmers busied himself with routine tasks. The work of the office, moreover, was changing in character; much of its original responsibility had passed to other government agencies. At his death in 1825, the post Chalmers had held for thirty-nine years was abolished.[19]

For most of these years the burdens of the clerkship were relatively light compared with the other tasks Chalmers had undertaken. His interests were primarily in research—at times historical,

18. Charles Cameron to Lord Bathhurst, 12 August 1817; and Edward Lack to Henry Goulburn, 22 January 1818, P.R.O., C.O.23: 64, 67.

19. Anna Lane Lingelbach, "William Huskisson as President of the Board of Trade," *The American Historical Review* 43 (1938): 759–74; Cockroft, *Public Life*, pp. 122–23.

often archaeological and scientific, sometimes literary. His chief preoccupation was Scotland, whose antiquities fascinated him. He collected its ballads, folklore, family histories, and anything else that would illuminate its past. Gathering the material he secured the help of old acquaintances living in Scotland, and searching for obscure data he carried on a correspondence with the great men of his time.[20] Many of his findings were published in *Archaeologia*, or given as papers before scientific or archaeological societies. In 1791 he was voted membership in both the Royal Society and the Society of Antiquaries, and a year later he became a corresponding member of the Scottish Society of Antiquaries. Over the years he often gave these organizations his latest speculations, but his most impressive undertaking in the field was *Caledonia: or, an Account, Historical and Topographic, of North Britain, from the Most Ancient to the Present Times*. Three massive volumes were published during his lifetime; an enlarged edition of eight volumes was prepared between 1887 and 1902 from his papers.[21]

On their surface, these volumes impressed his contemporaries, as they do his present readers, because they were based on a vast quantity of original documentation. His unceasing search for charters, detailed information, and local folklore was balanced by

20. William Robertson to Chalmers, 27 June 1791, Huntington Library MSS., 6566; Isaac Heard to Chalmers, 8 February 1796, Gratz Papers, Pennsylvania Historical Society. Walter Scott, David Laing, Joseph Banks, and Alexander Stenhouse were a few of his regular correspondents.
21. *Caledonia: or, An Account, Historical and Topographic, of North Britain, From the Most Ancient to the Present Times*, 3 vols. (London and Edinburgh, 1807–24); *Caledonia: or, A Historical and Topographical Account of North Britain . . .*, 7 vols. and index (Paisley, 1887–94, 1902). Chalmers was proud of his undertaking, and in the preface referred at least several times to the abundance of new material in *Caledonia*: "It is the common complaint of intelligent readers that there is nothing *new* in history, as the same facts are again served up in different forms with some interspersions of sentiments. It is very seldom, indeed, that any history contains so many new facts, new discoveries, and new documents, as the following account of North Britain discloses."

his presentation of data, his deductions, and his writing style. Chalmers was certainly a pioneer in exploring Scotland's antiquity. Public reception of his great study, however, was mixed because of his controversial evaluations, which his critics seized upon to point out his own shortcomings. But their sharp rebukes did not deter his antiquarian efforts: he wrote a *Life of Thomas Ruddiman,* a prominent Scottish librarian and writer; *The Life of Mary, Queen of Scots,* for whom he had an emotional attachment; and *The Political Remains of Some of the Scottish Kings,* which was published a few months before his death. The poems of Allan Ramsay and Sir David Lyndsay were also collected and edited by Chalmers and brought out in multivolumed editions.[22]

While these studies attracted wide audiences in England and Scotland who were sometimes critical of his scholarship, he frequently jumped into controversies which embarrassed even his admirers. In 1791, he published a satirical life of Thomas Paine, whose career he believed was an example for Englishmen to avoid. Chalmers decided to put Paine in his place, and belittled his accomplishments over the years. The spirit of the attack may be seen in these few lines from the biography: "Though the [Continental] Congress had wholly rejected our author, he did not totally reject the Congress; yet all that he could write, or others could do, did not prevent the bankruptcy of Congress. . . . But their ears were callous to the voice of the charmer. The pen had, however, ceased to influence. . . . Our author cheered them from time to time with another *Crisis,* till his *Crisis,* becoming common, was no longer a *Crisis.*" This bitterness toward Paine sharply

---

22. George Chalmers, ed., *The Poems of Allan Ramsay. A New Edition, corrected and enlarged, with a Glossary. To which are prefixed a Life of the Author* . . . , 2 vols. (London, 1800); George Chalmers, ed., *The Poetical Works of Sir David Lyndsay of the Mount, Lion King at Arms under James* V. *A New Edition, corrected and enlarged, with a life of the Author* . . . , 3 vols. (London and Edinburgh, 1806). Chalmers to Thomas Dibdin, 16 September 1808, Huntington Library MSS.

contrasted with his growing admiration of Burke, whose wisdom, zeal, and patriotism he praised.[23]

Chalmers also attacked Edmund Malone, who had exposed some Shakespearean documents which Chalmers and a group of London intelligentsia had publicly accepted as genuine. Chalmers admitted being deceived by the errors but assailed Malone just the same. While his logic was imperfect, he seemed to be making a case for free inquiry and emphasizing that there was much yet to be known about Shakespeare. He thought the publicity and public reaction to Malone's exposure of the frauds would do great harm to speculative scholarship. Chalmers's pride was apparently hurt, but his attempt to save face was justly criticized by journalists. Though the criticism irritated, he did not change his opinions. He took refuge in his own impressive scholarship and challenged those around him to do comparable work.[24]

During these years he edited and published Charles Smith's *Some Tracts on the Corn Trade and Corn Laws* (1790) and wrote a small tract of his own in 1795, *Useful Suggestions Favourable to*

23. [George Chalmers], *The Life of Thomas Pain, the Author of the Rights of Men, with a Defense of his Writings, by Francis Oldys* . . . (London, 1791), pp. 70–72. The biography had ten editions.

24. George Chalmers, *An Apology for the Believers in the Shakespeare-Papers, which were Exhibited in Norfolk-Street* (London, 1797); *Supplemental Apology for the Believers in the Shakespeare-Papers* . . . (London, 1799); *An Appendix to the Supplemental Apology for the Believers in the Suppositious Shakespeare-Papers* . . . (London, 1800). Chalmers devoted approximately 1300 pages of print to this controversy. Critics were harsh in their reviews of his books, but he received sufficient praise from the scholarly fraternity to continue his work. His essay on the English stage and his dating of the Shakespearean plays received recognition, and in 1803 his history of the English stage was reprinted by Isaac Reed in a new edition of Shakespeare's plays. Chalmers was a close friend of Henry John Todd, the editor of Spenser's works and a Milton scholar, and he moved near Todd in 1808. With Todd, Reed, and a half-dozen other scholars, Chalmers dined and joined in cultural activities in London. See Claude E. Jones, ed., *Isaac Reed Diaries, 1762–1804*, University of California Publications in English, X (Berkeley and Los Angeles, 1946), pp. 123, 176, 230, 298; Chalmers to Thomas Dibdin, 16 September 1808, Huntington Library MSS.

the Comfort of the Labouring People, in which he advised people to substitute vegetables for grain in times of severe shortages. He was active also in the defense of the homeland against the ravages of the French Revolution. Besides his early pamphlet against Paine, he wrote in support of measures to limit free speech to responsible people and backed the ministry of the younger William Pitt.[25]

In 1800 Chalmers entered the controversy over the authorship of the Junius letters. Chalmers was not alone in speculating on the authorship of these penetrating evaluations of British policy, but he was nearly alone in choosing Hugh McAulay Boyd as the author. He chose Boyd because his handwriting and literary style were similar to Junius's and also because Boyd's wife had accused her husband of being the author. From Chalmers's inside view of British politics, he speculated that Junius was some unimportant person with access to public information who was clever, witty, and an Irishman. Reviewers were brutally critical of Chalmers's logic, but he doggedly held his theory and published his findings again in 1817 and 1819 under the new title *The Author of Junius Ascertained.*[26]

Chalmers's life was thus full of books and controversy. At the time of his death in 1825 he had authored approximately fifty books and pamphlets and scores of articles. Most of what he wrote attracted public attention, and some of his archaeological and

25. George Chalmers, A *Vindication of the Privilege of the People, in Respect to the Constitutional Right of Free Discussion* . . . (London, 1796); *An Estimate of the Comparative Strength of Great Britain, during the Present and Four Preceding Reigns* . . . (London, 1794), p. xcix.

26. Chalmers added these ideas on Junius to his rebuttal of Malone on Shakespeare in his *An Appendix to the Supplemental Apology for the Believers in the Suppositious Shakespeare-Papers: being the Documents for the Opinion that Hugh McAulay Boyd wrote Junius's Letters* (London, 1800). *The Author of Junius Ascertained, from a Concatenation of Circumstances, Amounting to Moral Demonstration* (London, 1817). The new edition in 1819 included a postscript.

antiquarian studies were well regarded. His history of the English theater and his Shakespearean scholarship were highly valued in his lifetime, and even some modern Shakespearean scholars take note of his ideas.[27] He received much personal satisfaction from an impressive correspondence with learned friends and acquaintances, and he occasionally left his desk for visits with them.

Most of his life, however, was spent in London. Surrounding him in his home was an immense library of probably ten thousand books and packages upon packages of original letters, documents, and copied governmental reports. He and his nephew James and some secretarial assistants spent years transcribing documents and assembling them for future use. When his library was auctioned in 1841 and 1842, over six thousand items were listed. The range of books, newspapers, pamphlets, and documents was impressive, but the library contained a fuller assortment of English materials than of American, more historical than contemporary material.[28]

The sale of his great collection brought his heirs the modest sum of six thousand pounds. Since both George and his nephew had died without direct heirs, the money went to distant relatives in Scotland. His library today is well scattered, but important items are at the British Museum, the Library of Congress, the New York Public Library, and Harvard University. A few rare books and some manuscripts are also at the Huntington Library.

III

In 1845 the great editor Jared Sparks was responsible for publishing George Chalmers's *An Introduction to the History of the Revolt of the American Colonies*. He had discovered among the

27. Cockroft, *Public Life*, p. 199.
28. *The Catalogue of the Very Curious, Valuable and Extensive Library of the late George Chalmers* . . . (London, 1841–42). Three catalogues were issued, but the sales were conducted over a few weeks.

auctioned items in Chalmers's library a manuscript copy of the last part of Book Two. With this important addition, he published in two volumes Chalmers's entire history under a modification of the original title. In a short preface Sparks recognized the value of this history of the colonies, but he could not refrain from censoring Chalmers for his loyalism and unsympathetic attitude toward the rebellion. Sparks asked: How could anyone accuse Americans of being disloyal to Britain before the revolution? Certainly Chalmers had no proof of any disloyalty—"the whole mass of testimony, as the reader will see in this work, amounts to nothing more than an accumulation of suspicions, vented in moments of disappointment, vexatious defeat, or self-reproach for rash and abortive experiments." In fact, Sparks emphasized, the colonies at no time "acted with a direct view to independence, or even meditated schemes for such action, till very near the first conflict of arms which opened the war of the Revolution."[29]

Sparks's sunny view of American relations with Britain was definitely not held by Chalmers, who believed that while the colonies reflected the strengths and weaknesses of English rule their loyalty was left to chance. His summary of James I's rule typified his attitude, frequently expressed in the history. At the king's demise, he wrote, British colonists numbered 1980 despite the frightful loss of life through Indian massacre and the hardships of colonization:

It was his [James's] colonizing spirit which gave them existence . . . [and] nursed them in their childhood. . . . His colonial administration partook of that wisdom and impolicy, of that vigor and imbecility, which were the distinguishing characteristics of his rule in England. He governed both according to the maxims of his age. . . . The wisest lawyers regarded the plantations as territories gained by conquest; and thence inferred, without admitting the distinctions of circumstance, that the king might govern such newly-acquired countries by preroga-

29. Chalmers, *Introduction to the History of Revolt,* 1: x-xi.

tive alone. . . . [However,] the Commons justly claimed the privilege of superintendence and the power of legislation. . . . [But the colonies,] requiring support from the king during their infancy, . . . were too feeble to disobey the edicts of prerogative; and, though they talked, even in those days of "their ancient liberties," while they fled to the Commons for protection, they did not insist on inherent rights, since they had scarcely emerged from bondage.[30]

This denial of natural law was not accidental. Chalmers insisted that the colonies had always been subject to English law. They may have been disobedient over the years, they may have been permitted to escape the full vigor of the law because England was distracted at home by serious internal problems, but the law was imposed from time to time. Citing instance upon instance of English use of sovereign power and instance upon instance of colonial disobedience, Chalmers emphasized that the Board of Trade had warned about the danger of this inconsistency. The Board in January 1702, for example, had cautioned William III about the attitude of Massachusetts and advised him to reform the colony's charter, but other things had distracted the king and he returned the matter to the Board for further consideration.[31]

Discussing the problem of disobedience, Chalmers talked about English rights, their origin, content, and defense, but not in a consistent manner. At appropriate times in the history he carefully emphasized that Americans, like Englishmen, received rights as a gift of government and that political developments in England from earliest times determined their nature. But in England the process of definition involved the king, Parliament, and the courts, and the struggle for definition was almost completely English in character. Contrarily, the colonial struggle for local rule when in violation of English law was illegitimate and a sign of political corruption, according to Chalmers. English efforts to insure colo-

30. Ibid., 1:29–30.
31. Ibid., 1: 307–8.

nial dependency, however, Chalmers called "reform." For example, the disturbances in Virginia, South Carolina, and New Hampshire during Charles II's reign were branded "seditions," and the opposition of Massachusetts was called "refractory." To explain this behavior in the colonies, Chalmers pointed to the conduct of English politicians who provided bad examples. They were radicals, republicans, troublemakers who threatened the balance of power reestablished by the Restoration. Chalmers thus approved of Charles II's cancellation of the Massachusetts charter, a measure, he said, which "necessity rendered just and precedents made legal. But Charles II lived not to complete the plan of reformation."[32]

Chalmers revealed his attitude toward British rights again in his discussion of William III's reign. While he approved the results of the 1689 revolution, his approval was based first upon the "necessity" and popular acceptance of the revolution, and second upon the benefits England won by changing monarchs. His explanation blended prevailing philosophies, particularly those of Thomas Hobbes and David Hume:

The constitution was at length replaced on the solid basis of the social rights of mankind, of the special privileges of Englishmen. The various powers, legislative and executive, of each component person to it, were now defined, at least, were afterwards understood, with an accuracy hitherto unknown. And, by asserting the authority of the whole over every dominion of the state, that interesting event left a signal example to posterity of the omnipotence of the sovereign legislature and of the just submission of the governed.[33]

While Chalmers accepted the 1689 revolution on the grounds of expediency because it had benefited Englishmen, he was uncomfortable supporting revolution. His position was confused, if not ambivalent, and depended on issues, events, and politics. In his

32. Ibid., 1: 173–74.
33. Ibid., 1: 200–1.

pamphlets attacking Burke and Abingdon, he had taken the dangerous position that government was "a single, simple, bond of interest, of utility, and nothing else, which binds government to the people and the people to government." It was a "complicated machine." In A *Vindication of the Privilege of the People* . . . he touched directly on the 1689 revolution:

I consider *the Revolution* as *glorious;* not because much was done; but little was done; because none of the *old foundations* of our government were weakened, and none of the land-marks of the law were removed. I think *the Revolution* ought to be deemed *glorious;* because it was achieved by the good sense of Englishmen; because the Parliament sat quietly, and voted independently, what necessity demanded, and wisdom approved; because, when a mob presumed to interpose with premature tumult, King William signified to the mobbish chiefs, that he would not accept a scepter from such mean hands.[34]

But he recognized the dangers of revolution when government was based on utility and hastened to qualify his position. The question of who makes the decision for revolution was all-important. Obviously the people should make the decision, but this was simplicity. They did not exist as a corporate body: "They are the subject of government; but no such aggregate body as the people is known as a part of government." The people, he contended, were dependent upon government for their welfare, but government was not guided by a constitution or by a body of stated rights, only by a legislature. Chalmers was indeed all-embracing in his support of governmental supremacy: "The penetrating De Lome says with truth, that the legislative power of a state can change the constitution, *as God created the light.* Where then is the impious politician who will venture to define the constitution?"[35]

34. Chalmers, *Second Thoughts*, pp. 59–60. Chalmers, A *Vindication of the Privilege of the People*, pp. 66–67.
35. Chalmers, *Second Thoughts*, pp. 62–63.

From these remarks one receives the impression that governmental power makes right policy, but this position in his pamphlets was much too bold for Chalmers the lawyer, who actually favored law, custom, and balances of authority in setting guides for popular rule. However, he never clarified what he considered right conduct to be. In his discussion of the Protectorate he admitted his dislike for absolute power and a standing army, but he saluted the restoration of Charles II in 1660. That salutation was particularly warm: "Nothing could give more universal joy than a train of events, which restored that monarch to the throne of his ancestors; because with the king, that constitution, which the wise had approved and the brave defended, was again happily reestablished and improved."[36] Here Chalmers's concept of the constitution seemed to include the king, lords, and commons, interacting with tradition, in the government of England. The idea of balance was implied, but when was a governmental action illegal?

His discussion of George I's reign gave him opportunity to describe instances of imbalance when royal power improperly used endangered liberty. In a long footnote he laid down two principles: "A British subject must necessarily be entitled to British privileges, wherever he may reside within the British dominions; a British subject owes obedience to British laws and consequently submission to British government." When imbalances occur and when outright illegality is committed, what can be done? At this point Chalmers was not ready to do anything, except to urge reason and reflection and to cite events of the past "to teach moderation to the politicians of the present day, in their treatment of each other."[37] In short, this explanation gives the justification for his history—it was an appeal to reason.

Reason was undoubtedly not the solution to the imperial prob-

36. Chalmers, *An Introduction to the History of the Revolt,* 1: 97.
37. Ibid., 2: 105–6, 106n.

lem. Chalmers himself had repeatedly observed that the colonies had not been loyal and that a reformation of their institutions was absolutely necessary to bring them into a proper relationship with the mother country, but he was not able to set the standards of loyalty so that institutions could be reformed. Although he cited sufficient examples of turbulence, of leveling principles, and of resistance to British instructions to show the attitude of the colonies, he had balanced their actions against the conduct of British administrators, even admitting that these politicians had not grown in wisdom to understand the colonial relationship. His ideas were particularly well stated in his evaluation of Jonathan Belcher's governorship of Massachusetts in the 1730s: "During the foregoing period of degradation, while the authority of the nation, the king, and the laws had been sacrificed to mistaken policy, the principles of the people no less than opportunity introduced every species of internal irregularity and of illicit traffic."[38]

This theme of disloyalty and British weakness runs through the history. Balancing his criticisms, he tried to be fair-minded, but he did not please either side as a result. He did not admit that the colonies had a right to self-government that would make them independent of Parliament. Their rights were British rights, to be dependencies and to live under law. The British were obliged to be reasonable, to promise happiness, order, and prosperity, and to guard against arbitrary government.

IV

Chalmers was unlike most other loyalists. He accepted exile and made a new life for himself in England. Joining thousands of Scottish emigrants in London, he exploited connections of earlier immigrants to win himself patronage and honors. His bid for a

38. Ibid., 2: 141.

position had a constraining influence on his freedom as a writer, for he was careful to consult his superiors and take their advice.

He was plainly not an old Whig.[39] With little reverence for John Locke, James Harrington, and Algernon Sidney, he rejected many of their theories and criticized their successors who had governed England from 1689 to 1760.[40] He was also not particularly warm toward the monarchs who had ruled Britain during these years. Still, he accepted the position of Parliament as the core of British liberty and believed in a constitutional relationship between government and the people.

If Chalmers was ever a Tory, it was in the sense of his great reverence for Britain itself, its traditions, laws, and institutions; for the government "machine" that had developed through centuries of responsible government; for guaranteed happiness and order that Englishmen enjoyed. Like David Hume he had interest neither in searching the past for a contract of government, nor in speculating upon natural rights, nor in working out constitutional relations. It was enough to have Parliament, the laws, and a tradition of good government.

This emphasis upon the structure of government should not obscure Chalmers's genuine interest in historical and archaeological material. He believed that the spirit of a country could best be known from its earliest laws and experiences. He liked to gather details of charters, customs, ways of living, and biography, and he apparently had a feeling for historical accuracy. His documents in the *History of Revolt* are a good representation of official corre-

39. Chalmers, *A Vindication of the Privilege of the People*, pp. 77–79. Chalmers separates himself from the new, or modern, Whigs, but claims that he sympathizes with the old Whigs. "The old whigs were against innovation in the constitution of our government: the new whigs are for innovation in it: the old whigs were for supporting the balance of power in Europe, as of great importance to the weight of England: the new whigs are against any balance of power: . . . the old whigs were *patrons* of *free* discussion:—the new whigs are *persecutors* of *free discussion*."
40. Ibid., pp. 19, 61.

spondence—letters of governors and reports of the Board of Trade. Comparing his summaries with originals reveals an excellent ability to grasp important ideas without losing meaning.

His dependence on documents, however, did not prevent him from lashing out at the Puritans. They were intolerant people, separatists, and republicans; when England was occupied, they took advantage of the opportunity to expand their governmental powers. In these ideas he was not much different from other loyalist writers, like Joseph Galloway and Peter Oliver, except that he did not labor the point. The Puritans were one group among many who were disobedient to the mother country. Indeed, he found widespread disloyalty among Americans, and in Massachusetts he thought disloyalty was engulfing the people. This position, of course, a Peter Oliver or a Thomas Hutchinson could not support; they considered themselves victims of a conspiracy.

Chalmers did not treat the question of conspiracy directly in the history. Since his narrative broke off in 1760, he was spared the necessity of explaining why Americans finally revolted. In his report to the Loyalist Claims Commission he had described the way a group of people took over the reins of government and how he had planned to resist their activities. But he had never claimed, as Galloway had, that only a small segment of the public had supported the rebellion.

By not telling the story of the actual rebellion, Chalmers's history loses some of its potential. The 1760s and 1770s were obviously the most important decades of the colonial period. Chalmers's work has value, nevertheless, as a contemporary appraisal of the imperial problem; it reveals the great difficulty Chalmers had in freeing himself from his Whig inheritance; it provides a contemporary, authentic treatment of colonial history. Finally, George Chalmers, of all the loyalists, seems able to stand off from the dispute and assess responsibility, not for one colony but for all of them, as well as for the home government.

4.

Joseph Galloway's *Historical and Political Reflections*

JOHN A. SCHUTZ

Joseph Galloway ranks among the half-dozen most prominent loyalists who left their native land at the time of the American Revolution for exile in England. Galloway's loyalism was as much a mystery to him as it was to associates like Benjamin Franklin, who begged him to remain in Pennsylvania. For Galloway, a politician of twenty years' experience, the events leading to the revolution had an unreal, diabolical nature that spread over and engulfed America.

Less than three months before Galloway left public life, he appraised Pennsylvania politics: "I am happy in telling you, that the people of this province are altering their sentiments and conduct with amazing rapidity."[1] The tense politics of 1773 and 1774 had disturbed him, but his position as speaker of the assembly seemed secure, his influence as a politician was great, and his hope for a bright future was high. In February 1775 he could not have predicted either his departure from the legislature that summer or the misery he would experience from public criticism in the fall and winter. The momentous events of 1775 shocked

1. Joseph Galloway to William Franklin, 28 February 1775, in William A. Whitehead et al., eds., *Documents Relating to the Colonial History of the State of New Jersey*, 1st. ser. (Newark, N.J., 1880–1944), 10: 572–75.

and numbed him, as they did many other American loyalists, and he tried to separate himself from them.[2]

His sharp reversal of fortune during 1775 is difficult to understand. How could a speaker of the assembly for nine years and a legislator for nineteen so misjudge the political situation? Galloway would deny that he had misinterpreted public affairs. He would insist that a small group of demagogues had engineered a coup. This turn of events, he would emphasize, was "unnatural" and unpredictable.[3]

Galloway's attitude may reflect the secluded life of his country seat "Trevose." There he found refuge from day-to-day politics by letting the routine tasks of cutting hedges, planting trees, and cultivating herbs deflect his thoughts from greater matters. Living in isolation from the city, he lost touch with the realities of Philadelphia politics and the deepening distrust of British policy. His seclusion was reinforced by his attitude toward Britain—the greatest of nations, the most ideal of governments, the most humane and advanced of monarchies. Confirmed in the belief that nothing could be done to improve Britain, he admired its stability, long history, responsible leadership, magnificent constitution; he believed that no person, using his rational senses, would dare overturn this artistic creation of centuries.[4] America's best interest was

2. *Pennsylvania Gazette*, 17 May 1775; Galloway's testimony before the Loyalist Claims Commission, 20 September 1783, Old Claims, Public Record Office, Audit Office (P.R.O., A.O.) 12, 1: 68–71; Oliver C. Kuntzleman, *Joseph Galloway: Loyalist* (Philadelphia, 1941), pp. 134–35; Thomas Balch, ed., *Examination of Joseph Galloway, Esqr., by a Committee of the House of Commons* (Philadelphia, 1855), p. 51; Galloway to William Franklin, 25 November 1775, American Philosophical Society.

3. [Joseph Galloway], *An Account of the Conduct of the War in the Middle Colonies* (London, 1780), pp. 7–8, 11; Joseph Galloway to Lord Dartmouth, 23 January 1778; Benjamin F. Stevens, *Facsimiles of Manuscripts in European Archives Relating to America* (London, 1889–98), No. 2078.

4. Galloway to Richard Jackson, 20 March 1777, in Stevens, *Facsimiles*, No. 2051.

union with Britain, either by membership in Parliament or by a constitutional association. Union with Britain was the key to America's future.

His reveries were occasionally broken by the "irrational outbursts" in Boston, Providence, and New York, but he and his party of merchants in Philadelphia kept under control the "illness" that had disturbed other cities. While uneasy at times, Galloway felt these bilious attacks could be overcome by a reconstruction of imperial government through colonial reform—but revolution was unthinkable. Even as he took refuge inside British lines in 1776, he brushed away thoughts that he was witnessing anything more than a conspiracy.[5]

I

Few Pennsylvanians suspected Galloway's depth of feeling for Britain, that even surpassed his love for his native America and his adopted colony of Pennsylvania. His long association with Benjamin Franklin, his years of assembly labor, and his huge estate seemed to be inextricable ties to the colony. Even as the crisis with Britain mounted, the assembly insisted upon sending him to the Second Continental Congress and only removed his name from the list of delegates when he demanded that his wishes be respected. Franklin tried to advise him, and his legislative rival, John Dickinson, urged him to reconsider his decision. But Galloway persisted in withdrawing from Pennsylvania politics, and his exile followed from that decision.

Mobs gathered around his home, some threatened to hang him, but even in this crisis of personal safety friends rallied to protect him. For nearly a year these friends sought to change his mind as

5. [Joseph Galloway], A *Candid Examination of the Mutual Claims of Great Britain* . . . (New York, 1775), p. 31.

well as to shield him from his angry countrymen. However, he published a pamphlet in 1775 which examined the respective claims of authority of Britain and America and which had considerable circulation. The pamphlet convinced many people that he unalterably opposed independence, and yet his position seemed incomprehensible to them. "I am a friend of true liberty," he wrote. "I esteem it above all other temporal blessings, and *because* I esteem it, I disapprove of the independent measures of the congress."[6] Still he admitted that the colonies had serious and legitimate grievances which deserved a hearing in London. The colonists' course of action in Philadelphia, however, was wrong, Galloway said, because they denied Britain just rights of loyalty and obedience. Americans would become a conquered people because they listened to demagogues.

Galloway rejected most criticism of king and Parliament. Americans were deluded by ambitious men and should look back at their conduct and see how it had been disrespectful and insulting to the most benevolent of kings. Galloway convinced himself that submission was the only true course, to be followed by a union of the colonies with Great Britain. His Quaker heritage and associations had undoubtedly given him these ideals of reason and peace; nonviolent methods were infinitely better than suffering bloodshed and a loss of freedom.

His friends could not change his ideas. Franklin was unable to penetrate his consciousness and explain to him that Britain's corruption would contaminate American institutions. Galloway was unwilling to grant that Englishmen were at fault in refusing to receive American petitions, that their motives were hostile, that George III was vindictive. A proper attitude toward authority, he insisted, would bring a benevolent royal response.

6. Ibid., p. 48.

II

Galloway's admiration for England was gained through lifelong reading, not through personal contact, for he first went to the mother country as an American Tory in October 1778. Born in 1731 to Peter and Elizabeth Rigbie Galloway, who owned estates in tidewater Maryland, Joseph spent his boyhood in various parts of Maryland and probably knew Galloway relatives who had married into prominent Philadelphia families like the Pembertons, Chews, and Shippens. After his father's death, Joseph moved to Philadelphia and studied law. During the five years after 1749 he gained important clients and qualified for practice in the colony's highest court. His contacts and wealth grew. In 1753 he married Grace Growden, the daughter of Lawrence Growden, whose many estates near Philadelphia she eventually inherited. Grace and Joseph lived in an impressive mansion on the corner of Sixth and Market Streets. They moved among wealthy people, bought a carriage, held memberships in influential social clubs, and entertained royally. They had one daughter, Elizabeth, the center of their attention, and a host of relatives who were often house guests. Joseph occupied himself with his expanding law practice, his Maryland estates, and provincial politics.[7] In his business dealings he was well regarded by the Philadelphia merchants, who marked him a good man for the assembly.

His opportunity came in October 1756, when prominent Quaker members withdrew from the assembly in a compromise move to bring the colony into firmer support of the French and

7. Galloway's testimony before Loyalist Claims Commission, P.R.O., A.O. 12, 1: 68–71; 3: 404–5. There are a few studies of Galloway's activities. The most recent are Julian P. Boyd, *Anglo-American Union: Joseph Galloway's Plans to Preserve the British Empire, 1774–1788* (Philadelphia, 1941); Oliver C. Kuntzleman, *Joseph Galloway: Loyalist*.

Indian War. The Quaker-dominated assembly had resisted war measures and been severely criticized by the British government, which had considered disenfranchising pacifists. To prevent parliamentary scrutiny and interference, Quaker leaders gave way to less scrupulous Pennsylvanians; Galloway, backed by Quaker relatives and friends, was chosen one of the new assemblymen.[8]

Supporting the war effort, Galloway joined Franklin's faction and urged new taxes on all estates, especially on those of the proprietors who had long claimed exemptions. Indian raids, he said, had cost the colony hundreds of lives and thousands of pounds; a new military policy would halt these depredations and eventually assure peace and savings. The tax bill met with hostility from the governor and the proprietary faction and was returned to the legislature for amendment. Meanwhile Franklin and his friends had pressed other war bills, and Galloway achieved recognition in this effort. His talent for committee work and debate brought him closer to Franklin, who exercised unusual power in the assembly and the city and who had taken Galloway as a protégé. In 1757, when Governor William Denny refused to sign the defense bills, the assembly sent Franklin to London to protest this interference, leaving the management of party affairs in Galloway's hands.[9]

In giving these responsibilities to the young lawyer Franklin paid tribute to his abilities. The antiproprietary party was fighting the governor and proprietary interest on a wide front. Not only were defense policies perennial issues, but there were the problems of proprietary property taxation, Indian trade regulation, and legislative privilege. In managing the debates, Galloway showed his leadership, particularly in a contest against a critic of the assembly, Justice of the Peace William Moore. Charges were pressed against

8. Leonard W. Labaree et al., eds., *The Papers of Benjamin Franklin*, 15 vols. (New Haven and London, 1959—), 7: 29–30.
9. Benjamin Franklin to Galloway, 11 April 1757, ibid., 7: 179n.9.

Moore in early 1757, but proceedings dragged into the October elections and were not concluded until the next January. Galloway relentlessly pursued Moore; before he had secured his imprisonment, he also had Rev. Mr. William Smith before the assembly on charges of aiding Moore. Both defendants mobilized local support, but Galloway succeeded in having heavy penalties imposed on them. In time, Moore even lost his post as justice of the peace. The issue of legislative privilege was eventually heard in the Pennsylvania courts and the Privy Council in London. In both hearings the assembly lost its case and received much criticism for its ruthless disregard of human rights. Chief Justice William Allen of Pennsylvania, who was a partisan, accused Galloway and the party of being "violent & ignorant men," who claimed powers for the assembly that surpassed those of the House of Commons.[10]

But the assembly, despite its claims to power, remained unable to tax the proprietors' lands, and for Galloway this unjust restriction of its powers was a source of irritation. The eastern part of the colony bore the expense of war, often reluctantly, leaving the frontier without adequate money to maintain the forts. Each year the assembly tried to tax proprietary lands, and when the governor rejected the measures, used the occasion as an excuse for neglecting the frontier. This dangerous game continued as long as British troops garrisoned the frontier and became one basis for criticism of the Penn family.

The strategy helped Galloway and his associates to win annual reelection and bring calm to politics. Over the years, they avoided the risks of new policies, assured that the governor would veto their measures. Galloway became the most active member of the party and, except for Isaac Norris who was old and sick, was held next to Franklin in esteem. The calm in politics under Galloway

10. Theodore Thayer, *Pennsylvania Politics and the Growth of Democracy, 1740–1776* (Harrisburg, 1953), pp. 68–69; William Allen to Thomas Penn, Penn MSS, Official Correspondence, 9: 7, Pennsylvania Historical Society.

worried his opposition, who expected a shift of policy tactics upon Franklin's return to Philadelphia.[11]

But the calm was broken earlier than expected. When frontier Indian disturbances frightened the colony, the governor called the assembly into session, and together they responded to the immediate crisis. In September, the governor urged additional measures, and the assembly offered to raise funds through an issue of paper money. The governor objected, and the impasse delayed defense appropriations until after the October elections.[12]

When the new assembly met in December, Franklin was a member and John Penn was governor. Franklin backed a vigorous policy against the Indians, and with Galloway he urged taxation of proprietary lands. Their negotiations to secure Penn's consent continued well into 1764, resulting eventually in a compromise which taxed proprietary lands at the lowest rate of the poorest private lands. This did not end political bickering; Franklin and Galloway then insisted upon a new militia law, which would decentralize control and weaken proprietary power. They found not only an issue that the governor would fight, but also a critical one.

Hot heads in frontier areas, angered at the Indians, took revenge on domesticated Indians at Conestoga, near Lancaster. The murder of twenty Indians there led to fear of retaliation by the Six Nations. Anger and fear combined when the assembly ordered some peaceful Indians taken for protection to Philadelphia and the white murderers apprehended: how could the assembly favor Indians, many whites asked, when they ravaged the frontier? Some wild folk, known as the Paxton Boys, raised a force and threatened to kill the Indians held in Philadelphia, capture legislative leaders, and rule the city. The peril of the uprising caused panic. Many people were aroused, and men volunteered for military duty; but

11. Thayer, *Pennsylvania Politics*, pp. 78–79.
12. Ibid., pp. 81–82.

others, supporting the Paxton Boys, ridiculed the Quakers' pacifism and "love of Indians" and exploited the crisis for political gain.[13]

Franklin and Galloway condemned the proprietary government for creating the deadlock and urged establishment of a royal government. While his opposition to the Penns was not new, the violence at Conestoga convinced Galloway of the need for military force under royal officers to maintain law and order. He feared anarchy, but he worried too about a coup of Presbyterians and radicals who might seize power. In another crisis the city might not escape armed bands like the Paxtons. Galloway's critics, less afraid of anarchy, accused him of wanting a royal colony in order to make Franklin the colony's governor and himself its chief justice.[14]

This prolonged debate over civil peace and proprietary government, joined by other issues, caused an extremely bitter election battle in 1764. Pamphlets, broadsides, cartoons, and published speeches advertised the issues. Galloway, Franklin, and John Hughes were opposed by William Allen, John Dickinson, and Thomas Willing. Galloway argued boldly for royal government and traded diatribes with Dickinson. Galloway revealed an emotional attachment for the Crown which, he said, had no "private interest" to protect, had limits to its power, and inspired cooperation and unity. In Pennsylvania, he said, the proprietors have "so check'd and controled" the legislature that it was "almost annihilated. The Courts of Judicature are so dependent on Proprietary Influence, that wherever Proprietary Interest is in Question, the Stream of Justice becomes so turbid and thick, that it can no longer discharge its Duty, Security of Life and Estate is become an

13. Brooke Hindle, "The March of the Paxton Boys," *The William and Mary Quarterly*, 3rd Series, 3 (1946): 461–86; Franklin to Richard Jackson, 11 February 1764, in Labaree et al., *Franklin Papers*, 9: 67–78.

14. [Joseph Galloway], *The Speech of Joseph Galloway, Esqr.* . . . (Philadelphia, 1764), pp. 2–3; Joseph Galloway, "Americanus," *Pennsylvania Journal*, 29 August 1765.

empty Name, and the Spirit of Liberty, distrest and worn out, by ineffectual Efforts for her Preservation, is verging fast upon Dissolution. Nothing but a Royal Medicine . . . can possibly revive or restore her."[15]

The heat of this debate led John Dickinson to challenge Galloway to a duel. The assembly voted overwhelmingly, nonetheless, for royal government as the legislators took the issue to the electors in a very bitter campaign. On election day, large crowds turned out in Philadelphia and by a narrow vote unseated Franklin and Galloway, though elsewhere enough of their followers were returned to office to control the new assembly. They decided immediately to turn this attack on their leadership into a victory by sending Franklin to London with a petition urging the establishment of royal government.[16]

The debate over local issues deflected public attention momentarily from British measures to tax the colonies. Though the *Pennsylvania Journal* predicted the "serious consequences" of a stamp levy, threats of mob rule and continued proprietary government so concerned Galloway that he gave little thought to what harm the Crown might do to American liberty. Indeed, he thought of the king and Parliament as saviors who could use the tax money to assure law and order in the colony. In London, Franklin also saw nothing dangerous in the Stamp Act and nominated an important member of his party, John Hughes, as local stamp distributor.[17]

News of Hughes's appointment broke just as the colony became aware of the constitutional issue and the rising anger in other colonies. The press denounced both Franklin and Hughes and accused Galloway of trying to control public opinion. Galloway undoubtedly tried to block participation in a congress of the

15. Galloway, *The Speech of Joseph Galloway*, pp. 44–45.
16. Labaree et al., *Franklin Papers*, 11: 402n.6, 407–8.
17. Ibid., 12: 234–35n.2.

colonies at New York, and the newspapers exposed his efforts.[18] The notoriety, however, did not injure his chances to return to the assembly in September 1765.

During this crisis over British taxation, Galloway defended the Stamp Act in the newspapers, organized a force of nearly 800 men to protect Hughes and Mrs. Franklin, and helped moderate hostile action against Hughes. Like distributors in other colonies, Hughes was pressed to resign his commission. While he resisted the harassment, he assured the opposition that he would not distribute stamps unless the people requested him to do so. Both he and Galloway blamed the proprietary government for this outbreak of disloyalty to Britain; both blamed the Presbyterians for the disturbances. Galloway noted that the Presbyterians were using the turmoil "as a favorable opportunity" for establishing republican institutions. In his letters and newspaper articles, Galloway admitted the need for British taxes, emphasized that the results of the Seven Years War justified them, and urged obedience to Britain. He conceded, however, the emotional issue over the rights of taxation and proposed a legislative union as one solution to it. He was deeply loyal to Britain, even more deeply suspicious of disorder, and was willing to make concessions in order to restore peace. When the Stamp Act was repealed in 1766, he urged Philadelphians to adopt a sober, dignified attitude and authored the legislative address of 6 June which humbly expressed the province's appreciation.[19]

The address irritated some city radicals who, in a broadside,

18. Galloway to Franklin, 16 November 1765, American Philosophical Society.

19. Benjamin H. Newcomb, "Effects of the Stamp Act on Colonial Pennsylvania Politics," *The William and Mary Quarterly*, 3rd Series, 12 (1966): 257–72; Labaree et al., *Franklin Papers*, 12: 290n.4, 305; Galloway to Franklin, 13 January 1766, 23 May 1766, in Jared Sparks, ed., *The Works of Benjamin Franklin* (Boston, 1840), 7:303, 317–18; *Votes and Proceedings of the House of Representatives* . . . , Series 8 (Harrisburg, 1931–35), 7:5884.

urged his defeat in the October elections and his replacement by John Dickinson. It denounced him as an enemy of the people whom he "slandered, vilified, and traduced" and as an unstable leader whose antics in the assembly disgusted men of dignity and sense. This harsh and personal attack apparently rallied his supporters, and Galloway was returned to the assembly with an impressive vote and chosen by a majority of one as its speaker. His opposition, however, limited his power to appoint committees. In 1767, when he was unanimously elected speaker, the privilege of appointing committeemen was restored to his office; he was also permitted to regulate debate in the assembly.[20]

The Quaker party thus fully controlled Pennsylvania politics in 1767, and Galloway, seeking to widen the base of control, established the *Pennsylvania Chronicle* and enticed William Goddard of Rhode Island to become editor and partner. For a time Galloway and Thomas Wharton, his financial partner in the venture, controlled the editorial policy. Then Goddard launched forth on his own by publishing Dickinson's "Letters from a Farmer in Pennsylvania," which reflected radical views on taxation and resistance.

In Galloway's mind, Dickinson's opposition to British authority branded him a dangerous man because he encouraged mob activity and aroused emotion. Galloway wanted, instead, an accommodation with Great Britain—union in Parliament, the end of proprietary government, and a reduction of lawlessness in Pennsylvania. The new turbulence in 1767 and 1768, caused by enforcement of the Townshend duties, disturbed him as much as the protest over the Stamp Act, but he and his Quaker party counseled moderation, refused to be associated with the nonimportation agree-

20. *Votes and Proceedings of the House of Representatives*, 7:5938; Kuntzleman, *Joseph Galloway: Loyalist*, pp. 71–72.

ments, and resisted the popular clamor for an official protest to Parliament.[21]

The publication of Dickinson's letters by his own newspaper particularly stung Galloway, especially when they increased Dickinson's prestige throughout America and made him an unbeatable rival for Galloway's assembly seat. He tried to pressure Goddard, but the editor vented their quarrel in the *Pennsylvania Chronicle* and damaged Galloway's reputation with the city tradesmen. These bitter newspaper articles finally drove Galloway in 1770 to shift his political base from Philadelphia to Bucks County and to ponder retirement from politics. His attitude may have been reinforced by assembly politics, for his move to Bucks County gave Dickinson a chance to enter the assembly and an opportunity to organize opposition to the Speaker.[22]

Galloway's personal difficulties mirrored those of the Quaker party, which divided over a course of action to protest the Townshend duties. Some merchants bitterly opposed a nonimportation agreement because of its effect on their businesses. Most reacted to pressure from the mechanics who held public meetings and moved to turn back English ships. Galloway admitted that the party had lost the support of the mechanics and had weakened the loyalty of others, but he hoped that the hostility would soon dissipate as men recovered their reason. The opposition's effectiveness was brought home to him in 1772 when his friends were turned out of most of their assembly seats in the city and county of Philadelphia and when the press carried cartoons and criticisms that damaged his political image. The ever-antagonistic Goddard, in

21. John Dickinson to Richard Henry Lee, 22 June 1769, in *Memoirs of the Life of Richard Henry Lee and his Correspondence* (Philadelphia, 1825), p. 77.

22. David L. Jacobson, *John Dickinson and the Revolution in Pennsylvania, 1764–1776* (Berkeley and Los Angeles, 1965), pp. 65–67; *Votes and Proceedings of the House of Representatives*, 7:6583.

spite of court action and imprisonment, published additional slanders in the *Pennsylvania Chronicle*. Galloway's friends thought he could not endure the bitterness, but he kept control of the party, maintained his position as speaker, and entertained frequently enough at Trevose and at Greenwich Hall to make his presence felt among the politicians. Though worried about the personal attacks, he managed the assembly with a firm hand—a fact recognized even by his antagonists.[23]

But politics moved swiftly during these unstable times. When Britain passed the Tea Act and the East India Company commissioned agents to handle the tea, a new contest of strength began. The Philadelphia agents were compelled to resign, and one vessel with tea was forced to sail back to England. When Britain attempted to punish Boston for dumping its tea, some mechanics and merchants organized resistance in Philadelphia and put the colony behind a movement to hold an American congress. Fully aware of Galloway's power and the merchants' fear of radicalism, they called a convention of Pennsylvanians to apply pressure on them. The people responded favorably, and the convention, in which seventy-five delegates were present, voted to ask the assembly to send delegates to the Congress. In the meantime, the governor had convened the assembly, and the members quickly acted on the suggestion but chose delegates only from their own body and, except for John Dickinson who was later added to the delegation, picked moderates, including Galloway. Galloway apparently wrote the instructions which set the tone of the Pennsylvania protest. His own description of his attitude and actions during these critical days reveals his caution, hesitation, and apprehension:

23. *Pennsylvania Chronicle*, 26 September 1772. Dickinson retired from the assembly in 1771 and did not return until 1774. See Thayer, *Pennsylvania Politics*, pp. 150–51.

I went into Congress at the earnest solicitation of the Assembly of Pennsylvania—I refused to go, unless they would send with me, as the rule of my conduct, instructions agreeable to my mind;—they suffered me to draw up those instructions;—they were briefly, to state the rights and the grievances of America, and to propose a plan of amicable accommodation of the differences between Great Britain and the Colonies, and of a perpetual union; I speak now from the records of Pennsylvania, where the instructions are. Upon this ground, and with a heart full of loyalty to my Sovereign, I went into Congress—and from that loyalty I never deviated in the least.[24]

In making these plans for the Congress, Galloway and his Quaker supporters kept politics moderate—at least they kept the radicals from seizing control of the delegation.[25] The situation changed, however, when the Continental Congress convened in early September as arriving delegates fell under the influence of local radicals. Galloway suffered defeat in two strategic moves. He offered the State House for the meeting place, but the Congress selected Carpenters' Hall, a symbol of radicalism. The delegates then elected Charles Thomson, an opposition leader, to be secretary, thus giving radicals in the city an official position in the Congress.

These defeats put Galloway momentarily on the defensive, but he counted heavily on the support of South Carolina's delegates, who feared nonimportation, and on others who wanted to avoid antagonizing Great Britain. After a few days he noted that the members divided into two factions—one composed of men of property and principles and the other of debtors and republicans. The division among the delegates created suspicions and cliques,

24. *Votes and Proceedings of the House of Representatives,* 8:7100; [Galloway], *Examination of Joseph Galloway . . . Before the House of Commons,* pp. 47–48.
25. Galloway to Committee of Correspondence, 30 May 1774, Pennsylvania Historical Society.

and as a precaution Galloway kept his own opinions or confided them to a group of friends who shared some of his objectives. Anticipating the work of the Congress, Galloway had developed a plan of union and had the Pennsylvania assembly instruct its delegates to back colonial union. He had published a pamphlet, too, which analyzed the points in contention between the colonies and Great Britain. The pamphlet was withheld from general circulation when he became uncertain of congressional reaction. But on 28 September he presented his plan of union.

There are two versions of his speech before the Congress—one in Galloway's *Historical and Political Reflections* and the other in John Adams's notes. Undoubtedly the Adams version represents a more accurate statement—it was contemporary, while Galloway published his version six years later for a British audience. The Adams version was sharper in its attack on parliamentary taxation, more forceful in its use of words: "I am as much a friend of liberty as exists; no man shall go further in point of fortune, or in point of blood, than the man who now addresses you." Or as Galloway remembered these words: "desirous as I am to promote the freedom of the Colonies . . . I must intreat you to desert the Measures which have been so injudiciously and ineffectually pursued by antecedent assemblies."[26] Whatever his words, Galloway was regarded as a "sensible" speaker, sometimes using emotional expressions to convey his thoughts, but discreet in what he had to say. He had a positive personality—he could inspire support as well as raise opposition.

His plan of union was based primarily on the existing colonial system. The colonies would retain their present organization as royal or charter governments and would select delegates every

26. Galloway's speeches, 8 September and 28 September 1774, in *The Adams Papers: Diary & Autobiography*, 4 vols. (New York, 1964), 2:129–30, 141–42; Galloway, *Historical and Political Reflections on the Rise and Progress of the American Rebellion* (London, 1780), p. 79.

three years for an American legislature, a Grand Council. The Council would meet annually, or more frequently in emergencies, and have all the rights and privileges of the House of Commons. It would deal with all problems of defense, commerce, law enforcement, and administration that concerned two or more colonies. A governor general would head the administration and serve at the pleasure of the king, with power to veto bills and carry out the wishes of the Grand Council. Before bills could become law, however, action was required by Parliament. Indeed, bills could originate in either legislature, but passage by both was essential.[27]

Galloway had many reservations about his plan. It contained too many political and philosophical concessions for a permanent form of government and was offered in the spirit of compromise. Plainly an emergency proposal, it was offered as a first step in a general reformation of American institutions. He conceded later that basic reforms of colonial government were necessary before anything permanent was established. He wanted to see provisions for a balance of royal, aristocratic, and popular authority, a reformation of the Presbyterian church which he considered too republican in its philosophy, and the imposition of franchise restrictions so that only men of weight would qualify for the legislature.[28]

His plan had the backing of James Duane and John Jay of New York and Edward Rutledge of South Carolina; it inspired a spirited debate. Galloway spoke a second time at the end of the debate, urging the need for an immediate union of the colonies. "Our Legislative Powers extend no farther than the Limits of our Government. Where then shall it be placed. There is a Necessity that an American Legislature should be set up, or else that We should give the Power to Parliament or King." His plea brought forth considerable support but lost by one vote. The triumphant

27. The Plan is republished in Boyd's *Anglo-American Union,* pp. 112–14.
28. Galloway to Richard Jackson, 20 March 1777, Stevens, *Facsimiles,* No. 2051.

majority then had this dangerous suggestion of compromise and accommodation with Great Britain expunged from the minutes.

By the time Congress adjourned on October 26, the members had done many of the things Galloway feared. They had adopted a policy of nonimportation and nonexportation, approved the Massachusetts protest, and issued a statement of American rights. In short, they continued the aggravation of Britain begun at Boston in 1773; to Galloway they seemed to be "pushing on with precipitation and madness, in the high road of sedition and rebellion." He was angry over such irresponsible policies and decided to publish a pamphlet condemning them and take his arguments to the floor of the Pennsylvania assembly. Depending on the conservative merchants and politicians, he hoped to halt this reckless rush to destruction: "I spoke my Sentiments [to the Assembly] . . . without the least reserve. I censured & condemned the Measures of the Congress in every Thing—aver'd that they all intended to incite America to Sedition & terminate in Independence. . . . I stood single & unsupported, among a Set of Men every one of whom had approved of the Measures I was censuring. . . . The Opposition as I expected was violent & indecent. I kept my Temper unruffled & firm which gave me no small Advantage."[29]

His firmness was partly rewarded. The Pennsylvania assembly permitted him to continue debate on a proposal that the colony send a separate petition to the king. He hoped to detach Pennsylvania from the other colonies and to recover some of the ground he had lost in the Congress. While the petition was being written, false news from England gave the impression that the king had approved of the Congress and would consider its petition. In the turmoil that followed, Galloway's majority crumbled and the

29. [Galloway], *Candid Examination*, p. 2; Galloway to William Franklin, 28 February 1775, New Jersey Archives, Series 1, 10:573–74.

assembly supported Congress's petition. The bitter debate brought an exchange of pamphlets between Galloway and Dickinson, in which Galloway accused his opponent of being depraved, destitute of honor, and lacking in common sense. Dickinson replied in equally intemperate language. In defeat Galloway was angry, bitter, and stubborn, convinced that he should retire from politics rather than associate longer with unreasonable men. Since the winter session he had insisted that he would not serve again in the Congress and, despite private pleas from friends to change his mind, he prevailed on the assembly to remove his name from the delegation. From this time in May 1775 he came repeatedly under attack in the newspapers. He would soon find it necessary to abandon his place in the assembly.[30]

III

At Trevose he lived in semiretirement, hoping that he could escape further involvement in political discussion. But he had been in politics too long, was too prominent, and was too concerned about the approaching disaster that seemed to be pushing the colonies to the "brink of a precipice." He and his wife now entertained more than they had for many years past, and he had grown "fat and . . . hearty." They had house guests, so many that he had "Company every Day" for weeks, but his conversations with them only heightened his apprehension over the state of the colonies.[31] He criticized Dickinson, who shared his own conservative ideas, for approving the measures of the Continental Congress and its declaration of colonial rights. Whoever heard of

30. Galloway to William Franklin, 28 February and 26 March 1775, in New Jersey Archives, 10:572, 575, 579–86; Mrs. Theodore M. Etting, ed., "Some Letters of Joseph Galloway," *Pennsylvania Magazine of History and Biography* 21 (1897): 480–84.
31. Ibid., p. 484; Galloway to William Franklin, 25 November 1775, American Philosophical Society.

natural rights being the basis of anything, he asked friends? Englishmen receive their rights as members of the greatest of empires.

Politics grew increasingly more inflammatory, disturbing even his onetime opponent John Dickinson, who became worried about violence and the debility of colonial institutions as the movement toward independence took hold. Dickinson would fight for colonial freedom, but he hoped for reconciliation with Great Britain and the continuation of Pennsylvania's charter government. Events moved so rapidly, however, that he could not keep up with them. He could not understand the radicalism of the new men and decided to withdraw from the militia in September 1776. Two months later he left his political office.

As Dickinson retired to his estate in Delaware, Galloway escaped to British lines in New York City, thoroughly frightened by rabble bands who had harassed him at Trevose. Though his wife would remain at Trevose to look after their estates, Galloway now offered General Sir William Howe his services in what he thought would be a rapid suppression of violence.

In the safety of New York he pondered what was happening to America and offered one of his early analyses of the revolution. Its seeds, he wrote Richard Jackson,

have been planted in very different soils, and yet in their Qualities, have concur'd to promote the same End. . . . Some of them have been long planted, long in vegetation, and would, in a few Years, have arrived at a dangerous Maturity. They have been, notwithstanding, concealed in Religious Principles—in political Tenets—in various Forms of the American government . . . —in the too great Independence of the officers of the Crown on the Crown and their dependence on popular Favor—in the want of civil Discipline and an almost total Relaxation in the administration of the Laws—in that want of Respect for the Supreme authority of the State and its Representatives upon which all Obedience and Loyalty are founded—and in a too great Inattention in government . . . to extend . . . those Principles of

Policy that alone ever have or can bind the Members of a free Society together.

The plan he had presented to the Continental Congress was plainly inadequate to meet these fundamental causes of revolution, because it compromised with evils in American life. Now that the colonies had actually revolted, he felt Parliament should not bargain with them and should ascertain instead the bases for a permanent settlement and impose the plan as a condition of reunion. He emphasized the need for a "permanent" form of government, as if balances of power could be found, a structure devised, and a system of dependency worked out.[32]

As the months of 1777 passed, Galloway was convinced that the rebellion was "in its last languishing stage, and in another year must be ended provided vigorous and proper measures are pursued." General Howe had taken Philadelphia and had invited him to accompany the expedition as an adviser. His advice, however, was not heard at some critical times, and Galloway felt that the war was prolonged as a result. In his role of adviser he was commissioned colonel of some loyalist American troops and permitted to engage in a few raids on enemy strongholds in the countryside; but when he planned a daring raid on Trenton where the New Jersey governor and legislature were sitting, he was refused permission. The general gave him, however, a freer hand in the management of Philadelphia's police and port facilities.[33]

He imposed price controls, regulations for cutting firewood, standards of sanitation, and a curfew. Much of what he did encouraged criticism for the occupation and himself, but he labored unselfishly to help the poor, reduce irritations, and mobilize Tories for military service. He was badgered by the revolu-

32. Galloway to Richard Jackson, 20 March and 28 March 1777, Stevens, *Facsimiles*, Nos. 2051, 2055.
33. Galloway to Lord Dartmouth, 3 December 1777; *Pennsylvania Evening Post*, 4 December 1777, in Stevens, *Facsimiles*, Nos. 2069, 2075.

tionary press for doing the dirty work of the military occupation, and he was warned that he would be allowed to wear himself out in this work and then be cast aside. Galloway had that feeling, too, for he accused his military superiors of bungling their opportunity for easy conquest. He urged the arming of Tories, the employment of more British troops, the commencement of military operations early in the season, and direct attacks on Washington's army to bring a quick end to the war.[34]

When he heard that the British army was going to evacuate Philadelphia, he was shocked. He feared for the safety of his wife who was still living at Trevose, for their daughter, and for their estates. In desperation he tried to convince British officers that in the city and countryside nine-tenths of the people were Tories and that ten thousand men could easily be raised for a loyalist army if only the British would release the arms. Placing his arguments before General Howe and Lord Dartmouth, he revealed his great anxiety for the loyalist cause, but he was advised by Howe to make peace with the rebels or prepare to face exile. His feelings were naturally bitter, particularly toward the rebels and the British army, and he decided his only alternative was a personal confrontation with the authorities in London. In the last weeks of his stay in New York, he wrote these sentiments to his wife:

In the present Situation of our Affairs every Friend we have advises me immediately to go for England. I am sure I need not tell you that this involves me in great Distress not only on your Account but that of our dear and only Child. The thought of leaving you in your present State, destitute of Friends, and among my Enemies, is at Times more than I can well Support myself under, especially when I reflect it is not in my power to relieve you. And the necessity I find myself under of taking our dear Child with me and of carrying her farther from you, with the reflection that this will add to your Distress gives me still greater Pain. I wish I knew how to avoid it. It was at first my resolu-

34. Galloway to Lord Dartmouth, 24 March 1778, ibid., No. 2098.

tion to leave her. It was also my inclination to stay. But with whom. Could I leave her in a Strange Place destitute of either father or mother. . . . Everyone here thinks of nobody but themselves; and friendship is not to be found. . . . Can you my dearest . . . bear the double stroke of parting with us both for a Time—I hope not longer than the Spring when we shall either return to you or you will come to us. . . . If the Congress will not treat, I have every reason to believe the War will be carried on with Vigor and Spirit—I feel much for my Country and fear its Distress is not yet half felt.[35]

Except for this absence from his wife, Galloway found British life exciting. He and Betty visited relatives and traveled to historic places; then they settled down in a rented flat near the governmental offices. "We wait with great anxiety for Events on your Side of the Water," he wrote his wife in 1779. "Should they prove favorable we shall lose no Time in coming over to you—if otherwise and no hope shd remain, you will undoubtedly come over to us, that we may spend the Short remains of Life together, which will be to me the greatest of all Temporal Blessings."[36]

Though the reality of their separation was ever in his thoughts, Galloway kept himself unusually occupied. He regularly met with fellow loyalists like former Massachusetts governor Thomas Hutchinson, had frequent dinners with members of the aristocracy, and often issued pamphlets on British policy. Soon after his arrival, however, he attacked General Howe. His first assault appeared in the *London Chronicle,* but he reserved his most telling evidence for an appearance before Parliament when it inquired into American military affairs. On two occasions he accused the general of being incompetent, a blunderer, and a liar, and aroused not only Howe but the general's friends. But the investigation of Howe's conduct was much too damaging for the military, which

35. George Galloway to Grace Galloway, September 1778, Galloway Papers, Library of Congress.
36. George Galloway to Grace Galloway, 2 April 1779, Galloway Papers, Library of Congress.

forced an end to the hearings. Galloway again took his attack to
the newspapers, though at the risk of being considered controversial by the government and the Tories. In repeating his charges,
he was obviously counting upon the protection of powerful ministers who benefited from Howe's embarrassment. He was, nonetheless, morbidly serious, insisting that few Americans were rebels and
a majority of them would welcome the destruction of Washington's ragged army and an offer of union.

Galloway's other preoccupation was the formulation of a new
plan for British-American union. He drastically amended his 1774
plan of union—so drastically that he removed most of the concessions which he felt necessary for colonial acceptance. Now his plan
would be imposed upon the colonies and would carry out the
necessary structural changes in American government that would
permit a permanent union. He increased the Crown's powers by
making most local officials appointive at the Crown's pleasure, by
turning all colonies into royal governments, by putting the calling
and proroguing of the legislature in the president general, and by
creating a second legislative house whose members would have life
tenure.[37] In his explanation, Galloway stressed the balances of
Crown, aristocracy, and democracy, and the reservation to the
British government of imperial affairs. Those peculiarly American
would be managed by an American legislature whose powers were
to be checked to insure dependency.

In 1780 and 1781, while Galloway again modified his plans for
union, he issued pamphlets which reviewed the causes of the
revolution, the inept military conduct of the war, and the principles
of sovereignty and empire. His most imposing work was the
*Historical and Political Reflections on the Rise and Progress of
the American Rebellion.*

37. Boyd, *Anglo-American Union*, pp. 115–26.

IV

Like most Tory pamphleteers, Galloway believed that the war was a conspiracy of a few individuals—certainly no more than a tenth to a sixth of the total population—and that this minority, using trickery and compulsion, dominated the overwhelming majority of Americans. By holding legislative positions, controlling the press, and using mobs, they appeared to possess far more strength than they actually had. They exploited the naturally retiring character of loyalists and, in times of crisis, moved aggressively to attain their objectives.

But Galloway also felt that all Americans were naturally inclined toward disobedience and disloyalty because of their development as a people. From earliest times they were subjected to republican ideology. The Calvinist religion, based upon republican principles, spread disloyalty to the Crown and organized public opinion in the form of a conspiracy. Some republicans organized mob protests and others joined with smugglers to undermine the law, resulting in a diminished sense of loyalty. The protest against the Stamp Act united republicans in England and America, and both conspired to keep the home government from imposing corrective measures on the colonies. But American institutions were always imperfect because they had never infused royal and aristocratic power with republican. At their founding nothing was done to establish proper principles, and Americans lived under governments which lacked precautions against radicalism. This danger was not fully realized so long as the colonies were threatened by French Canada, but when Britain drove France from North America in 1763, the colonies were free to go their own way. Soon thereafter nascent radicalism appeared in the Stamp Act protest, then in the organization of Presbyterian synods, and later in a new type of colonial leader.

The development of radicalism astonished Galloway because it seemed to him without cause. Britain had always treated the colonies benevolently, and they had, in turn, always acknowledged British rule as beneficial. Britain had saved them from suffering in the Seven Years War and had paid the wartime costs of military operations. Even when the colonies had to bear the burden of their own defense, Britain searched for a painless way of raising money. Both the Stamp Act and the Townshend duties were equitable levies—in fact, Galloway believed that "no law within the compass of human wisdom could be found more just and adequate to its purpose" than the Stamp Act, and he praised the Tea Act not only because it cut the price of tea by fifty percent, but also because it was reasonable. In short, Galloway could find nothing seriously wrong with British-colonial relations and noted, in addition, that George III reigned "without one act of oppression or injustice."[38] If anything, the king was too solicitous, too benevolent, and too hesitant to do Americans harm. This state of affairs the colonists had universally recognized, and most of them even in 1775 were content to be his loyal subjects. In 1780, most Americans still wished peace with Britain instead of the perils of military rule by a ruthless American faction.

Galloway's regard for British rule was reflected in his attitude toward human rights. These were primarily guaranteed by representative institutions, but they were vested in the will of the legislature and in the structure of government. Rights derived from one's relationship with others, one's dependence upon the Crown, and one's submergence in a British way of life. The Crown, Parliament, and church were fountains of justice, and drinking at the fountains secured one's happiness. In less figurative language, Galloway emphasized the need for total control by the "supreme legislative authority over every member and part of a society, in

<hr />

38. Galloway, *Historical and Political Reflections*, pp. 12, 17–18, 111–12.

respect to every matter susceptible of human direction, [as an]
. . . essential in the constitution of all states." Rights were attained, therefore, by total submergence, loyalty, and obedience,
and were not attached to the individual nor derived from nature.
But the essence of freedom, he emphasized, was representation in
the supreme legislature.[39] Without this voice in lawmaking, the
government would become despotic.

The form of government thus gave content to freedom—much
more important than popular education and wealth in assuring
stability. Galloway believed, moreover, that the state became
healthy through proper balances of power and that when these
balances were disturbed, the state became sick. Instability (in the
form of change and innovation) was serious because it threatened
vested rights—the established rights of Crown, aristocracy, and
people. Any change in balances created uncertainties and led to
injustices.

This fear of change was reflected in Galloway's other ideas
about government. He clung to the ancient belief of unstable
institutions and circular change. Governments followed a predict-
able pattern of evolution, but mixing the pure forms could retard
indefinitely the rate of instability. The British mixture seemed
ideal, for the great blessings of peace and prosperity were enjoyed
more abundantly in England than anywhere else in the world. All
this was sacrificed in America by mob rule, republicanism, and
independency. He was unwilling to grant that America could have
a better destiny as an independent nation than it enjoyed as a
British dependency.

This lack of appreciation for reform was a basic aspect of his
thought. Since Britain had reached a state of perfection, the only
course for America to follow was to unite with it.[40] He was appar-

39. Ibid., pp. 122, 125–26.
40. Ibid., pp. 131–32.

ently not aware of the many significant changes that had taken place in British life in the century since the Puritan Revolution. Though aware of the religious nature of that revolution, the turbulence of the Civil War, and the politics of the Restoration, he did not think that they changed the basic structure of society, but only prevented for a time the course of British politics. The revolution of the 1640s was regrettable, a source of present republicanism, and a pernicious evil to be avoided at all costs.

Galloway's knowledge of these events was not very deep. He had not read much history and the little he had read was not helpful in understanding English life. He quoted from Thomas Hutchinson's *History of Massachusetts Bay*, was familiar with Roman politics, and may have seen Edward Gibbon's work, but institutions as growing things did not impress him. He had little feeling for jurisprudence or the common law, even though he had read Locke, Grotius, Puffendorf, and Burlamaqui. His work showed little interest in literature and was less sophisticated than the writings of John Adams, Benjamin Rush, or Thomas Jefferson. Still, he was rarely intemperate, and his works indicated analysis of problems, much reflection, and a knowledge of government organization.

Galloway was utterly loyal to king and Parliament—indeed more British than a native Englishman, and he believed firmly in the goodness of Britain. Britain and America united insured the greatness of the empire. Perhaps his recommendation for a colonial union best revealed his practical education and his scholarly reflection. While his many plans of union now seem cumbersome, they did provide ways for keeping both countries under the same king and Parliament. This recommendation was his chief contribution as a Tory theorist.

His essay, modest in size and content compared with the works of Tories like George Chalmers and Thomas Hutchinson, resembled in organization and ideas, though not in humor and style of writing, Peter Oliver's *Origin & Progress of the American Rebel-*

lion. They may easily have exchanged ideas during one of their dinner meetings. Like Oliver, Galloway accepted conspiracy as the principal cause of revolution, but Oliver believed the whole colony of Massachusetts was tricked by vile and mean men, while Galloway held that only a minority of Pennsylvanians even wanted revolution. Both men, however, wanted to ascertain the causes of the revolt. They saw the evils of Puritanism, Presbyterianism, and republicanism and drew upon history and experience in making their judgments. But unlike Hutchinson and Chalmers, Galloway was primarily a lawyer and legislator who witnessed the destruction of his society and was baffled by it. He would resort to British arms and a plan of union to bring peace, while these fellow Tories were convinced that a general reformation of American life was absolutely necessary before peace was possible.[41]

V

Galloway never tired of presenting his case for British-American union and wrote nearly a dozen additional pamphlets between 1780 and 1785. Besides he carried on a correspondence with Americans, kept in contact with fellow Tories, and petitioned the British government from time to time on American policy. He was granted a pension of £500, which he considered too low, and agitated for an increase.[42]

As the years passed, he realized that he could not return to America nor be reunited with his wife, who had remained in

41. *Peter Oliver's Origin & Progress of the American Rebellion*, ed. Douglass Adair and John A. Schutz (Stanford, Calif., 1967); George Chalmers, *An Introduction to the History of Revolt of the American Colonies*, ed. Jared Sparks (Boston, 1845); Thomas Hutchinson, *The History of the Colony and Province of Massachusetts-Bay*, ed. Lawrence Shaw Mayo (Cambridge, Mass., 1936).

42. Loyalist Claims Commission, P.R.O., A.O. 12, 3:404–5.

Pennsylvania to look after the family interests.[43] He arranged a marriage for his daughter Elizabeth with a British army officer and reconciled himself to exile in England. In his old age he kept busy writing pamphlets, but he now found the prophecies of the Bible a more engaging topic. He moved from London to Watford, in Hertfordshire, and died there on 24 August 1803.

43. Galloway to Thomas McKean, 7 March 1793, McKean Papers, Pennsylvania Historical Society.

5.

Jonathan Boucher's *Causes and Consequences*

Michael D. Clark

Jonathan Boucher was not a typical loyalist of the American Revolution. His peculiarly ultraconservative political assumptions, best articulated in *A View of the Causes and Consequences of the American Revolution,* placed him in a class almost by himself.

Historians have agreed that Boucher's position was extreme, while recognizing the intelligence of its expression. Moses Coit Tyler in 1897 admired Boucher's character and courage and believed that his *Causes and Consequences* was probably the ablest and most comprehensive "presentation of the deeper principles and motives of the American Loyalists. . . ." Vernon Louis Parrington characterized Boucher as "the high Tory of the Tory cause in America." Boucher's political philosophy, said Parrington, was "the voice of seventeenth-century Cavalier England, speaking to an alien people, bred up in another philosophy of government." Yet Parrington, who was not always so kind to Tories, also found Boucher fearless, capable, outspoken, and "above all of independent mind." In a similar tone, Leonard Labaree acknowledged Boucher as "altogether the most emphatic and prolific spokesman for a conservative and even reactionary point of view anywhere in the Southern Colonies." William H. Nelson, more recently, found no Tory writer more profound, and Allen Guttmann, though not impressed by Boucher's message, granted that "he ought to be remembered as an authentic, if somewhat exaggerated, representative of what the majority of his contemporaries were not."[1]

Despite such recognition, Boucher has not received the systematic attention commensurate with his significance as an observer and interpreter of the revolutionary struggle. "Toryissimus"[2] as he may have been, Boucher was not divorced from reality, and his perceptions were often acute. From his own perspective, Boucher clearly discerned the nature of the eighteenth-century break with the past in which the American Revolution was an incident.

Jonathan Boucher was born in the village of Blencogo, Cumberland County, England, in 1738. He cited in his *Reminiscences* the legend that the Bouchers had come from Normandy with William the Conqueror, thereupon receiving a grant of land in the North of England. During the seventeenth century, however, family fortunes had drastically declined. A Boucher had taken the side of Parliament in the Civil War and had forfeited a large part of his estate in consequence—as he deserved, according to his conservative descendant. (Boucher suggested that his forebear was "seduced probably by the Sir John Bourchier, whose name appears to the warrant for the execution of the King, and who called my ancestor his *dear cousin*. . . .") As if to reinforce this object

1. Moses Coit Tyler, *The Literary History of the American Revolution, 1763–1783*, 2 vols. (New York, 1957), 1:320; Vernon Louis Parrington, *The Colonial Mind, 1620–1800* (New York, 1927), pp. 214–15, 218; Leonard Woods Labaree, *Conservatism in Early American History* (Ithaca, 1959), pp. 63, 128; William H. Nelson, *The American Tory* (Oxford, 1961), p. 74. Speaking of the New York loyalist Charles Inglis, Nelson says that "only he and Boucher were able to raise the Tory argument, for more than a moment, from the level of politics to the higher ground of philosophy, there to discover between themselves and the revolutionists an unbridgeable chasm." Allen Guttmann, *The Conservative Tradition in America* (New York, 1967), pp. 17–18.

2. Richard M. Gummere, "Jonathan Boucher, Toryissimus," *Maryland Historical Magazine* 55 (June 1960): 138–45.

lesson in the fruits of rebellion, Jonathan at the age of eight was taken to witness the execution of several leading Jacobites.[3]

Boucher's father, having failed in business, earned a scanty living as village schoolmaster during Jonathan's childhood. His son recalled that the family "lived in such a state of penury and hardship as I have never since seen equalled, no, not even in parish almshouses." With the pride of a self-made man, Boucher noted that "there is no kind of labour at which I have not often worked as hard as any man in England, and, I may add, I have fared as hard." His parents, however, were determined to educate their children. His father early taught him to read, and at six he began studying Latin at a nearby free school. Ten years later Boucher himself began a career as a schoolmaster. He particularly profited from his association with the headmaster of Saint Bees School, Rev. John James, who not only employed Boucher as a teacher, but polished his still spotty education.[4]

Although struggle against hardship dominated Boucher's youth, a large element of chance affected his young adulthood. Hearing through Reverend James of a position as private tutor in Virginia, Boucher emigrated and landed near the mouth of the Rappahannock River in July 1759.[5]

Boucher's entry into the Anglican priesthood was equally fortuitous. Following an abortive commercial venture, he unexpectedly received the offer of Hanover Parish in King George's County, Virginia, and returned to England in 1762 to be admitted into holy orders by the Bishop of London. Boucher cannot, however, be dismissed as a mere placeman. His respect for religion was

---

3. Jonathan Boucher, *Reminiscences of an American Loyalist 1738–1789*, ed. Jonathan Boucher (Boston and New York, 1925), pp. viii, 2–3. (The editor is Boucher's grandson.)

4. Ibid., pp. 5, 8–10, 15, 21–22.

5. Ibid., pp. 23–25.

genuine and deep. A diligent study of Scripture and a strong effort
of will settled him in an orthodoxy from which he never deviated.
All evidence indicated that Boucher sincerely regarded the Church
of England, as he wrote to James in 1770, as "with all her Imperfections . . . ye Glory of ye Reforma'n." In his own priestly
office, Boucher considered himself "as *a city set on an hill,*" an
active example for good or ill.[6]

In addition to his ecclesiastical duties, Boucher expanded his
tutoring activities into a boarding school for thirty boys, among
them John Parke Custis, stepson of George Washington. "A very
particular intimacy and friendship," as Boucher recalled it,[7] was
established between the schoolmaster and Washington, the future
archrebel. Whether or not Washington regarded the association in
the same terms, the two men did remain friendly until the War
for Independence, despite some differences over "Jackie" Custis's
education. Boucher thought Custis inclined to be "indolent and
voluptuous"—"one would suppose Nature had intended him for
some Asiatic Prince"—and urged Washington to send master and
student on a tour of Europe. Washington was dissuaded from the
project by Boucher's talk of heavy expenses and by his own feeling
that Custis was too immature to profit from it.[8]

Boucher recounted in his *Reminiscences* a chance meeting with
Washington in 1775, as the general went north to command the
Continental Army. According to Boucher, Washington assured

6. Ibid., pp. 28–32, 43–45; Boucher to Rev. John James, 25 August 1770,
in "Letters of Rev. Jonathan Boucher," *Maryland Historical Magazine* 8
(June 1913): 174; Jonathan Boucher, *A View of the Causes and Consequences
of the American Revolution* (London, 1797), p. 574.

7. Boucher, *Reminiscences*, p. 48.

8. Boucher to George Washington, 9 May, 21 May, and 18 December
1770, 4 July 1771, in Worthington Chauncey Ford, ed., "Letters of
Jonathan Boucher to George Washington," *The New-England Historical and
Genealogical Register* 52 (1898): 176, 330–34, 461–63; Douglas Southall
Freeman, *George Washington: a Biography*, 7 vols. (New York, 1951),
3:254–55, 263, 272, 285–86.

him that if the clergyman ever heard of his being involved in any
scheme for independence, he might "set him down for everything
wicked." The friendship was soon sundered by a bitter letter from
Boucher informing the American commander that "a man of
honour can no longer without dishonour be connected with you."
Later, in a more judicious frame of mind, Boucher remembered
Washington as temperate, cautious, and honest, but lacking any
extraordinary penetration or generosity of nature. Boucher's dedication of *A View of the Causes and Consequences of the American Revolution* to Washington, and "a very handsome letter from
the late President of the United States of America" in response,
closed the rather curious association.[9]

Boucher moved to Maryland in 1770, having obtained the
parish of St. Anne's in Annapolis—then, as he remarked, "the
genteelest town in North America." He had already achieved
success during his short residence in America, and his fortunes
now were at flood tide. He owned land and slaves. When he
married Nelly Addison of Virginia in 1772, he later estimated, he
was worth about £1000 sterling, and his wife £2500.[10] He quickly
became prominent in the "court party" in Maryland politics, a
friend of Governor Robert Eden, and first president of the
Homony Club, one of several Annapolis weekly social and literary
societies meant to "promote innocent mirth and ingenious hu-
mour." King's College in New York conferred on him in 1774 an
honorary degree of Master of Arts, in recognition of his "services
. . . to Church and State."[11]

Boucher's love for America and Americans was qualified by the

9. Boucher, *Reminiscences*, pp. 50, 109, 141; George Washington to
Boucher, 15 August 1798, Boucher to James Maury, 17 February 1799,
Maryland Historical Magazine 10 (June 1915):123–24.

10. Boucher, *Reminiscences*, pp. 65, 77.

11. Philip A. Crowl, *Maryland During and After the Revolution* (Baltimore, 1943), p. 20; Charles Albro Barker, *The Background of the Revolution
in Maryland* (New Haven, 1940), p. 60; Boucher, *Reminiscences*, pp. 67, 100.

political bitterness of his last years in the country; yet there is no reason to doubt the plaintive assertion of his farewell sermon that America was the land of his choice. His marriage, property, friends—his very success in life—were American and comprised strong "ties of attachment."[12] Boucher had been very young when he emigrated, and by his own account he had adapted quickly to America. He was startled by the "obscene Conceits and broad Expression" that enlivened Virginian manners and at first could not think of settling permanently. But he found the people hospitable and generous, and his criticisms of American society were from the beginning offset by evidences of affection.[13] Boucher confided in 1767 that he sometimes thought of returning to England—particularly when he felt slighted—and accepting a "comfortable Independence" there. On balance, however, he saw "infinitely superior" advantages in remaining where he was. In view of his later emphasis on order and authority in church and state, it is interesting that he explained to his English correspondent, as one reason that America was "ye Country for Me," that "We are much less under ye Controll of dogmatis'g Superiors here than you are. . . . I do not think my Pride w'd suffer Me now to act in a subordinate Capacity to any Man whatever. . . ."[14] By 1772, Boucher contentedly contemplated a life in America. "I flatter myself," he wrote, "I may quietly repose myself for the Remainder of my Life, under my own Vine, Bless'd with that Ease, Competence & Independence, which I have so long been in search of."[15]

12. Boucher, *Causes and Consequences*, pp. lxxxix, 593.

13. Boucher, *Reminiscences*, p. 26; Boucher to James, 7 August 1759, 14 September 1759, in *Maryland Historical Magazine* 7 (March 1912):4–5, 14.

14. Boucher to James, 9 March 1767, 28 November 1767, ibid., 7 (December 1912):338, 352–53.

15. Boucher to James, 10 July 1772, ibid., 8 (June 1913):181. After returning to England, Boucher wrote sadly: "Wou'd to God, I had been in Circumstances never to have emigrated; but, since that was not my Lot, am I to be

Approaching the crisis that would destroy these happy prospects, Jonathan Boucher was in his mid-thirties, vigorous enough physically to knock down an impudent blacksmith and gain a useful reputation as "a d——d fellow, equally in favour with Mars and Minerva." His wife affectionately described him as awkward of manner, "a thorough gentleman as to internals and essentials, tho' often lamentably deficient in outward forms." Occasionally self-analytical, Boucher admitted that vanity was his "prevailing foible." He suggested that "there was nothing quite ordinary or indifferent about me; my faults and my good qualities were all striking. All my friends (and no man ever had more friends) really loved me; and all my enemies as cordially hated me."[16]

On balance, Boucher's character and ability stand up well. In the heat of political controversy, some Whig opponents professed a low opinion of him,[17] but there seems little reason to cast doubt on his integrity. At the same time, his personal qualities embroiled him in controversy. He was determined and obstinate, and Parrington was hardly hyperbolic in describing him as another Increase Mather in his love of domination, directness of purpose, and strength of will. But willfulness combined with a sensitive strain in his personality; his quickness in suspecting and resenting a slight did not help him to weather Maryland's political storms, nor did his eagerness to strike back. Amiability and ambition also contended in his nature. Boucher was not the "puritan" suggested by Parrington's comparison of him with Mather. He was a warm if

blam'd, that I have cultivated those Talents chiefly, which were adapted to the Land in which my Lot seem'd to have fallen, or that, of Course, I am fit only for America. There, I have some Character & Note—here, every Body I see eclipses Me" (Boucher to unknown recipient, *Maryland Historical Magazine* 8 [December 1913]:345).

16. Boucher, *Reminiscences*, pp. 2, 80, 114–16. Boucher thought that "this opinion alone saved my bacon on many occasions" (ibid., p. 116).

17. See "Extracts from the Carroll Papers," *Maryland Historical Magazine* 15 (March 1920):56–57; William Paca, open letter to Boucher, *Maryland Gazette*, 11 March 1773.

sometimes demanding friend and could be markedly sentimental, especially about his first wife. Capable of ponderous whimsicality, he wrote his projected father-in-law an elaborate letter asking for his daughter's hand through an allegory based on the purchase of a choice piece of land.[18]

This geniality, however, did not obscure his drive to accumulate and to succeed. He could be opportunistic in both personal and political matters. He expressed with eighteenth-century frankness his satisfaction at finding a rich second wife after the death of his first, and he advocated the rights of "Papists" in Maryland largely in an effort to keep them loyal to the Crown.[19] Boucher's personal qualities which make him an interesting historical figure, also made him a formidable antagonist in the crisis that preceded the revolution.

Jonathan Boucher could not be confidently described as a "Tory personality." His eventual commitment to the loyalist cause seems due less to temperament than to his role as an Anglican priest and to his social and political ties in Maryland. Indeed, Boucher's energies could have been employed on the opposite side of the struggle. He never slavishly admired British policies, and in 1765 he vehemently condemned the Stamp Act as "in every Sense, oppressive, impolitic & illegal." The Americans' "best & dearest Rights," he then thought, "w'c, ever like Britons They are anxiously jealous of, have been mercilessly invaded by Parliament, who till now, never pretended to any such Privileges. . . ." As late as 1769, Boucher described the American opposition as "the most warrantable, generous, & manly, that History can produce"; protesting members of the Virginia Assembly, it seemed to him, "like

18. Parrington, *Colonial Mind*, p. 214; Boucher, *Reminiscences*, pp. 82–91.
19. Boucher, *Reminiscences*, pp. 181–83; Boucher, *Causes and Consequences*, pp. 241–42.

ye Druids of old," had "really learn'd Eloquence as well as Knowledge beneath Their trees. . . ."[20]

Yet there was a crucial distinction between his criticism of British policy and his later indictment of the American reaction to it; the British might have erred in judgment, but American Whigs strayed from moral duty. "Error in them," he told his congregation in 1774, "is no excuse for guilt in us. . . ." Boucher contrasted the honorable means of effecting repeal of the Stamp Act with the dishonorable methods of more recent American "Ahitophels." Only at the last, apparently, did Boucher regret his earlier defense of "Licentiousness" in the guise of "Constitutional Liberty."[21]

Explaining his gravitation to the Tory side, Boucher emphasized the religious issues in Maryland during the 1770s. He strenuously opposed Whig attempts to limit the Church of England's power in the province. As a conscientious priest, Boucher took seriously his oath of allegiance to the king, and was aware that Anglican Church authority depended, quite properly in his view, on its relationship with the government. His sermon against "Schisms and Sects," which he used more than once, indicated his zeal for the religious establishment.[22] His strong advocacy of an American

20. Boucher to James, 9 December 1765, 25 July 1769, in *Maryland Historical Magazine* 7 (September 1912):295; 8 (March 1913):44.

21. Boucher, *Causes and Consequences*, pp. 371, 418, 590. But as late as 4 May 1775, Boucher could write to Dr. William Smith, Provost of the College of Philadelphia: "Surely the Americans have most wofully mismanaged their Cause; and, as Things are now carried on it is not easy to say to which side a real Friend to Liberty, Order and good Government would incline. For my Part I equally dread a Victory on either side." (*Maryland Historical Magazine* 8 [September 1913]:240). Boucher probably tailored his remarks to Smith's uncertain political position, but they suggest that while he dutifully supported submission to authority, he was less decided in his own mind about the rights of the immediate issues.

22. Boucher, *Reminiscences*, p. 104; Boucher, *Causes and Consequences*, pp. 46 ff.

episcopate placed him among militant Anglicans. To deprive
Americans of bishops, he thought, not only denied the church
"Consequence & stability," but amounted to the only real denial
of religious liberties in the British dominions.

Boucher was thrust into a direct confrontation with Maryland
Whigs by the attempt of Samuel Chase and William Paca to
reduce the poll tax for ecclesiastical salaries. (The legal pretext was
highly technical; Chase and Paca argued that the 1702 law which
provided for the clergy was invalid because the governor had
signed it in the name of William III, who had died some weeks
before.) Boucher actively opposed this antiestablishment scheme,
and was drawn into what he described as "a long, keen and weari-
some newspaper contest with the two chief demagogues, viz.
Messrs. Chase and Paca. . . ." The churchman held his own.
Charles A. Barker remarked that Boucher "made his plea as logical
and vigorous as any in Maryland history." Whatever the merits of
the case, however, the practical issue went against Boucher, for the
Whigs in 1773 enacted a law "estimated as likely to have reduced
clergy incomes from one-fifth to one-half."[23]

Maryland politics, of which these religious questions were a
part, divided into "court" and "country" parties. The country
party, according to Philip A. Crowl, "were for the most part
planters, merchants, and lawyers—men of means and well-
established social and political positions within the Province."
Traditionally opposed to the proprietary government, they now
fought king and Parliament. The court party included the gover-

23. Boucher to James, 16 November 1773, *Maryland Historical Magazine*
8 (June 1913):184; Boucher, *Causes and Consequences*, p. 137; Barker,
Revolution in Maryland, pp. 360–64, 366; Boucher, *Reminiscences*, pp. 70–
71. Boucher appeared to score a telling point when he asked his opponents
how they could continue to act as vestrymen of St. Anne's parish, concurring
in assessments on its taxpayers. Paca and Chase replied that the authority of
vestrymen was not grounded on the 1702 law (*Maryland Gazette*, 31 December 1772, 14 January 1773).

nor and his council, "a mass of petty officials appointed by the proprietor or his governor; and finally the Anglican clergy, whose livings were mostly bestowed by proprietary favor." Many of these, though not all, became loyalists.[24]

Boucher's associations and interests clearly placed him among the "courtiers." He attributed his "being set down as a Government-man" largely to his "confidential intimacy" with Governor Eden. "With no other man," Boucher remarked, "did I ever live half so long in such habits of the most unreserved friendship and confidence." Boucher was also described as a "protégé" of the Dulany family, which was predominantly loyalist during the revolution. The Dulanys had helped bring Boucher to Annapolis from Virginia, and several younger members of the family had been educated in his school. The Dulanys belonged to Boucher's Homony Club (which included members of both country and court parties), and Eden was an honorary member.[25]

Personal and political associations, combined with his staunch Anglicanism, committed Boucher in 1775. He chose sides regretfully but of necessity. Civil disobedience, as Leonard Labaree has noted, was the point of no return for many conservatives who believed British policy mistaken but for whom submission to law was an inescapable duty. Boucher, moreover, was faced with personal intimidation and violence. As early as 1772, when he moved from Annapolis to Queen Anne's parish in Prince George's County, he was threatened with "the fate of St. Stephen" after "a turbulent fellow had paid eight dollars for so many loads of stones

24. Crowl, *Maryland*, pp. 19–20. Wallace Brown points out that some members of the court party became patriots or remained neutral (*The King's Friends: the Composition and Motives of the American Loyalist Claimants* [Providence, 1965], p. 170).

25. Boucher, *Reminiscences*, pp. 54, 67, 104. This friendship endured despite Boucher's strong support of an American Episcopate, which in the view of the proprietary government would have been contrary to the Maryland charter (Barker, *Revolution in Maryland*, p. 359). Aubrey C. Land, *The Dulanys of Maryland* (Baltimore, 1955), pp. 281, 299–300.

to drive me and my friends from the church by force."[26] Two
years later he opposed aiding recalcitrant Boston and was called
before the Provincial Committee in Annapolis, accused, he complained, by "a Papist and two Presbyterians" of lack of sympathy
with America. His eloquence procured his acquittal by his own
account, but Boucher preached at the end with a pair of loaded
pistols at his side. He recalled escaping from a mob only by seizing
its leader by the collar and threatening to blow his brains out.
Boucher later wrote bitterly of "the countless Insults Indignities &
Injuries I have long suffered in America, solely on account of my
Loyalty. . . ."[27]

The war made his personal position untenable, and Boucher
sailed for England in the summer of 1775, expecting to be absent
six months. He left in America about £5000 worth of property in
land and slaves which were confiscated, though he eventually
received some compensation from the British government. Among
his parting shots were "Quaeries addressed to the people of Maryland," which excoriated Whig committees as unconstitutional and
unrepresentative, and a letter "To the Honble The Deputies in
Congress from the Southern Provinces." In the letter Boucher
warned that independence would benefit only the North; it was as
natural for "the wolf and the lamb to feed together," he thought,
"as Virginians to form a cordial union with the saints of New
England." Northerners, he predicted, would become the Vandals
of America and seize the best lands of the South.[28]

26. Labaree, *Conservatism*, p. 17; Boucher, *Reminiscences*, pp. 73–74;
Boucher, *Causes and Consequences*, p. 589.
   27. Boucher, *Reminiscences*, pp. 105–8, 113, 123; Boucher to James, 31
October 1775, in *Maryland Historical Magazine* 8 (September 1913):242.
   28. Boucher, *Reminiscences*, pp. 126–36; Boucher to unknown recipient, 8
January 1776, in *Maryland Historical Magazine* 8 (December 1913):346. Another loyalist, Joseph Galloway, similarly predicted that the northern colonies,
like the ancient Saxons and Danes, would "carry devastation and havoc over
the Southern." (*A Candid Examination of the Mutual Claims of Great
Britain and her Colonies: With a Plan of Accommodation, on Constitutional
Principles* [New York, 1775], p. 59.)

In England, Boucher confidently expected that the rebellion would be crushed; the real difficulty, he believed, would be to make good subjects of the colonists again. Contemptuous of Whig leaders as "a Catalinarian Combination of individual Scoundrels," he attributed early American successes to British mismanagement and irresolution. Detecting in the Battle of Long Island evidence of Yankee cunning in leaving southern troops badly exposed, he expressed a grim satisfaction that "Our Maryland Fools suffered the most; many of my Parishioners & quondam Persecutors being knock'd in the Head." Boucher offered political and military advice to British officials, emphasizing that American dissension if nothing else would doom the rebellion. Bewildered by American persistence and shocked by speeches in Parliament "which would have been thought licentious, seditious & treasonable, in America, even when I left it," Boucher concluded that the British government was "rotten at the Core." "Hereafter," he wrote after the Battle of Saratoga, "I give up all Faith in History; seeing, as I do, a greater event than it has ever yet recorded likely to be brought about by the most unlikely of all human Means."[29]

The outcome of the revolution precluded Boucher's return to America, where "everything . . . is turned topsy-turvy: Mankind have lost all Principles of Religion & every Thing else, by which Societies are held together. . . ." His later life in England was comparatively tranquil. For a time, beginning in 1779, he served as assistant secretary to the Society for the Propagation of the Gospel in Foreign Parts. His old desire to tour Europe, which George Washington had declined to sponsor, was realized in 1785 when he accompanied two young gentlemen to the continent. Boucher amply recouped his lost fortunes, partly through his second wife who was worth nearly £14,000 at their marriage in 1787. He owned

29. Boucher to James, 23 December 1777, in *Maryland Historical Magazine* 10 (March 1915):27; Boucher to James, 23 October 1776, 21 November 1776, ibid., 9 (September 1914):232, 236.

a library, at this time, of over ten thousand volumes.[30] In his later years Boucher indulged a longstanding interest in etymology. In America, he had composed a pastoral poem (reminiscent, according to one critic, of Ebenezer Cooke's *The Sot-Weed Factor* of 1708), "written solely," he said, "with the view of introducing as many of such words and idioms of speech, then prevalent and common in Maryland, as I conceived to be dialectical, and peculiar to those parts of America." His research resulted in *Boucher's Glossary of Archaic and Provincial Words*, intended to supplement the dictionaries of Samuel Johnson and Noah Webster and published posthumously in 1832.[31]

In 1785, Boucher obtained the living of Epsom in Surrey and resided there for the rest of his life. After the death of his second wife, he married a third time and, though he never before had children, at this late stage of his life fathered eight. Jonathan Boucher died at Epsom, 27 April 1804.[32]

II

Publication of thirteen of his American sermons as *A View of the Causes and Consequences of the American Revolution* was historically most significant project of Boucher's later life. He was concerned about the book's reception. It won approval in England, and the author declined a Doctor of Divinity degree from a "Scots University." He naively believed that the book would also be well received in America, except among "Jacobins." After all, George Washington approved of his efforts, the sensitive Tory reminded an unenthused American correspondent (although

30. Boucher to James, 10 November 1779, ibid., 10 (March 1915):35; Boucher, *Reminiscences*, pp. 152, 178–80, 183.

31. Allen Walker Read, "Boucher's Linguistic Pastoral of Colonial Maryland," *Publications of the American Dialect Society* 6 (December 1933): 353, 358–59, 362–63.

32. Boucher, *Reminiscences*, pp. x, 198.

Washington, in his proper letter of thanks for the dedication, noted that he had not read the book and so could not comment on its political contents).[33]

A *View of the Causes and Consequences of the American Revolution* grew naturally out of Boucher's personal experiences in America. It recorded the evolution of a Tory point of view—in some ways typical, in others idiosyncratic—from the peace with France in 1763 to the Anglo-American rupture of 1775, and from that revolution's preface to the grand aftermath of the French Revolution. The book was the product of the need to argue a case. If not a lawyer's brief, it was an Anglican priest's plea before the bar of divine justice. Boucher acknowledged that his sermons were of interest chiefly because of their circumstances and that he had begun to think seriously of their subject matter only when events made it necessary.[34]

The product of political exigencies, the *Causes and Consequences* was also the product of a self-made intellect. Far from the centers of thought and learning, Boucher "sat down," he told us, "to explore the truth." Had he been a university scholar, he would not, in the second half of the eighteenth century, have found the highest embodiment of political truth in the writings of Sir Robert Filmer. Boucher knew that Filmer was not fashionable; such doctrines, he had heard, were fit only for tyrants and slaves. But as Parrington noted, Boucher was independent-minded, and Filmer best explicated traditional political principles as his American disciple understood and accepted them.

If this seems provincial, it should be recalled that American Whigs also studied a seventeenth-century political philosopher whose doctrines were past their prime in England. J.G.A. Pocock

33. Boucher to James Maury, 17 February 1798, *Maryland Historical Magazine* 10 (June 1915):121–22; Boucher to Maury, 17 February 1799, ibid., 124–25.
34. Boucher, *Causes and Consequences*, p. xxiii.

suggests that "in the eighteenth century [John Locke] was a writer largely for those who were situated somewhat outside the established order and wanted to appeal against its practice to its somewhat remotely perceived principles—Anglo-Irishmen, Americans, Dissenters."[35]

Locke, of course, plausibly rationalized American needs; Filmer did not. But Jonathan Boucher, to whom political truth was an absolute transcending time and place, was not deterred by this practical difficulty insofar as he perceived it. He was tenacious in his opinions, once they were formed. "The ground I have taken, I am aware, is deemed untenable," he told his congregation in 1775, "but, having now just gone over that ground with great care, I feel a becoming confidence that I shall not easily be driven from it." He was successful enough in its defense that Filmer's modern editor, Peter Laslett, attributed to Boucher "the best common-sense defense of Filmer that ever was made."[36]

Boucher's acceptance of a doctrine so inapplicable to American realities as Filmer's divine right of kings, and his concomitant rejection of Locke and of the American conceptions of society and government symbolized by Locke, made him seem the alien voice of the Cavalier. But he did recognize in the American Revolution, especially from the perspective of 1797, a fundamental challenge to an older and more enduring social ideal than Filmer's version of it. Boucher did not necessarily support those who believed in the uniqueness of the American experience or who emphasized the

35. Ibid., p. 591; J. G. A. Pocock, "Machiavelli, Harrington, and English Political Ideologies in the Eighteenth Century," *William and Mary Quarterly*, 3rd Series, 22 (October 1965):581. W. H. Greenleaf notes the more pervasive and enduring influence of Filmer's ideas outside England (*Order, Empiricism and Politics: Two Traditions of English Political Thought, 1500–1700* [London, 1964], p. 87). I have compared Boucher to American Lockeans in this aspect of provinciality ("Jonathan Boucher: The Mirror of Reaction," *The Huntington Library Quarterly* 33 [November 1969]: 19–32).

36. Boucher, *Causes and Consequences*, p. 501; Sir Robert Filmer, *Patriarcha: and Other Political Works*, ed. Peter Laslett (Oxford, 1949), p. 41.

revolutionary social aspects of the War for Independence. Despite his observation that "every thing in America had a republican aspect," Boucher did not believe that the issues were defined by the opposition of the Old World to the New. He rather interpreted the American Revolution as a party contest within the British Empire. He believed that loyal American people had been misled by demagogues and persuaded himself that Presidents Washington and Adams, though they would resent being called Tories, had become "in practice at least as much so as I avow myself to be in principle." With evidence that Americans were returning to true principles of government, Boucher could hope in 1799 for an Anglo-American alliance against revolutionary France—"the common enemy of the human race." Yet while believing the challenge to the social order to be international in scope, and attributing the American Revolution itself to "the loose principles of the times," Boucher did attribute a seminal role to America. From the perspective of the 1790s, the French Revolution seemed only the "first-born, in direct lineal succession, of a numerous progeny of revolutions, of which that of America promises to be the prolific parent. . . ."[37]

By "the loose principles of the times" Boucher referred to current ideas which challenged the traditional moral and social order. He used the metaphor of harmony to describe this assumed order. There could be no society, he explained, without government; "nor, without some relative inferiority and superiority, can there be any government. A musical instrument composed of chords, keys, or pipes, all perfectly equal in size and power, might as well be expected to produce harmony, as a society composed of members all perfectly equal to be productive of order and peace." The schoolmaster's definition of education clearly reflected this con-

---

37. Boucher, *Causes and Consequences*, pp. vi, xliii; Boucher to Maury, 17 February 1799, *Maryland Historical Magazine* 10 (June 1915):125–26; Boucher, *Causes and Consequences*, pp. xliv, lxiv, lxxiii.

cept. "Whatever qualifies any person to fill with propriety the rank and station in life that may fall to his lot," Boucher thought, "is education."[38]

In contrast to traditional social harmony, the spirit of "republicanism" seemed to Boucher to be that of monotone. Philadelphia was its true embodiment:

> The city is disgusting from its uniformity and sameness; one street has nothing to distinguish it from another, but that one is the first, and another the second, and so on. There are no squares, no public edifices of any size or dignity; the situation is flat and level; and, in short, everything about it has a quakerly or rather, a Republican, aspect.

Boucher was aware that social bonds were weaker in America than in the Old World, but he drew no clear connection between this sociological factor and the nature of American politics.[39] The difficulties seemed to him largely those of structure and form. Shortly after leaving America he wrote that it was chiefly a lack of "*form & Comeleiness*" in the American governments—and especially a lack of "Pith & Energy" in their executive branches—which had given the advantage to the "republican Spirit." The relative lack of ceremony in America was itself significant. As a priest of the Church of England, Boucher understood that men were not satisfied solely with "Abstract Excellence" in religious or civil institutions; "Externals," he knew, ". . . are of Moment in both."[40]

Boucher's conception of society as an organic whole was incompatible with the divisions and compartments recognized by modern institutions. The alliance of church and state, in particular, seemed natural and essential: "Each is a part of each: each a part of the constitution: and an injury cannot be done to the one

38. Ibid., pp. 156, 515.
39. Boucher, *Reminiscences*, pp. 99, 101.
40. Boucher, "possibly" to William Knox, undersecretary of state, 27 November 1775, *Maryland Historical Magazine* 8 (September 1913):247–48.

without the other's feeling it." The converse principle was the "fundamental maxim of modern revolutionists." Boucher's emphasis on the mutual dependence of church and state undoubtedly derived from his position as an Anglican priest. Similarly, his hostility to political parties and religious sects, which he regarded as different manifestations of the same phenomenon, owed much to his bitter experience with colonial Whigs and dissenters. On principle, the matter went deeper. As a "sinful schism" was a "needless separation from a church, which has all the requisites and characteristics of a true church," so a political party was a separation from true government, for Boucher believed that parties seldom pursued the real interests of their country. Of course, many Whigs agreed on the evils of faction. But unlike James Madison, Boucher thought political or religious division necessarily tainted with sedition: "A sect is, in fact, a revolt against the authority of the Church, just as a faction is against the authority of the State; or, in other words, a sect is a faction in the Church, as a faction is a sect in the State; and the spirit which refuses obedience to the one, is equally ready to resist the other."[41]

Obedience was the heart of the matter. Once highly critical of British policies, Boucher by 1775 believed that the rebellion was based on trivial causes, such as "an insignificant duty on tea" which most Americans would have no occasion to pay. But Boucher knew that it was not enough to argue the merits of immediate issues. The doctrine of the right of resistance to government must be countered, especially the Lockean version popular among Americans. Neither here nor elsewhere was Boucher an original thinker, but he did deliver, in the opinion of Leonard Labaree, "the best and fullest exposition of what were the essentially Tory principles of obedience and nonresistance pro-

41. Boucher, *Causes and Consequences*, pp. lxxix, 56, 80, 102, dedication (unnumbered).

duced in colonial America." These principles, Labaree added, represented the extreme conservative view in both England and America. But they were also, as the conscientious priest was aware, sound tenets of his church. Dependent on the monarchy for its existence, "the Church of England taught nonresistance as the condition of its own survival," Harold J. Laski noted.[42]

Boucher argued that government by its nature was irresistible; the assumption that governmental prescriptions could legally be defied was absurd. From the Christian subject's point of view, furthermore, to resist a lawful government was to oppose the ordinance of God. But Boucher did not, as his enemies charged, advocate unlimited obedience. Unlike modern totalitarianism, a theistic system of authority had to admit that the state could command something forbidden by God. Accordingly, "passive obedience" might be necessary: in a conflict, the subject must obey God, but he must also conscientiously submit to whatever civil penalties this entails.[43]

This doctrine of obedience answered Boucher's needs in the crisis of 1775. But though he was aware of the hazards of Locke's right of revolution, he could hardly have anticipated the revolutionary potential of "passive obedience." The difference between passive obedience and passive resistance rested more on temper than on principle. In much the tone of twentieth-century advocates of nonviolence, Boucher attributed to "nonresistance" a dignity superior to that of doctrines which led to "disputes and debates which admit of no decision, and of wars and fightings which are almost as endless as they are useless. . . ."[44] But for Boucher, of course, this was a conservative rather than a reforming principle.

42. Ibid., pp. 554–55; Labaree, *Conservatism*, pp. 128–30; Harold Joseph Laski, *Political Thought in England: from Locke to Bentham* (New York, 1920), pp. 83–84.
43. Boucher, *Causes and Consequences*, pp. 423, 517–18, 545, 546, 593.
44. Ibid., p. 543.

Boucher's acceptance of passive obedience and nonresistance, despite his disclaimers, made him appear to American Whigs as an advocate of unlimited submission to imperial authority. His rejection of Lockean precepts more accurately defined him as an extreme Tory, setting him apart from moderate loyalists like Joseph Galloway and Peter Van Schaack, who accepted Locke but denied that he justified the American rebellion. Boucher saw that the right of revolution, however Locke had meant to circumscribe it, could be invoked to sanction any uprising. Whatever expediency such a principle had in vindicating the "Glorious Revolution," it subverted authority.[45]

Locke's social compact was likewise inadmissible. Boucher believed that government founded on consent implied the possibility of withdrawing consent at any time; such government could never be safely established. It was ironic that a traditionalist could argue against the social compact hypothesis as well as an eighteenth-century rationalist. By Boucher's time, after all, the social compact idea had been undermined by David Hume and others, and after Edmund Burke it would cease to be a vital influence on political speculation. Boucher produced no systematic refutation of the idea, but he posed commonsense objections to the social compact as a literal explanation of the origins of government. The weight of historical evidence, he thought, was on his side.[46]

Boucher's fundamental objections were not to Locke's historical plausibility but to his concept of society. Boucher glimpsed in Locke a pattern for "republican sameness" as he thought of it. The social compact, Boucher inferred, rested on the principle that

45. Galloway, *Candid Examination*, pp. 13, 27–32; Nelson, *American Tory*, pp. 121–23; Boucher, *Causes and Consequences*, pp. 482–84.

46. Ibid., pp. 516–17; David Hume, *A Treatise of Human Nature*, ed. L. A. Selby-Biggs (Oxford, 1958), pp. 540–41; David Hume, *An Enquiry Concerning the Principles of Morals*, ed. Charles W. Hendel (Indianapolis and New York, 1957), p. 21; Laski, *Political Thought*, pp. 71–72; Boucher, *Causes and Consequences*, pp. 515–18, 525–28.

men were born equal, with no man naturally inferior or subject to another. Yet to Boucher it seemed axiomatic that "man differs from man in every thing that can be supposed to lead to supremacy and subjection, *as one star differs from another star in glory.*" Even more to the point, a government formed with the reserved right of resistance made social cohesion impossible: "Such a system . . . can produce only perpetual dissensions and contests, and bring back mankind to a supposed state of nature; arming every man's hand, like Ishmael's, against every man, and rendering the world an *aceldama,* or field of blood."[47]

This gloomy picture more readily suggested Thomas Hobbes's state of nature than Locke's, but this may be, not because Boucher was confused, but because he placed the two philosophers on the same level. Boucher found Hobbes no more acceptable than Locke, although Hobbes supported political authority in a way more plausible to the modern than Sir Robert Filmer's patriarchalism. Hobbes portrayed human nature as a beast "fiercer than either wolves or bears"; Boucher abhorred this as he did the philosopher's materialism. Boucher recognized in both Hobbes and Locke the prophecy of a society incompatible with his own notions—a society atomistic, relentlessly competitive, deducing (as C. B. MacPherson says of Hobbes) "political rights and obligations from the interest and will of dissociated individuals." Hobbes and Locke alike, in MacPherson's opinion, were exemplars of the "political theory of possessive individualism."[48]

With a Lockean or Hobbesian approach ruled out, Boucher turned logically to Sir Robert Filmer. Filmer's *Patriarcha: a Defence of the Natural Power of Kings Against the Unnatural Liberty of the People* was written about 1640, although not published until 1680. Filmer supported the divine right of kings with

47. Boucher, *Causes and Consequences*, pp. 514–15, 518.
48. Ibid., p. 332; C. B. MacPherson, *The Political Theory of Possessive Individualism: Hobbes to Locke* (Oxford, 1962), p. 1 and *passim*.

an exposition of the patriarchal origin of government. Kings, he held, were supreme fathers. Granted by God to Adam, the authority of kingship had descended through successive heads of families. Over every aggregation of people, consequently, someone ruled with the right of a father. Filmer has frequently been viewed as an easy foil for Locke's *First Treatise of Government*, but Filmer's argument was more sophisticated than Locke or many later critics acknowledged. "The crux of the matter was not an historical argument at all, but an analogy or correspondence between the king of a people and the father of a family and between the authority of each." This argument from correspondence was an accepted part of the old school of political thought based on the order and harmony of the world and of society.[49]

Boucher's own understanding of the patriarchalist argument was similarly sophisticated. His assertion in 1775 that "kingdoms and empires are but so many larger families," to which the fifth commandment applies, made better sense as an argument from correspondence than it did as a literal statement. At the same time, he carefully pointed out that the patriarchal origin of government not only was supported by historical evidence, but also was "by far the most natural, most consistent and most rational idea." Thus even without divine prescription men "would naturally have been led to the government of a community, or a nation, from the natural and obvious precedent of the government of a family."[50]

Although Boucher in his 1797 footnotes asserted that his opinion had not changed in twenty-two years, he seemed at the later date to shy away from a literal interpretation of the origin of kingly power. He qualified his defense of Filmer, admitting that the old patriarchalist had "entertained some very extravagant notions on monarchy, and the sacredness of kings" and had dis-

49. Greenleaf, *Order, Empiricism and Politics*, pp. 56, 87, and *passim*.
50. Boucher, *Causes and Consequences*, pp. 525–26, 528–30.

paraged the supremacy of law. Boucher now adduced historical and anthropological evidence, giving a more modern and scientific tone to Filmer's hypothesis that government derived from the family. He acknowledged that Locke had effectively ridiculed Filmer's less tenable points, but Boucher maintained that Locke had not answered Filmer's basic argument. "The leading idea or principle, of Sir Robert Filmer's Patriarcha," he finally concluded, "is, that government is not of human, but divine origin; and that the government of a family is the basis, or pattern, of all other government."[51] This was all that Jonathan Boucher's understanding of human society required.

Boucher had found in Filmer a rationale for a conservative point of view. Patriarchalism, he assumed, was adequately embodied in the British constitution, to which Boucher in 1773 could apprehend no danger except perhaps the weight of its own grandeur. Like many contemporaries he still believed that constitution to be a true expression of mixed government, though by 1776 he was disturbed by "the Preponderancy of the Popular Scale, even in England." The lack of any effective "Counterpoise" to the popular element he took to be the great weakness of American governments, and he finally accused Americans of a premeditated attack on the British constitution. Boucher's view of the constitution as "unalterable" fitted well with his hostility to political innovation. His constant targets were those who waged war against everything that was "established, venerable, and good," and he could say in 1771 that "there is danger, even in the notion, that religion and government admit of improvement; much of their influence and efficacy depending on the persuasion that they are already perfect."[52]

51. Ibid., pp. 527n.–532n.
52. Ibid., pp. 101, 217, 307; Boucher to William Eden, 3 January 1776, *Maryland Historical Magazine* 8 (December 1913):341; Boucher to James, 10 July 1776, ibid., 9 (March 1914):67; Boucher, *Causes and Consequences*, pp. 203, 323, 362.

Yet nothing in Boucher's philosophy precluded amelioration within the established order, and he occasionally championed reform. His suggestion that Indians be regarded "as human beings, capable of civilization" was liberal in 1763, and his "abhorrence" of slavery showed some awareness of the evils of that institution. Although he did not deny its legality and believed it to be relatively humane in America, he recognized that it debased both slaves and their masters and was "injurious to society at large." Priding himself on being a kind master and on having baptized hundreds of Negroes, he exposed the hypocrisy of American Whigs—"the most clamorous advocates for liberty [who] were uniformly the harshest and worst masters of slaves." Boucher's early conclusion that a freed slave could never exist on equal terms with the free white man confirmed the deep roots of American racism.[53]

Boucher was an even less likely libertarian than reformer, but he has been depicted as "a man eager to preserve and increase human freedom." Such an interpretation seems incompatible with Boucher's strict understanding of liberty ("True Liberty, then, is a liberty to do everything that is right, and the being restrained from doing any thing that is wrong") and with his animadversions upon "schisms and sects."[54] But Robert G. Walker correctly asserted that Boucher supported toleration of dissenters—as distinct from religious indifferentism by the state. Boucher made this clear in arguing for the toleration of "Papists." He believed that "no man was ever made a convert to any opinion by compulsion." This position was apparently sincere, although his support of Catholic rights was designed to encourage their loyalism. Boucher entertained no such animosity for Roman Catholicism as he did for

53. Ibid., pp. 13, 39–42, 186n.; Boucher, *Reminiscences*, pp. 57–58, 96–97.
54. Robert G. Walker, "Jonathan Boucher: Champion of the Minority," *William and Mary Quarterly*, 3rd Series, 2 (January 1945):13; Boucher, *Causes and Consequences*, pp. 60ff, 511.

Puritanism; indeed, his social and political views inclined him to sympathize with it. Despite his condemnation of Catholic "error," he anticipated that he would be accused of *"edging towards Popery"* for proposing that Catholics be put on an equal footing with other Dissenters in Maryland.[55] Boucher's proposal for a reunion of Catholics, Anglicans, and Presbyterians "on almost any terms" may have been conservative in intent, as was his plan for universal peace and order under an Anglo-American-Indian federation. Neither proposal, however, showed an inflexible mind—nor did his suggestion that the seat of the British Empire be transported to staunchly unrepublican Asia.[56]

III

A View of the Causes and Consequences of the American Revolution touched on major issues and problems of the revolutionary period. As a priest of the Church of England, Boucher discussed at length the religious aspects of the Anglo-American conflict, which have received increased attention in recent years. He represented, of course, an ultra-Anglican position on such specific issues as ecclesiastical salaries and the American episcopate. But he also expressed an ultra-Anglican *Weltanschauung* which provided an interesting historical foil for the revolutionary Calvinist impetus that Alan Heimert found in the Great Awakening. Certainly Boucher, in common with many loyalists, recognized and despised New Englanders as archenemies of the values he held dear and directly associated the Puritan tradition with a republican and rebellious spirit. Religious contempt was the basis of

---

55. Walker, "Jonathan Boucher," p. 8; Boucher, *Causes and Consequences*, pp. 255, 259–61, 270, 288, 577–578. No one, said Boucher, should suffer pains merely for being a religious dissenter. "More than this, no reasonable, well-informed, or well-principled Dissenter will ask, and less, no Christian State can consistently think of granting" (ibid., p. 259).

56. Ibid., pp. lxvii–lxxxiii, 264.

Boucher's ardent sectionalism; his contention that the southern colonies were inveigled into rebellion by a people "for whom they entertained an hereditary national disesteem, confirmed by their own personal dislike," is worth mention in the history of North-South antagonism.[57]

Aside from questions of religion and the ultimate question of submission to authority, Boucher did not seriously discuss the immediate issues of the revolution—the Tea and Coercion Acts, for instance, or the basic constitutional issue of parliamentary taxation. He dealt with the revolutionary crisis either on a personal and local level or on an abstract plane where universal forces of authority contended with those of sedition. Reading of Boucher's maltreatment as the defender of unpopular views, we gain some insight into the role of personal grievances in revolutionary situations. Boucher was aware of this personal factor, as shown by his comments on Benjamin Franklin. But he professed to understand the American Revolution as "merely" a party contest. (The "merely" seems inappropriate, since he referred to transatlantic Whig and Tory parties and blamed the Whigs for unleashing the monster of revolution which seemed to be devouring European civilization as Boucher wrote the preface to his *Causes and Consequences*.[58]) And he reminded us that to the traditionalist—to the man threatened in Maryland with Whig "terror"—the American and French Revolutions seemed essentially alike as expressions of a historical movement.

Although no more objective than David Ramsay and other contemporary historians he criticized, Boucher did, as he had

57. E.g. Carl Bridenbaugh, *Mitre and Sceptre, Transatlantic Faiths, Ideas, Personalities, and Politics, 1689–1775* (New York, ·1962); Alan Heimert, *Religion and the American Mind from the Great Awakening to the Revolution* (Cambridge, 1966); Boucher, *Causes and Consequences*, pp. xxxiv–xxxv, 102–4, 472–74; Nelson, *American Tory*, pp. 51, 180.
58. Boucher, *Causes and Consequences*, pp. vi–vii, 445–47.

hoped, make easier a fair appraisal of the American Revolution. As a profound and articulate spokesman for the loyalists, he made loyalism more comprehensible. Other Tories might not follow him back to Sir Robert Filmer, but they agreed with him on such points as the weakness of American social and political institutions and the close connection between Puritanism and revolution.[59] Boucher's Toryism was more often hyperbolic than unrepresentative.

It is tempting to present Jonathan Boucher as an American counterpart to Edmund Burke. Certainly if a counterpart is required, Boucher makes a more plausible one than John Adams, who has sometimes been assigned that role. Boucher and Burke disagreed, of course, on the character of the American rebellion and on the distinction, if any, between it and the French Revolution. But Boucher frequently applied the same strictures to the earlier conflict that the great Whig reserved for the upheaval of 1789. Parallel sentiments are easily found: reluctance to sweep aside proven political institutions in pursuit of imaginary perfection, consciousness that the accreted work of centuries could be quickly destroyed. Boucher's belief in the value of sound prejudices was reminiscent of Burke's dictum: "Prejudice renders a man's virtue his habit." Although their political philosophies were not identical (Burke was not a Filmerian), both belonged to a school of political traditionalism which "had existed for so long," according to Pocock, "that it was itself traditional."[60]

But Boucher could not be an American Burke, if only because

---

59. Ibid., pp. ii–v, xxii–xxiii; Nelson, *American Tory*, pp. 51, 172.

60. Allen Guttmann points out the fallacy of equating Adams and Burke (*Conservative Tradition*, pp. 23–27); Boucher, *Causes and Consequences*, pp. 208, 246, 356; Edmund Burke, *Reflections on the Revolution in France*, ed. Charles W. Eliot (New York, 1909), pp. 235, 244, 316. I have compared Boucher and Burke at somewhat greater length ("Mirror of Reaction," pp. 26–27, 30–31). J. G. A. Pocock, "Burke and the Ancient Constitution—a Problem in the History of Ideas," *The Historical Journal* 3 (No. 2, 1960):126.

British society was not duplicated in the American colonies. Burke's traditionalism was related to the ancient and well-established order he knew. While American political institutions and ideas were patterned on British models, Boucher's own traditionalism was less applicable in a relatively fluid and unstructured society. Boucher never entirely grasped this problem; he saw only that everything in his adopted country "had a republican aspect." Believing that his fortunes were cast in America, Jonathan Boucher became an exile for beliefs alien to his countrymen.

6.

Israel Mauduit: Antirevolutionary Pamphleteer

ROBERT J. TAYLOR

Israel Mauduit, son of a dissenting minister, was born in 1708, probably in Bermondsey, London.[1] Educated in the Dissenters School at Taunton, he preached for a while in England and abroad, but he soon left the ministry to go into trade with his brother Jasper as a woolen-draper in Lime Street. Yet Israel never lost his interest in the dissenters; toward the end of his life he accepted a place on the board of the Society for the Propagation of Christian Knowledge. He was elected a fellow of the Royal Society in 1751.

Mauduit first came into political prominence in 1760, during the Seven Years War, as the author of a highly praised pamphlet advocating that England give up its alliance with Prussia against Austria in the Silesian campaign. As a naval power, England ought to devote its energies, he felt, to seizing the lucrative French West Indies. *Considerations on the Present German War* demolished the popular assumption that partnership with Prussia would help Protestantism or that loss of Hanover would hurt England. Essentially a study in power politics conceived in terms of population and resources, the pamphlet was remarkably persuasive. It earned for its author a customs post at Southampton.

1. Biographical details are from *DNB*; *The Gentleman's Magazine* 57 (June 1787):549; *The European Magazine and London Review* 11 (June 1787): 383–84 and 12 (July 1787):6–8; and Robert J. Taylor, "Israel Mauduit," *New England Quarterly* 24 (June 1951):208–30.

Israel's brother Jasper in 1762 had been named colonial agent for Massachusetts, partly because of his dissenting religion and partly because other candidates suffered from factional hostilities. From the first, Israel assisted in the agency, and Jasper, whose health·was not good, sought unsuccessfully to make his brother's role as assistant an official one. Israel lobbied to get Massachusetts its reimbursements for military expenditures, a reduction of the proposed duty on foreign molasses, and a reduction of the duty on whale fins to encourage the whale fishery. Israel knew many influential men of the day, and his pen was active. In May 1764, after George Grenville had mentioned in Parliament a stamp tax on the colonies, Israel was among the agents who met with Grenville to get more detail about what he had intended. Israel said that without "the particular heads of the Bill," the minister was asking the colonies "to Assent to they did not know what."[2] When he published his account of the meeting between Grenville and the agents, he pictured Grenville offering the colonies a genuine opportunity to suggest alternatives to the stamp tax.

Jasper Mauduit lost the Massachusetts agency to Richard Jackson in January 1765, before the rift really opened between the colonies and Great Britain over parliamentary taxation. Thus Israel never faced the practical question of which side to take. Had he been forced to choose, he would not have hesitated, for he firmly believed in parliamentary supremacy. While he worked to secure economic benefits for his brother's colonial employers, he never questioned parliamentary authority, and he could not forgive those who did. For him, the lesson of history was clear: Englishmen in removing James II from the throne had established Parliament as supreme. No power in the British Empire could withstand the king acting through Parliament. As early as 1774 he concluded that Massachusetts was in rebellion. Mauduit took a

2. Edmund S. Morgan, ed., *Prologue to Revolution: Sources and Documents on the Stamp Act Crisis, 1764–1766* (Chapel Hill, 1959), p. 27.

simplistic view of the colonists' theoretical arguments, never going beyond charter interpretations to look into theories of representation, distinctions between taxation and legislation, possibilities of a commonwealth scheme, and other ideas that challenged men on both sides of the Atlantic.

During the revolution, Mauduit stayed active, exerting his influence on behalf of those whom he approved and writing an occasional pamphlet. In 1778 he wrote a pamphlet advocating independence for the colonies. He may have been acting for Lord North, who perhaps wished to sound out public sentiment after the news of the treaty between France and America. North himself publicly opposed granting independence, but he sent the pamphlet to the King, telling him that a number of friends of government feared that Great Britain would be "overmatched" in a war with France, Spain, and the United States.

A few weeks later, Mauduit began a new undertaking—publicly dressing down General William Howe and Admiral Richard Howe for their timid and inept leadership of British forces in 1776 and 1777. His five pamphlets' knowledge of tactics and terrain suggested that someone with inside information supplied him with details. Since North and the king were not hostile to the Howes, Worthington C. Ford has suggested that Mauduit may have been working for Lord George Germain, who as American secretary and thus secretary at war could furnish him with technical information.[3] Germain probably feared that he himself would be blamed for the strategical blunders that contributed to General Burgoyne's failure. Mauduit himself had anxious moments over his bold attack on the Howes, a failure of nerve that friends like Hutchinson could not understand. He breathed easier when the ministry began to suffer criticism for mismanagement of the war and his

3. Worthington C. Ford, "Parliament and the Howes," Massachusetts Historical Society *Proceedings* 44 (1911):130.

diatribes against the Howes no longer threatened his standing with ministers who were themselves under attack.

When Mauduit died in 1787, newspapers praised his firm support of the British cause and his effectiveness as a pamphleteer. A number of Tories exiled in London had cause to be grateful for his influence, and men in high places had found him useful on occasion. He was never, of course, a prime mover, but neither was he a mere tool for sale to the highest bidder. He deeply believed in the supremacy of king and Parliament; for him· the colonies were defiant children, scandalously setting at naught proper submission to the mother country.

Mauduit's *History*

A Short View of the History of the New England Colonies originally appeared in 1769, without the author's name, as *A Short View of the History of the Colony of Massachusetts-Bay with Respect to Their Original Charter and Constitution.* The change of title in 1776 did not signify broader coverage; Massachusetts remained Mauduit's sole concern. Here and there he talked about charters or used a plural pronoun, but Connecticut, Rhode Island, and New Hampshire received little mention. Mauduit saw Massachusetts and its leaders as particularly offensive and wrongheaded in the argument between the colonies and the mother country, and he sought to show the speciousness of relying on their charter to justify their claim that Parliament had no right to tax them.[4]

4. Between the 1769 and 1776 editions, however, changes occurred in content. The publishing history of *A Short View* is, in fact, extremely complicated. In 1769, a title page reading "second edition" was printed, although this and the first edition were printed from the same typesetting at the same time. Another edition from the same typesetting also appeared in 1774, but to this was added the first Massachusetts charter printed without marginal annotations. The charter was also printed separately with its own pagination for those who already had earlier editions. Also in 1774 came a new typesetting of

Mauduit directed much of his attack at two newspaper articles which he quoted at length in the early editions of his pamphlet. From the *Boston Gazette* cf 5 September 1768, he had extracted an anonymous piece signed "Clericus Americanus," which asserted that the land of Massachusetts belonged originally to the Indians and was purchased from them by settlers without help from the Crown, that the connection between Massachusetts and Great Britain was solely one of compact embodied in the charter. The essay then called for an assembly of representatives to meet because Governor Francis Bernard refused to call the General Court into session. (Lord Hillsborough, the American secretary in London, had ordered the Court's dissolution for its refusal to rescind the Circular Letter.) Bernard's inaction contravened the charter. "Clericus Americanus" implied that under the circumstances the colonists probably returned to a state of nature, but a persistent note of utter loyalty to the king's person ran through his discourse.

An extract from the *Boston Evening Post* of 19 September 1768 included resolutions adopted by Boston on 12 and 13 September and Boston's letter to Massachusetts towns urging them to elect representatives to a convention to meet on 22 September. Bostonians were exercised over three matters: Bernard's refusal to assemble the General Court on the ground that he lacked instructions from Great Britain; a report that three British regiments

---

the text, which eliminated fourteen and one-half pages of excerpts from two Boston newspapers. With this shorter text was included a new printing of the charter with marginal annotations; this was called the third edition. The fourth edition, with altered title, appeared in 1776 in two forms. One was the third edition with two paragraphs added to the body of the text, and with an account of a meeting between George Grenville and the colonial agents tacked on after the charter. The other fourth edition was a second resetting of the type of the body of the text and included the account of the meeting and the charter which had appeared earlier with its own pagination and without marginal annotations. I am indebted to Thomas R. Adams for help in getting straight the differences among the various editions. See his "The British Pamphlets of the American Revolution for 1774: A Progress Report," *Mass. Hist. Soc. Proceedings* 81 (1969): 50–52.

would be quartered in the Boston area; and Parliament's attempts to tax the colonies. All three actions were held to violate constitutional, charter, and natural rights. Mauduit wished to attack the appeals to the charter.

Citing Massachusetts history from the Pilgrims' landing to the charter granted by William III in 1691, and acknowledging his heavy dependence on Daniel Neal's *The History of New England* and Thomas Hutchinson's *The History of the Colony of Massachusetts-Bay*, Mauduit strove to establish several facts. The earliest settlers had no idea of independence from England or of the importance to them of representative institutions. The latter emerged for practical reasons when increasing size made a primary assembly inexpedient. Charter claims put forward by eighteenth-century colonists respecting their elected assembly could be based only on the first Massachusetts charter of 1628, granted when the extent of Stuart sovereignty was uncertain. Clearly the charter of 1691, granted by a king fully cognizant of Parliament's power, could not make Massachusetts independent of Parliament's right to tax. Along the way, Mauduit underscored the limited nature of the seventeenth-century franchise, when church membership was a prerequisite for voting. This restriction showed how far Massachusetts people then were from the principle of no taxation without representation, which their eighteenth-century descendants claimed was inherent in their charter. Mauduit found instances when Massachusetts accepted subordination to the king as one element of the British legislature, and accepted the House of Commons's assumption that it could legislate for Massachusetts.

When Mauduit discussed the efforts of Increase Mather and other Massachusetts agents to get King William to reinstate the old charter, he outlined the legal objections made by eminent lawyers—Solicitor General John Somers, Attorney General George Treby, and Edward Ward. The original Massachusetts charter contained no provisions for a body of deputies, for courts, for taxing nonresidents, and for other powers essential to government. The colony had simply taken on these powers, an impropriety sufficient to have voided the charter. Mauduit's conclusion was emphatic: exemption from parliamentary taxation could not be derived from charter rights.

Drawing on source materials available in Hutchinson's *History*, Mauduit knocked holes in the charter argument. Massachusetts had made a fetish of the charter, reading into it what could not be found there. Cogently Mauduit pointed out awkward facts that could not be reconciled with the charter as guarantor of virtual self-government under the king. But as a polemic, *A Short View* ignored the coupling of the charter argument with appeals to the British constitution and to natural rights. This defect was compounded when the pamphlet was reissued in 1776, after the colonists had dropped appeals to the charter. Moreover, omission of the excerpts from Boston newspapers in the 1776 edition made the emphasis on the charter argument even more puzzling.

The fourth edition also contained two additional paragraphs. The first was an unflattering comparison between those who fled England, albeit for religious liberty, and those who stayed at home, enduring "the much greater Hardships of a Civil War for the Common Deliverance" to preserve "the Freedom of this Country and of America both." When England was "enthrall'd under a popish Tyrant," the colonists remained passive, reserving "all their active Powers to rebel against the mild Government of Laws" under George III. Mauduit chided the colonists at this point, forgetting his later admission that Massachusetts did indeed rise up against Sir Edmund Andros and establish an interim government.

The other additional paragraph noted the grateful entrance in Massachusetts General Court records in 1642 of Parliament's action foregoing customs duties on goods going to and from New England "until the House of Commons shall take further Order therein to the contrary." Mauduit saw this as a perfect example of accepting Parliament's right to tax the colonies. But he ignored the careful distinction colonists made in the 1760s between taxation for revenue and imposts for trade regulation.

Chief justification for the fourth edition of *A Short View*, of course, was the addition of Mauduit's account of the meeting between George Grenville and the colonial agents. Actually, Mauduit's account of the meeting, which took place while Grenville considered a stamp tax, had been before the public for some time, since it had first appeared in the newspapers in 1775. Mauduit ostensibly was answering Edmund Burke's charge in April 1774, in a speech on American taxation, that Grenville had never given the colonies the alternative of taxing themselves. Mauduit's long delay in answering suggested that he had another purpose. Edmund S. Morgan believes that Mauduit's account prepared the way for Lord North's conciliatory resolution, offered on 20 February 1775, which would have permitted the colonies to tax themselves with the approval of king and Parliament.[5]

Mauduit contended that Grenville had genuinely proposed self-taxation to the colonies if they wished to avoid a parliamentary tax. Their failure to respond proved, Mauduit felt, that their main object was to avoid taxation, not to support a principle. Thus Mauduit sought to answer Burke's charge that Grenville had not given the colonies an alternative to the Stamp Act. Polemic zeal caused Mauduit to forget that he himself had recognized the vagueness of Grenville's words at his meeting with the agents, that he had asked in vain for more particulars about the proposed tax and had been put off by the minister.

Historians differ in interpretating Grenville's purpose. Professor Morgan is convinced that no sincere offer was intended; Michael G. Kammen feels that Grenville might have intended a requisition system as a real alternative to the stamp tax, but that in any case

5. Edmund S. Morgan, "The Postponement of the Stamp Act," *William and Mary Quarterly*, 3rd series, 7 (July 1950):384–85.

he was not sincere; and Jack M. Sosin feels that Grenville's offer can be called hollow only if a requisition system was his alternative, but that Grenville in fact expected the colonies to propose alternative parliamentary taxation.[6] At any rate, Mauduit felt that the corroboration of William Knox, agent for Georgia and author of *The Controversy between Great Britain and her Colonies Reviewed*, and the approval of Edward Montague, agent for Virginia, gave sufficient weight to Mauduit's version, although Professor Morgan has shown that Knox's pamphlet was not consistent with one he wrote earlier.[7]

Trying to make a whipping boy of Massachusetts, Mauduit failed to grasp the scope and profundity of the revolutionary arguments. A *Short View* contributed to Englishmen's misunderstanding of what was bothering the American colonists.

The Hutchinson Letters

Like A *Short View*, Mauduit's pamphlet bringing together letters of Thomas Hutchinson, remarks by Mauduit, and the proceedings of the Privy Council has a complicated publishing history. According to Thomas R. Adams, who is preparing a bibliography of British pamphlets of the revolutionary period, the Mauduit compilation appeared in at least five different forms in 1774.[8]

Copies of the letters of Hutchinson, Andrew Oliver, and others

6. Edmund S. and Helen M. Morgan, *The Stamp Act Crisis* (Chapel Hill, 1953), pp. 91–92; Michael G. Kammen, *A Rope of Sand* (Ithaca, 1968), pp. 109–10; Jack M. Sosin, *Whitehall and the Wilderness* (Lincoln, Neb., 1961), pp. 84–86, and *Agents and Merchants* (Lincoln, Neb., 1965), pp. 51–53.

7. Morgan, "Postponement of the Stamp Act," pp. 378–79.

8. Adams, "The British Pamphlets," pp. 54–55. The exact title of Mauduit's pamphlet is *The Letters of Governor Hutchinson, and Lieut. Governor Oliver, &c. Printed at Boston. And Remarks Thereon. With the Assembly's Address, and The Proceedings of the Lords Committee of Council. Together with the Substance of Mr. Wedderburn's Speech Relating to Those Letters.*

had appeared in American and English newspapers in 1773, well before Mauduit reprinted them; in America they had been circulated in a variety of pamphlets.[9] Mauduit's edition was designed to publicize both his own views and a harsh attack on Benjamin Franklin by Alexander Wedderburn before the Privy Council. Mauduit was serving the interests of the ministry, as he did on several occasions, but he acted also out of genuine revulsion for the way Hutchinson was treated.

The general outline of the Hutchinson letters episode is well known. Through means he never divulged, Franklin came into possession of letters written in 1767, 1768, and 1769 by Hutchinson and Oliver to Thomas Whately, a member of Parliament and formerly a secretary at the Treasury who held no government post at the time the letters were written. The letters described anti-British activities in Massachusetts and suggested strong responses from London. Franklin sent these letters to Speaker Thomas Cushing of the Massachusetts House of Representatives, suggesting that they be circulated among a select few and stating that he had no permission to publish them. Despite Franklin's caution, Samuel Adams and others published the letters after first carefully hinting in the press of forthcoming scandalous revelations touching persons in high office. When Hutchinson and Oliver wrote these letters, they were lieutenant governor and secretary of Massachusetts respectively; at the time of publication they were governor and lieutenant governor, the two highest royal appointees in the province. In a petition to the king, the House of Representatives requested dismissal of both men for alienating the affections of the king for Massachusetts, for turning the royal administration against the province, and for bringing troops and a fleet to Boston.

The House petition was drawn up in June 1773 and transmitted

9. Ibid., p. 54, and Thomas R. Adams, *American Independence: The Growth of an Idea* (Providence, 1965), p. 72.

by Franklin on 21 August to the Earl of Dartmouth, the American
secretary, but the ministry delayed formal consideration until
December. Before a committee of the Privy Council could report
on the request of the Massachusetts House, Mauduit petitioned to
be heard with counsel on behalf of the accused officials. Thus the
stage was set for a trial of the issues, which, according to the
province's attorneys, John Dunning and John Lee, was not Massachusetts's intention. They argued that the petition demonstrated
the dissatisfaction of Massachusetts people with their royally
appointed officials. Dunning and Lee saw it, as Franklin did, as a
political matter to be settled by the king as he saw fit. There was
no need for charges, proof, and the legal trappings of a trial. But
a trial it became—mainly a trial of Benjamin Franklin, who sat
silent through Wedderburn's passionate condemnation of him.
The Privy Council, finding nothing reprehensible or unworthy in
the letters, dismissed the Massachusetts petition and characterized
it as "groundless, vexatious, and scandalous."

Since the hearing took place a day or two after the shocking
news of the Boston Tea Party, Wedderburn's severe attack on
Franklin and the joy it roused in many who packed the council
chamber was understandable. What puzzles the modern reader is
why Massachusetts patriots made such an issue over the letters of
Hutchinson and Oliver. A check of the Hutchinson letters against
extant letterbook copies shows that they were printed virtually
verbatim; there were no editorial deletions or colorful additions.[10]
Obviously the letters were seized on as an excuse to be rid of men
hated for their offices, their views, their pretensions. But read
dispassionately, the letters offer no surprises, and their publication
seems a weak tactic. People in Massachusetts did not read them

10. For interesting speculation on a possibly significant change in wording
from *Liberty* to *English liberties*, see Malcolm Freiberg, "Missing: One
Hutchinson Autograph Letter," *Manuscripts* 8 (Spring 1956):179–84.

dispassionately, of course, and key phrases were lifted out of context and flaunted as proof of perfidy.

The six Hutchinson letters referred to "highly criminal" things spoken and written by some of the common people, to the "ill-natured and impotent" result of the Massachusetts convention of September 1768, to "the licentiousness of such as call themselves Sons of Liberty," and to a wish for more support from England than "some declaratory acts or resolves." But Hutchinson also expressed a desire to avoid "the least degree of severity beyond what is absolutely necessary to maintain . . . the dependence which a colony ought to have upon the parent state." He saw an end to such dependence as utter ruin. In the passage most often cited, Hutchinson called for an "abridgment of what are called English liberties," which sounded ominous enough. He fleshed out his meaning, however, with explanations ignored by his enemies: that in going from a state of nature to government, natural liberty must be restrained; that a colony three thousand miles from the mother country could not expect as much liberty as existed at home; and that restraint of liberty was preferable to a breach that would bring ruin. Rather than scheming to curb American liberty, Hutchinson was expressing traditional conservative fears of drastic change.

Oliver's letters suggested more specifics for reconstructed government in the colonies. He urged the creation of a local aristocracy of landed gentlemen, freed of service in the lesser but demanding offices of the province, who could serve on the legislative council. He thought members of this superior order might choose council members, subject to the governor's veto, and thus avoid the disadvantages of either popular choice or royal mandate. In turn, the governor would fill the ranks of the honorary order by naming additional men from time to time with the advice of the council. Oliver also suggested a privy council of some or all of the legislative council plus distinguished men from the House of Representatives. Appointing men to such a council would be another way for the governor to recognize "the better sort." Oliver felt it important to maintain a balance between the popular part of government and an independent royal authority. Such a balance approximated the legislative system of Great Britain in which the House of Lords played a significant role. A number of conservatives in the colonies—usually to their cost—had outlined such schemes.

Besides advocating such aristocratic devices, Oliver strongly approved the suggestion (made in a pamphlet he had received from Whately) that colonists elect representatives to Parliament. *The Present State of the Nation*, published in 1768 and attributed to William Knox, advocated representation not because Parliament could not tax those who were unrepresented, but because the colonies' extent, population growth, and valuable trade demanded "that more attention should be paid to their concerns, by the supreme legislature, than can be expected from it, so long as the colonies do not elect any of the members of which the house of commons is composed." Oliver noted that William Bollan, agent for the Massachusetts Council, and former governor Thomas Pownall both favored representation; yet the colonies, in the Stamp Act Congress of 1765, had emphatically denied that they could be represented in Parliament.

Oliver's calm scheming with Nathaniel Rogers, Hutchinson's nephew, to fill the offices of lieutenant governor and secretary, with its overtones of nepotism and influence-seeking, irritated the readers of these letters. Even to the modern reader the timid calculations and selfish considerations, however familiar, make protestations about the good of the province ring hollow.

Mauduit's defense of these and other published letters consisted of three main points: the correspondence was private; publication of the letters was an excuse to attack and try to remove the royal governor, as royal governors had been attacked in the past and would be in the future; Boston's interpretation of English liberties came from a false reading of the Massachusetts charter, a reading wholly inconsistent with the British constitution.

Whether or not the correspondence was private was a significant question. Franklin had justified sending the letters to the province on the grounds that they were written by public officials on public matters and handed to other officials for the purpose of affecting public measures. Taking his cue from Wedderburn, Mauduit noted that the letters were written when Thomas Whately was merely a member of Parliament who voted in opposition to government policies. Whately had given up his position with the Treasury two or three years earlier. Certainly Lieutenant Governor Hutchinson could have written directly to the ministry to influence policies had that been his purpose; moreover, Hutchinson had openly criticized Whig views in Massachusetts. In January 1773, for example, he had rejected the position of the Boston Committee of Correspondence when it claimed exclusive taxing powers for the General Court. Hutchinson declared that any government could have only one locus of sovereignty, that separate and independent representative bodies under a single king could lead only to separate states—a defense of the Augustinian conception of sovereignty that Mauduit quoted with approval.

Mauduit's contribution to the debate over the General Court's powers was his interpretation of the charter phrase guaranteeing the people of Massachusetts that they were to "have and enjoy all Liberties and Immunities of Free and natural Subjects within any of the Dominions of Us . . . to all Intents Constructions and purposes whatsoever as if they and every of them were borne within this Our Realm of England." This grant of English liberties did not mean, as Bostonians had contended, that the Massachusetts General Court had full power to levy taxes for the support of provincial government, including the salaries of judges, or that the General Court was virtually coordinate with Parliament. Mauduit insisted "that single clause . . . grants them nothing while they are *in* the province, but only provides for their good reception *in all parts of the King's dominions, when* they go *out* of it."

Within the province, Mauduit argued, the legislative power of the colonists was limited by the Charter's requirement that their laws must be consistent with the laws of England; this meant they could not act contrary to the statutes of Parliament. Mauduit returned to this point in the copy of the first Massachusetts charter included with his third edition of *A Short View;* he called attention in a footnote to the difference in language between the Massachusetts charter and the first Virginia charter. The latter specified that the colonists would enjoy all liberties "within any of our *other* Dominions" (Mauduit's italics). Mauduit believed that the word *other* was implied in all such charter clauses. If by English liberties the Massachusetts people meant full right to legislate for themselves, then their liberties did indeed need abridgment.

Besides his own comments on the letters, Mauduit's pamphlet included enough of the Privy Council proceedings to give a proper backdrop to the trenchant harangue of Alexander Wedderburn. Solicitor General Wedderburn had been an intimate friend of Thomas Whately and felt keenly the dishonor that had fallen on the Whately heirs who for a time had been thought guilty of giving Franklin the letters. But more than personal animus fired Wedderburn. The ministry knew, through Franklin's communications to his constituents, that Franklin encouraged colonial resistance to parliamentary measures. The letters gave Wedderburn an opportunity to publicly besmirch Franklin's character—an opportunity he intended to make the most of.

Wedderburn scoffed at the contention of Dunning and Lee that there was no need for a trial. He treated the Massachusetts petition as a series of unfounded charges, demolishing each in turn in lawyerlike fashion. But he devoted most of his energy to castigating the behavior and assumptions of Franklin, casting doubt on his credentials as agent and falsely accusing the colonist of writing anonymously to Speaker Cushing. At some length he portrayed Franklin "as inventor and first planner of the whole contrivance," as the man who taught the doctrines which the Boston Committee of Correspondence had circulated to the Massachusetts towns in an effort to stir up resistance against alleged encroachments by Parliament on the charter. He had even brought out an English edition of the Boston statement. Behind it all, Wedderburn thundered, lay a plot to make Franklin governor and to create an independent American republic.

At the end of Wedderburn's denunciation Franklin chose not to be examined. His silence seemed to his opponents an admission of guilt, to his supporters an expression of contempt. The Privy Council immediately asked for dismissal of the Massachusetts petition, and the ministry enjoyed its triumph. Franklin lost his position as colonial postmaster and faced a suit in chancery brought by William Whately.

Some who heard Wedderburn castigated his speech as scurrilous and inhumane, but Franklin noted that Wedderburn had frequently been interrupted with loud applause. When Mauduit's pamphlet appeared, Franklin charged that "the grosser parts of the abuse are omitted, appearing, I suppose, in their eyes too foul to be seen on paper, so that the speech, compared to what it was, is now perfectly decent."[11] If Franklin was accurate, Mauduit edited as well as compiled.

Mauduit's pamphlet did not contribute to the discussion of constitutional issues dividing Americans and Englishmen, but it

11. Opinions on Wedderburn's speech and Franklin's comment on Mauduit's editing of it are quoted in Carl Van Doren, *Benjamin Franklin* (New York, 1938), pp. 473, 476.

did titillate that part of the public which enjoyed seeing a great American brought low. Some Englishmen sprang to Franklin's defense, of course, and in America his reputation was only enhanced. Chiefly the pamphlet increased the smugness of those Englishmen who thought that Americans were wrong and that the ministry had been too lenient. Thus it helped create a suitable atmosphere for the passage of the Coercive Acts in the spring of 1775.

7.

Alexander Hewat's *Historical Account*

GERALDINE M. MERONEY

Alexander Hewat's *An Historical Account of the Rise and Progress of the Colonies of South Carolina and Georgia,* published anonymously in London in 1779, is clearly within the Enlightenment tradition of historical writing and more precisely within the Scottish school represented by William Robertson. The eighteenth century viewed history not as events studied for their own sake, but as intellectual and moral instruction for men striving to overcome the destructive forces of ignorance and passion. The progress of civilization was measured by the degree to which man's sense of order and moral justice prevailed over unreason in his nature and his society.

To this concept of history, William Robertson added the "dignity of history." By this he meant that history "should be written about dignified events and characters." To preserve this noble purpose, the historian should concentrate on "those transactions which necessarily demand attention because of their inherent interest, or because of the instruction to be derived from them."[1] This left to the historian's judgment the choice of relevant and informative events and transactions. William Douglass included in his histories such a variety of curious detail that his selection seems either indiscriminate or lacking in purpose.

1. John Bennett Black, *The Art of History. A Study of Four Great Historians of the Eighteenth Century* (London, 1926), p. 131.

Robertson also included a variety of informative details, but he used them to support his analyses of causal relationships. He was among the first to recognize that environmental factors such as geography, climate, customs of barbarian peoples, and unique dangers or advantages of an environment, were relevant to the historical development of a society.[2]

Alexander Hewat proposed in his Preface "to present the world with a particular, but imperfect, detail of its [South Carolina's] most memorable and important transactions."[3] He wanted to inform his readers of conditions in the southern colonies so that the British might better understand the colonies' importance to Britain and that the colonists might better understand their own history and Great Britain's importance to them. Like Robertson, Hewat included detailed descriptions of climate, geography, animals and insects, rituals and customs of neighboring Indian tribes, conditions of slavery, and all the environmental dangers or advantages experienced by southern colonists in America. He considered these details instructive for those unacquainted with them and supportive for his analyses of causal relationships in the progress of colonial society.

Although Hewat did not have Robertson's skill in organizing and integrating his supportive materials, his work was superior to that of William Douglass. He cannot be fairly criticized for rambling "widely from his subject, frequently interrupting his historical narrative to give long digressions on natural history, religion, or economics," or of interspersing his political narrative with "social history, as well as some natural history . . . rarely related to the

2. William Douglass, A *Summary, historical and political, of the first planting, progressive improvements, and present state of the British settlements in North America* (Boston, 1752); Michael Kraus, A *History of American History* (New York, 1937), pp. 102–3; Black, *Art of History*, pp. 135–38.

3. [Alexander Hewat], An *Historical Account of the Rise and Progress of the Colonies of South Carolina and Georgia*, 2 vols., (London, 1779), 1:iii.

theme of politics."[4] Hewat was not writing a political history or a chronological narrative. He used a periodic framework, but his narration was analytical rather than chronological and his theme was more dignified than simply that of political development. What may seem irrelevant to modern historians was included to support analyses of causes and mutual relationships—that is, the struggle of man's rational and moral activities against the destructive forces in nature and society.

Eighteenth-century historians had a passion "for accuracy, completeness, and impartiality." Robertson was particularly concerned with accurately determining and presenting events or conditions so the historian could make an objective and judicious analysis of "their mutual connection and dependence" and show "how the operation of one event or one cause prepared the way for another and augmented its influence."[5] Hewat reflected this same concern when he explained: "Many long speeches, petitions, addresses, etc. he might no doubt have abridged; but as these were his principal vouchers, for his own sake, he chose to give them entire." A critic in *The Monthly Review* commended Hewat's diligence in collecting materials and his fidelity in using them: "Though the work is extremely deficient in the graces of historical composition, and though in the detail of facts it is often tedious, it will probably be preserved as a valuable collection of materials, from whence future writers of superior abilities may derive assistance in forming a general History of the Colonies."[6]

4. Elmer D. Johnson, "Alexander Hewat: South Carolina's First Historian," *The Journal of Southern History* 20 (February 1954):52; Kraus, *History*, p. 123.

5. Ralph H. Bowen, "The Heavenly City: A Too-ingenious Paradox," in *Carl Becker's Heavenly City Revisited*, ed. Raymond O. Rockwood (Ithaca, N.Y., 1958), p. 147; William Robertson, "A View of the Progress of Society in Europe," *The History of the Reign of the Emperor Charles the Fifth*, 3 vols. (Philadelphia, 1883), 1:25; see also Black, *Art of History*, pp. 118–21.

6. *The Monthly Review* 61 (December 1779): 444.

Hewat's sources included colonial records, printed accounts, newspaper articles, family papers, oral traditions, and personal testimonies by participants in recent events in South Carolina and Georgia. Although he seldom identified his sources, it is easy to recognize his use of early accounts written by John Archdale, Francis Yonge, and Governor Glen. Hewat paraphrased these and other authors and often reproduced official documents word for word. His friendships in Charleston with Lieutenant Governor William Bull, Superintendent for Indian Affairs John Stuart, and other prominent men gave him access to many personal and official records. Estimating the accuracy of Hewat's history, Edward Mc-Crady said that when "Dr. Hewat speaks from tradition he does so from the very best source of information."[7] Considering that many materials, such as the Shaftesbury papers, were unavailable and that he was the first to collect available sources into one comprehensive narrative, Hewat accomplished a remarkable task with impressive care and accuracy.

Most eighteenth-century historians claimed an impersonal objectivity in handling historical materials, but few attained it. Robertson, more than most, judiciously handled factual materials and analyzed causes and mutual relationships of events. But total objectivity defeated the purpose of eighteenth-century history; if history was to instruct men in their moral struggle, then the historian must be on the side of reason. Hewat revealed a fairness of mind that resembled Robertson's dispassionate attitude, but he firmly opposed slavery, fanaticism, religious intolerance, and other irrational aspects of society. His objectivity was superior to that of William Douglass, who claimed impartiality but displayed animosity and bias, and to that of George Chalmers who, though

7. B. R. Carroll, ed., *Historical Collections of South Carolina*, 2 vols. (New York, 1836), 2:85–120, 141–92, 193–272; Edward McCrady, *The History of South Carolina under the Proprietary Government, 1670–1719* (New York, 1897), p. 17.

outstanding in his use of sources and in his literary abilities, indulged in "the warmth of political disputation" and thereby lost "the dignity of history."[8]

Many authors found the American Revolution a propitious occasion to publish historical accounts of the colonies in order to declare their own partisan views, but Hewat did not enter the controversy, though exiled as a loyalist from South Carolina while writing his history. Only the last few pages of his history dealt with the causes of the rebellion. He believed that both the colonies and Great Britain would benefit if their community remained intact. His purpose in writing was not to expound the royalist view, but to resolve the controversy through instruction and to give weight to reason in the struggle against forces of destruction.

Contemporary historians in Great Britain regarded Hewat highly. George Chalmers, whose study of the American colonies was also published in 1779, sought Hewat's advice on some of his later writings. William Robertson, then principal of the University of Edinburgh, probably recommended the Doctor of Divinity degree that the University granted Hewat in 1780.[9]

Among American historians, Hewat's loyalist sentiments indicted his credibility. David Ramsay, historian of South Carolina and Hewat's contemporary, warned that although Hewat's earlier accounts were reliable, his treatment of prerevolutionary years could not be trusted because of his Tory prejudice. But historians

8. Black, *Art of History*, pp. 123–28; Kraus, *History*, p. 102; *The Monthly Review* 62 (June 1780):465.
9. Letters from Alexander Hewat to George Chalmers, National Library of Scotland, Adv. MS. 81.9.8, ff. 13–14, Adv. MS. 21.1.12, ff. 19–20; David Laing, *Catalogue of the Graduates . . . of the University of Edinburgh* (Edinburgh, 1858), p. 245; Hew Scott, *Fasti Ecclesiae Scoticanae* (Edinburgh, 1928), 7:382. In a letter dated 2 October 1969, Charles P. Finlayson, Keeper of Manuscripts, Edinburgh University Library, suggested that since their copy of Hewat's book, received under the Copyright Act from the Stationer's Office, was anonymous, Hewat might have sent a personal copy to Principal Robertson.

of South Carolina and Georgia used his work despite some animosity against him, and other historians, like George Bancroft, used
Hewat's materials for lack of a better source. Southern historians
tempered their views of Hewat after the American Civil War, and
Edward McCrady found Hewat less biased than had earlier historians. However, the first to accept Hewat's historical perspective
as valid were the "Imperialist" school of American historians.
They found his work free of the chauvinism which marred many
American histories of the revolution, and it served them as a
primary source for social and intellectual history.[10]

Hewat's first volume analyzed the failure of proprietary government in South Carolina. To Hewat, this form of government had
no rational relation to colonial conditions. He warned that "there
is danger of error, where speculative men of one country attempt
to sketch out a plan of government for another, in a different
climate and situation." Although he recognized the abilities and
merits of the author of the Fundamental Constitutions, "yet his
fine-spun system proved in effect useless and impracticable . . .
the inhabitants, sensible of their impropriety, and how little they
were applicable to their circumstances, neither by themselves, nor
by their representatives in assembly, ever gave their assent to them
as a body of laws." He found irrational a situation where a government unsuited to the governed, and by its very nature unable to
adapt to their needs, imposed demands or expected success. As
long as the proprietary government existed, the destructive elements of colonial society would prevail and no progress could be
expected.

One important destructive element in the colony was the religious dissension which grew out of the proprietors' guarantee of
religious freedom. "From the various principles which actuated

10. "Belknap Papers," Massachusetts Historical Society *Collections*, 6th
Series, 4:568–69 (13 March 1794); Kraus, *History*, p. 124; Johnson, "Alexander Hewat," pp. 55–62.

the populace of England, and the different sects who composed the first settlers of Carolina, nothing less could be expected, but that the seeds of division should be imported into that country with its earliest inhabitants." The rigid morals and sober life of dissenters "were made the object of ridicule" by high-Anglican royalists, while the dissenters, having suffered from high-Anglicans in England, "could not bear to see the smallest share of power committed to them in Carolina." To this religious division Hewat attributed early difficulties in framing laws, in distributing justice, and in maintaining public order and tranquility. Religious differences complicated political obedience, and proprietary governors usually found themselves in untenable positions. If they carried out the proprietors' orders, they met with rebellion from at least one religious group; if they satisfied the needs of both groups, they often found themselves recalled. There was no remedy. The fault lay in the nature of proprietary government, which could not cope with colonial problems and was in turn weakened by them.

The Indians Hewat saw as another force threatening the progress of the colony and gaining in destructive power because of the structure of government. To protect themselves and to gain commercially, colonists pitted one tribe against another and trafficked in Indian slaves to the West Indies. The proprietors, however, insisted on protecting the Indians by forbidding their enslavement and controlling their trade. Had Hewat judged policies solely on their merit, he would have supported the proprietors, for he had deep sympathy for the Indians and despised slavery. But however fair and moral the proprietors' policy, it was antithetical to the needs of the colonists and neither settled Indian problems nor alleviated growing antagonism toward the proprietors.

The proprietors, unwilling to spend their fortunes to protect the colony from the Spanish on the frontier, also left the colonists to raise their own militia and build their own forts. Governor Moore's costly expedition to St. Augustine, taken on his own initiative, forced the colonial assembly to discharge the debt by issuing its first paper currency. Hewat saw a causal interaction in the Spanish and French threat, the presence of Indians, the practice of slavery, and religious dissension. The Spanish, allied with Indians, fomented trouble among African slaves, encouraging rebellion or escape. Huguenots in the colony received harsh treatment because of English fears of the French: "English settlers began to revive the odious distinctions and rooted antipathies of the two nations, and to consider them [Huguenots] as aliens and foreigners, entitled by law to none of the privileges and advantages of natural-born subjects."

Some environmental influences aided the colony's progress. Common European crops did not flourish in the soil and climate of South Carolina, but colonists turned this to advantage. Abundant pine trees made possible production of tar, pitch, and turpentine; silk and cotton could be produced for European markets; rice and indigo, cultivated by African labor, brought wealth to the colony and the empire. Climate also affected the growth of Charleston; wealthier planters retreated from the low country in unhealthy seasons and built homes in the city, making it a center of the planter economy and a place of beauty and charm rather than a manufacturing or commercial city.

The proprietors attempted to reduce religious dissension in the colony by establishing the Church of England. Hewat recognized that their motive was good, though in one of his less temperate comments he described the Palatine, Lord Granville, as a "bigoted zealot for this mode of ecclesiastical worship and government." And when discriminatory laws removed the civil liberties of dissenters, agitation in the colony reached serious proportions. But Hewat did not see this quarrel as merely between dissenters and Anglicans. "Many wise and religious men of all denominations condemned . . . the acts of assembly, as unreasonable in themselves, repugnant to the principles of Protestants, and robbing many of the colonists of their most valuable privileges, for their difference in religious opinion." Open rebellion was averted only by the urgent need to repel a French and Spanish attack; everyone rallied to the defense under the leadership of Governor Johnson. Although deploring Johnson's role in the religious controversy, Hewat praised his military leadership and found him "a man of courage, and skilled in the arts of war" whose presence inspired the colonists with "fresh confidence and resolution." Despite colonial opposition to a Church of England establishment, the new Palatine, Lord Craven, accomplished it with "lenity and toleration, which in general have been productive of peace and union, while rigour and persecution have seldom failed to excite discord and promote superstition in every community."

To the antagonism of colonists toward the proprietors over the religious establishment was added the horror of the Yamassee War, begun "at the instigation of the Spaniards at Augustine." Although the Yamassees were defeated and expelled, the colony was weakened by the large debt incurred and the drop in trade and credit. No help came from the proprietors, and even hopes of gaining Indian lands were "frustrated by the Proprietors" who claimed the lands for themselves, "insisting on the right of disposing of them as they thought fit." With this impasse and the colony on the verge of disaster, there was no alternative but rebellion: "Therefore, sick of the feeble proprietary government, the people, after many violent struggles and convulsions, by one bold and irregular effort entirely shook off the yoke, and a revolution, fruitful of happy consequences, took place, to their great relief and unspeakable satisfaction."

This crisis focused Hewat's analyses of all earlier events and conditions. His accurate detail preserved the dignity of the event. Hewat used the narrative of Francis Yonge, a member of the council and agent chosen to present grievances to the proprietors and to the Crown. He did not adopt Yonge's point of view, but made his own judgment of the causes of the rebellion.[11] A man who despised passion as a destructive element in society, Hewat had no sympathy with rebellion, but he admitted its necessity at this time for the colony's survival and prosperity.

Hewat's two volumes have balance and integrity of purpose. The second volume, which analyzed the nature and quality of the colony's progress under royal government, logically followed and intentionally contrasted with its predecessor. The first volume had shown the success of destructive forces under the unrational proprietary government; the second volume showed how royal government mitigated or eradicated these same forces. The treaty with the Cherokees insured peaceful relations and encouraged trade; the availability of rich lands, previously possessed exclusively, encouraged new settlers; new laws increased commerce and expanded credit; religious tensions became unimportant. Colonial government functioned smoothly, even under Governor Johnson, who had been the victim of colonial rebellion as proprietary governor. The British constitution, unlike the Fundamental Constitutions,

was not a plan of systematic rules . . . but . . . the result of many ages of wisdom and experience. Its great object is the public good, in promoting of which all are equally concerned. It is a constitution which has a remedy within itself for every political disorder, which when properly applied, must ever contribute to its stability and duration.

Nothing in the first volume was as optimistic as the opening lines of the second: "A new aera commences in the annals of that country, which may be called the aera of its freedom, security, and happiness."

The colony's only serious threat remained the French and Spanish near the frontier. But the royal government, with interests

11. Carroll, ed., *Historical Collections*, 2:141–92.

identical to those of the colonists, alleviated this threat by establishing the buffer colony of Georgia. Although approving this action, Hewat did not approve of a government by trustees holding a charter from the Crown. He felt this was as unsuitable as proprietary government had been in South Carolina. Although he admired the benevolent and generous purposes of the trustees of Georgia, he thought their idealistic regulations had no rational relation to need: "The imagination of man could scarcely have framed a system of rules worse adapted to the circumstances and situation of the poor settlers, and of more pernicious consequence to the prosperity of the province." Only Oglethorpe's wisdom and ability mitigated the impropriety of this type of government, and Hewat devoted most of his early history of Georgia to discussing Oglethorpe's effectiveness in establishing a successful buffer colony.

Following his usual pattern of analysis, Hewat looked for the interrelationship of events and conditions in discussing the war with Spain. Although the Indian treaties held firm, the Spanish successfully fostered a slave insurrection in South Carolina which brought terror to the colony.

At this point Hewat analyzed the institution of slavery in South Carolina. (He had introduced the subject in his first volume with a discourse on the origins of the slave trade, which he viewed as "one of the most odious and unnatural branches of trade the sordid and avaricious mind of mortals ever invented.") Since the African was better suited physically than the European to clear and improve the land in the sultry climate of southern colonies, little progress could have been made in agriculture without African labor. Hewat felt that the trustees had retarded progress in Georgia by excluding Africans. But he carefully distinguished between the value of African labor and the evils of slavery, for he felt that Africans should have been allowed to come freely as servants and settlers: "Every argument that can be brought in support of the institution of slavery, tends to the subversion of justice and morality in the world."

In his description of the treatment of slaves, Hewat reflected a deep indignation against turning helpless human beings into legal property: "Their natural rights as human creatures are entirely disregarded . . . they are exposed defenceless to the insolence, caprice, and passions of owners, obliged to labour all their life without any prospect of reward, or any hope of an end of their toil until the day of their death." Describing the punishment meted out to slaves, Hewat thought such treatment would "fire them with desires of liberty and vengeance" and give their oppressors grounds for fear. He also condemned the neglect of religious instruction for the slaves: "It would strike a stranger with astonishment and indignation, to hear . . . planters . . . tell you they [Africans] are beings of an inferior rank, and little exalted above brute creatures; that they have no souls, and therefore no concern need be taken about their salvation." After a short essay on the benefits of the tempering influence of Christianity, he indicted slavery: "To keep the minds of human creatures under clouds of darkness, neither disciplined by reason, nor regulated by religion, is a reproach to the name of Protestants especially in a land of Christian light and liberty." Even Catholics pitied "the miserable condition of negroes living among the protestant colonies" and offered them the "advantages of liberty and religion at Augustine" to induce them to revolt.

Having discoursed on the immorality of slavery, Hewat turned to domestic matters of happier consequence. Using the account of the colony written by Governor Glen, Hewat showed the advances made in the economic life of South Carolina by midcentury and reflected on the advantages it enjoyed from its political and commercial connections with Great Britain.

In sharp contrast was Georgia's poor condition under the trustees. Hewat described the increasing poverty and the intensity of the colonists' grievances. But the crisis in Georgia was resolved without rebellion when "the Trustees of Georgia finding that the province languished under their care, and weary of the complaints of the people, in the year 1752 surrendered their charter to the King, and it was made a royal government."

With fine disregard for chronology, Hewat next gave an account of George Whitefield's mission into Georgia. But his discussion of Whitefield at this point served as a transition to an analysis of the developing colonial unrest against British rule. Although Hewat recognized the effectiveness of Whitefield's evangelism, he disliked religious zeal and the problems it created in a society.[12] Among Whitefield's followers Hewat found the first appearance of a spirit of rebellion.

Hewat now considered the growing discontent within the colonies. He felt it could be alleviated by instruction and reason. He explained the privileges and advantages every class of society enjoyed within the British community. Even restraints on domestic manufactures served the advantage of the colonists: "However much such a system of policy might affect the more northern colonies, it was at this time rather serviceable than prejudicial to Carolina." He explained the colony's monopolistic advantage in selling staple products to the world market under British protection and the disadvantages of entering manufacturing in competition with the more advanced and efficient merchants of Britain. "I mention these things because many of the colonists are ignorant of the privileges and advantages they enjoy; for upon a general view of their circumstances, and a comparison of their case with that of

12. Journal of Rev. Archibald Simpson, cited in George Howe, *History of the Presbyterian Church in South Carolina*, 2 vols. (Columbia, S.C., 1870–83), 1:319. Simpson noted that Hewat and several other Presbyterian ministers spent the evening of 6 January 1768 criticizing Mr. Whitefield and "ministers of his stamp." The manuscript of Simpson's Journal is in the Charleston (S.C.) Library Society.

their fellow-subjects in Britain and Ireland, they must find they had much ground for contentment, and none for complaint."

Having analyzed South Carolina's economic relationship within the British community and having countered complaints with rational explanations, Hewat took up the colonies' political relationship to each other and to the mother country. First to be considered was the French and Indian War. Great Britain, though aware of the French threat to colonial frontiers, expected that since the English colonists outnumbered the French, "they would unite among themselves, and raise a fund for the common defence." Instructions to royal governors recommended an association for defense, but many colonies had reached "a considerable degree of opulence and strength" and were so divided "in their views and interests, that it was found impossible to unite them altogether." The more imminent the threat, the less legislatures seemed able to cope with the problem or to act in unison. Each colony therefore looked to Great Britain for protection.

While the war was being fought in northern colonies, South Carolina and Georgia were at peace. The Cherokee treaty made many years before proved helpful, and in 1755 Governor Glen held a congress with Cherokee chieftains and gained a cession of Indian lands to build frontier forts. Then a skirmish over stolen horses between some young Cherokees and a few Virginia settlers caused trouble on the frontier. In Hewat's view, Governor Lyttleton so aggravated the situation by his dishonorable treatment of Cherokee chieftains that they launched full war against the colony. Hewat's belief that the war could have been avoided but for Lyttleton's mistakes probably reflected the viewpoint of Lieutenant Governor William Bull, who governed the colony after Lyttleton's departure and later became one of Hewat's close friends. The details of the campaigns and of John Stuart's escape from Fort Loudon were probably also obtained from William Bull and perhaps from Stuart as well, whom Hewat later knew in Charleston.

Although this war was happily settled, the presence of regular troops in South Carolina had created ill feeling. A quarrel between Colonel Grant, commander of the royal troops, and Colonel Middleton of the provincial regiment exemplified the scorn of British regulars for colonial militia and aroused resentment. "From this period a party-spirit appeared in Carolina. . . . Prejudices were contracted, cherished, and unhappily gained ground among the people." Although forces of unreason began to gain strength, Hewat was convinced, even at the time he wrote his history in 1779, that reason and progress would prevail under the British constitution.

Hewat's final chapter, which described the prosperity and well-being in South Carolina and Georgia after 1763, provided one of the best available descriptions of southern colonial life. Royal governors received orders to grant lands to those who had served in the war, bounties encouraged new settlers, Indian treaties fixed the boundaries of their hunting lands and prevented encroachment: "His Majesty evidently made a distinction between the rights of sovereignty and those of property; having excluded his governors from all manner of jurisdiction over those lands." Instead, an office of Superintendent for Indian Affairs for the Southern District was established, and at the request of the Indian chieftains John Stuart was appointed. Hewat felt that the government wanted the Indians as allies not only to keep the frontier peaceful, but to expand trade for the colonies. He made no comment about the resentment of new settlers at their exclusion from Indian lands.

Removal of the Spanish threat in Florida and containment of the Indians within fixed boundaries gave Georgia its first opportunity to flourish. Governor Wright opened the lowlands to cultivation and increased credit and trade. Growing exports of rice, indigo, and naval stores brought wealth to the colony, attracting settlers from Europe and from other colonies. "No province on the continent felt the happy effects of . . . public security sooner than the province of Georgia."

In South Carolina, a burst of prosperity made that colony one of the richest in America. Hewat felt that few colonies had "in the space of an hundred years, improved and flourished in an equal degree." Charleston was a beehive of activity tempered by an aura of leisure, pleasure, kindness, and well-being: "Travellers could scarcely go into any city where they could meet with a society of people more agreeable, intelligent and hospitable than that at Charlestown." Details drawn from Hewat's own experience enriched this description, and his affection for his adopted home was evident.

Hewat devoted the closing pages of his history to a "slight view of the causes of that unhappy quarrel which at this time began . . . and afterwards proceeded to such a degree of violence as to threaten a total dissolution of all political union and commercial intercourse." He had anticipated these causes earlier in his history and built his analysis on what had gone before. The dissenters, the majority of the early colonists in America and the exclusive settlers of New England, had always been averse to monarchy and "have not always been found the most peaceable members of society." This aversion to monarchy, continuing through generations and reinforced by the evangelism of Whitefield, now supported republican forms of government in church and state. The natural bonds of affection toward the mother country had understandably weakened in later generations, a tendency encouraged as the colonies increased in wealth and power. Americans were becoming jealous of their liberties, proud of their strength and wealth, and sensible of their importance to Britain. Hewat found the essential cause of the rebellious spirit not in any series of events or limitations of freedom, but rather in changed colonial conditions which the British did not understand.

The first overt agitation, according to Hewat, grew out of Britain's attempt to stop colonial merchants from trading with the French and Spanish and smuggling the goods into America. The perpetual debt owed to English merchants, which Hewat had earlier argued offered an advantage to southern colonies, irked the commercial colonies of New England. Although Hewat believed that merchants were loyal only to the country best serving their monetary advantage, he honestly presented their argument: restrictions against trade with France and Spain cut off their sole source of gold specie with which to pay debts to England.

The next agitation arose when the British government proposed a stamp tax on the colonists to raise money for their protection. Since the people in Great Britain were already burdened by the costs of the recent war and the colonists had been reimbursed for their expenditures, the government felt it only fair that Americans contribute to their own defense. Hewat, without questioning the right of Parliament to tax the colonies, thought it would have been good policy at this time to create a common council in the American colonies to raise revenue. New Englanders, engaged to a greater extent in trade and manufacture than others and "advanced to such a degree of strength as rendered troops unnecessary for their defence," openly affirmed "that the King, Lords and Commons had formed a design of enslaving them." They formed associations to boycott British goods and to encourage home manufactures and sought the cooperation of other colonies. "They pretended that they were driven to such measures by necessity; but in reality they had nothing less in view than their favourite plan of independence, for the accomplishment of which it required time to secure the union and help of other colonies."

Hewat did not consider the Stamp Act as the cause of rebellion, but only as a government blunder used by those long opposed to monarchy to bring about republican government and independence. Hewat thought the British government made a serious mistake in consulting the colonies before passing the Stamp Act and in hearing suggestions for another kind of tax without taking any measures to prevent opposition. By doing this, it gave opportunity to the "few discontented persons" in the colonies to question the "jurisdiction of Parliament over their properties." When Parliament finally passed the Stamp Act, "bold and seditious speeches were made [in New England] to stir up the people to resistance," declaring that silence in these circumstances was a crime. These "flames, kindled in New England, soon spread through all the capital towns along the coast." In South Carolina, Lieutenant Governor Bull "manifested a desire of complying with the act . . . but wanted power sufficient for maintaining the dignity and authority of his government, and carrying that act into execution." Hewat felt that a small military force in the colony at this time would have secured obedience to legal authority. He blamed the "imprudence of ministers, the faction in parliament, and the weakness of the civil power in America" for the spread of the rebellious spirit.

The colonial policy of nonimportation created sufficient reaction in England to change the government. Pitt, anxious to avoid detrimental consequences to commercial interests even while defending the right of Parliament to impose the tax, pushed through repeal of the Stamp Act. Hewat felt that repeal not only promoted among colonists a doctrine subversive of all good government, but that it also "exposed the real friends of government to popular prejudice, and rendered their affections more cool, and their future endeavours in support of government more feeble and ineffectual." It very soon appeared that "the power of Great Britain in America had received a fatal blow, such as she would never be able to recover without the severest struggle and boldest exertions." Here, with the year 1766, Hewat ended his history.

In his analysis of the causes leading to rebellion in the colonies, Hewat maintained a dispassionate viewpoint. This was the more remarkable because he wrote his history in England, having been exiled by the South Carolina revolutionary government in 1777 for his refusal "to denounce his Allegiance to the King and swear Fidelity to the Congress."[13] Hewat had stated at the beginning of his second volume that the British constitution had a remedy within itself for every political disorder. He also recognized that that remedy was not being applied to stifle these forces of unreason, these "seeds of disaffection which had sprung up in New England [and] spread through the other colonies, insomuch that multitudes became infected with republican principles, and aspired after independence." Formation of a common colonial council to tax the colonies might have avoided the constitutional problem of Parliament's right to tax. However, if Parliament insisted on this power without enabling royal officials to enforce the laws, and retreated in the face of disobedience, it gave credence to radical demands and created wider disaffection. Hewat indicted those in the government who had the remedy for disorder in their power and did not use it. He analyzed the causes of rebellion, not to serve partisanship, but to teach wisdom, to give weight to the elements of reason against the forces of passion and unreason.

Hewat's views of the origins of the American Revolution have particular historical value since he lived in Charleston from 1763 to 1777 and witnessed colonial reaction to the Stamp Act and its repeal. One could wish that he had carried his narrative to the outbreak of hostilities, for it would have been a rare account. But

13. The Memorial of Alexander Hewat, Public Record Office, A.O. 12/47, Loyalist Transcripts, Manuscript Divison, New York Public Library, 53:584–585. The Memorial states that Hewat had been "deprived of his Benefice since the year 1777" and this date is substantiated in Hewat's testimony as witness to the Memorial of James Brisbane in Hugh Edward Egerton, ed., *The Royal Commission on the Losses and Services of American Loyalists, 1783–1785* (Oxford, 1915), p. 296.

that he did not do so was consistent with his view of the responsibility of the historian. It would have been difficult, perhaps impossible, for him to secure authentic information to support an accurate history of this period. Nor could he have made a dispassionate judgment of the events, for "while he was employed in arranging [already collected] materials, being in a town agitated with popular tumults, military parade, and frequent alarms, his situation was very unfavourable for calm study and recollection."

An account of Hewat's life throws some light not only on the history he wrote, but on the history he could not write. He was a young man of about twenty-four when he arrived in Charleston in 1763 as minister of the Scots (First Presbyterian) Church there.[14] He had received his early education at Kelso Grammar School in Scotland and had attended the University of Edinburgh. On the recommendation of "the College at Edinburgh," Hewat "was appointed by the Ellection of the [Scots Presbyterian] Society" in 1763. Since the Scots Church usually commissioned several distinguished persons in Scotland to seek out and recommend a candidate, Dr. William Robertson, the historian and principal of the University of Edinburgh, was possibly responsible for selecting Hewat.[15]

14. Hewat's name appears on a list of Charleston ministers drawn up by Rev. Elam Potter in 1767 as "Mr. Huit, aet. 28, Edinburgh," cited in Howe, *Church History*, 1:363. *The South-Carolina Gazette*, 13 November 1763, notes the arrival the preceding week of "Rev. Mr. Hewett for the Scots meeting in this town." Judge Mitchell King, whose biographical record of Hewat forms the basis for later accounts, noted that in the church records, in what King believed to be Hewat's handwriting, was a notation that Hewat had presided as moderator at the meeting of the session on 20 March 1763. Since Judge King never knew Hewat and the church records were destroyed in the American Civil War, it is not possible to verify King's statement or to reconcile the discrepancy between his statement and the notice in *The South-Carolina Gazette*. Judge King's sketch forms the chapter on Hewat in William B. Sprague, *Annals of the American Pulpit*, 9 vols. (New York, 1857–69), 3:251–53.
15. Hewat refers to his study at Kelso in his *Sermons*, 2 vols. (London, 1803–5), 1:386. According to University records, Hewat attended the 1755–

Hewat's congregation in Charleston numbered about seventy families, many of whom were leading merchants and planters. He received a salary of £250 sterling per year, plus the rent of a house worth £35/14/2, all of which came to about £2,000 Carolina currency, not an inconsiderable amount for an unmarried man with thrifty habits. Hewat soon became an influential member of the presbytery and a man of prestige and dignity in the Charleston community.[16]

Shortly after his arrival in Charleston he was elected to the St. Andrew's Club, an organization of native-born Scotsmen formed to promote sociable and charitable enterprises. This society included some of the colony's leading men, among them Sir Alexander Cumming, Bart., whose curious treaty with the Cherokees Hewat described in his history; Alexander Skene, a member of the Council when the proprietary government was overthrown; John Fraser, trader among the Yamassee whose experience with the Indian Sanute prior to the Yamassee War was recounted by Hewat; and, as honorary members, all the royal governors of the colony. When Hewat was invited to join, the membership included John Stuart, Superintendent of Indian Affairs for the Southern District; James Wright, royal governor of Georgia; Chief Occonastota of the Cherokees; Robert Wells, editor of the *South-Carolina and American General Gazette*; and a number of royal officials and members of the Council and Common Assembly.[17] Through these associations, Hewat also came to know other

---

56 session and studied logic and metaphysics under Professor John Stevenson. Letter of Charles P. Finlayson, Keeper of Manuscripts, Edinburgh University Library, 2 October 1969; Memorial of Alexander Hewat, Loyalist Transcripts, 53:593. When in 1792 the Scots Church again needed a minister to succeed Hewat, Dr. Robertson was one of those commissioned, along with Dr. Alexander Hewat and a Dr. Blair. Sprague, *Annals*, 3:251–52.

16. Howe, *Church History*, 1:319, 363; Memorial of Alexander Hewat, Loyalist Transcripts, 53:594.

17. J. H. Easterby, *History of the St. Andrew's Society of Charleston, South Carolina, 1729–1929* (Charleston, S.C., 1929), pp. 21–22, 25–26, 45–

leaders of the colony, among them Lieutenant Governor William
Bull, whose family had been among the first settlers of Charleston
and whose father had worked closely with Oglethorpe in the early
settlement of Georgia. The Bulls were probably the single most
politically prominent family in South Carolina.

Hewat's interest in the history of the southern colonies must
have been aroused by these friends. A man of learning and culture—the only requisite for an eighteenth-century historian—
Hewat had the chance to secure authentic evidence and firsthand
experience for his historical narrative. He had the unique opportunity of knowing the participants in many recent events of South
Carolina's and Georgia's history and those who preserved an oral
tradition not far removed from the events themselves. His association with royal officials gave him access to official documents
which he used in his history. In their company, he had the vicari-
ous experience of being a man of affairs, familiar with the work-
ings of government and commerce. He observed firsthand the
customs and conduct of neighboring Indians, traveled into
Georgia, and probably visited the Purrysburg settlement on the
Savannah river. During his fourteen years in Charleston, Hewat
also experienced the dangers of the climate and on at least one
occasion left Charleston to recover his health.[18] His experiences
and travel in the two colonies were reflected in his precise descriptions of their physical features, Indian customs, system of slavery,

46, 50–52; *The South-Carolina Gazette*, 26 November 1763: "The entertain-
ment . . . was elegant . . . his Excellency the Governor [Thomas Boone],
the members of his Majesty's Council, and many other gentlemen of note
. . . being invited thereto."

18. Memorial of Alexander Hewat, Loyalist Transcripts, 53:597. In 1766 he
had to leave the colony "in a very bad state of health," according to the
Journal of Rev. Archibald Simpson, cited in Howe, *Church History*, 1:319.
James Simpson, a witness for Hewat before the Loyalist Commission, stated
that Hewat was "much Beloved by his Parishioners inso much that finding it
necessary to come to Europe some years before the Troubles for his Health
They paid his Exps. and continued their Subscriptions as before." Memorial
of Alexander Hewat, Loyalist Transcripts, 53:595.

and debilitating climate. He used all these factors in his analyses of causal relationships.

Hewat found Charleston a most agreeable place, and his description of life in that city, of which he was himself an intimate part, formed a significant portion of his history. He seemed to have had every intention of settling permanently, for in 1772 he purchased one thousand acres of land in Craven County, and in 1777 he bought three hundred acres of unimproved land in Colleton County on the Savannah River near Augusta for his brother Andrew, who was at that time in Nova Scotia raising a company to fight for the king.[19]

The "popular tumults, military parade, and frequent alarms" that Hewat mentioned in his preface began in 1774 with the formation of the revolutionary provisional government in South Carolina. By May 1775, when the news of the battle of Lexington reached Charleston, the provisional government demanded that royal officials resign and leave the colony. Since the new governor, Lord William Campbell, was shortly to arrive, Lieutenant Governor Bull ignored the demand. But in July, John Stuart, Superintendent of Indian Affairs, fled the colony rather than risk being charged by the revolutionary government with conspiring to launch an Indian attack. Lord William Campbell, upon arrival, could not enforce his authority and escaped for safety to a British ship in the harbor. The provisional government had demanded that everyone sign an Association for the defense of the colony or face expulsion. Hewat probably subscribed, since many people did so who did not support the revolutionary cause but felt that discretion at this time was the wiser course.[20] Lieutenant Governor

19. Ibid., pp. 591–92.
20. John Drayton, *Memoirs of the American Revolution*, 2 vols. (Charleston, S.C., 1821), 1:292–96, 313–17; Alexander Hewat's statement as witness to the Memorial of James Brisbane, in Egerton, *Royal Commission*, p. 296. James Simpson, witnessing the Memorial of William Carsan, stated he believed there were not forty persons in Charleston who refused to sign it (ibid., pp. 147, 315).

Bull, however, in the face of threats and intimidation, retired to his plantation; other officials soon left the colony. The departure from Charleston of those who had provided Hewat access to official documents added another dimension to his preface statement that "his means of information . . . were not so good as he could have desired, and even from these he was excluded before he had finished the collection necessary to complete his plan."

Although Hewat took no overt action against the revolutionary government, he tried to give "an Example of a stedfast adherence to his King and Country" and claimed singular success in "preserving those under his Influence steady and Loyal almost to a Man which however in event proved the Occasion of much harsh treatment to himself and severe persecution and Dispersion to his Parish." When the British fleet under Admiral Parker arrived at Charleston in the summer of 1776, many people, including some members of Hewat's congregation, were imprisoned for refusing to take up arms against the British.[21] When Hewat, along with other Charleston ministers, was ordered on 3 August 1776 to pray no more for the king, he "changed the form to 'those in Lawful Authority over us' which gave great Offence," but complied with the letter of the order. Despite the dispersion of his congregation and the absence of many friends, Hewat remained in Charleston until the summer of 1777. When the revolutionary government required that he renounce his loyalty to the king and give open support to Congress, he refused to do so. Given sixty days to leave

21. Memorial of Alexander Hewat, Loyalist Transcripts, 53:585. An elder of his church, Robert Rowand, was imprisoned until the threat was over and then confined to his plantation until banished in 1778. (Memorial of Robert Rowand, Loyalist Transcripts, 54:298–301.) Other members included William Ancrum, Robert Philp, Dr. Robert Wilson, and William Glen, all of whom were ultimately banished and their property confiscated in the Act of 1782. Lorenzo Sabine, *Loyalists of the American Revolution*, 2 vols. (Boston, 1864), 1:475; 2:471, 566, 597. See also *Centennial Celebration of the Dedication of the First Presbyterian Church, Charleston, South Carolina* (Charleston, S.C., 1915), p. 123.

the colony or suffer imprisonment and perhaps death, Hewat left his congregation and his property and took passage to Nantes; from there, he went to London. Before leaving Charleston, Hewat had secured a testimony of his loyalty to the king from James Henderson, moderator of the Presbytery of South Carolina, and upon arrival in London he secured testimonies from Governor Lord William Campbell and from Lieutenant Governor William Bull. With these testimonies, Hewat secured a temporary Treasury allowance of £100 per year until he could return to Charleston.[22] He now devoted himself to completing his history, which he published anonymously in 1779.

Like other loyalists, Hewat assumed that the troubles would soon end and he could return to Charleston and resume his old life there. He may have published his history anonymously in order to avoid indicting his work of many years with the partisanship of his temporary political exile. Charleston had been recaptured by British forces by the time Hewat received the honorary Doctor of Divinity degree from Edinburgh University on 12 July 1780. Hewat obviously expected to return to his home, for he signed the Laureation Book of the University as a resident of "Charlestown, South Carolina."[23]

When Lieutenant Governor Bull departed for South Carolina on 1 December 1780, all subsistance allowances being paid to South Carolina loyalists in Britain were withdrawn "upon the Presumption of the Province returning to its Allegiance." Hewat, now without funds and "having Encouragement to Return to his Living," applied to the government for a "sum of money to enable him to return to Charlestown." He was advanced £100 under the government policy of assuring its military gains by the presence of loyal subjects in South Carolina. Hewat booked passage in a fleet

22. Memorial of Alexander Hewat, Loyalist Transcripts, 53:590–91; Public Record Office, A.O. 13/129, Nos. 568, 575, 577; A.O. 12/99, p. 175.
23. Laing, *Catalogue*, p. 245.

sailing from Torbay in the summer of 1781, which was taking many royal officials and exiled loyalists back to America. But before sailing, Hewat learned that "There would be no use going out" because his congregation in Charleston had scattered and he would have no income. With the financial support of his brother and "another Gentleman a Merchant of London," he remained in Britain and tried to secure another congregation. In the summer of 1782, he went to Scotland to preach at the chapel of his old school at Kelso, but he soon returned to London.[24]

At the end of the war, Hewat considered returning to his church in Charleston, since the legislature there showed signs of being lenient toward returning loyalists. However, a letter from William Ancrum, a loyalist member of his congregation who had returned to Charleston, gave him no encouragement since "most of his congregation were loyalists and therefore dispersed," and the church could not pay Hewat's salary arrears. On 9 April 1783, Hewat applied to the Loyalist Commission for compensation for his loss of benefice and property in America and was granted a temporary allowance of £60 per annum, later increased to £100. In July 1788, when the allowance was replaced by a life pension of £120 per annum, Hewat testified that this was his only income.[25]

On 7 November 1785 Hewat presented to the Loyalist Commis-

24. Memorial of William Bull, Loyalist Transcripts, 57:16; Public Record Office, A.O. 12/52, A.O. 13/129, No. 569, A.O. 12/99, p. 175; *The Royal Georgia Gazette*, 1 November 1781, dated "Charlestown, October 16 [1781]," announced the arrival the day before of a British fleet bringing many royal officials to South Carolina and "the Rev. Alexander Hewat." Since Hewat did not sail with this fleet, his name must have still remained on the passenger manifest when the fleet arrived in Charleston. The Journal of Rev. Mr. Simpson states that Hewat's church was being used as a "place for the Royalists from the country to live in." Cited in Howe, *Church History*, 1:474; *The Centennial Celebration of . . . the First Presbyterian Church*, pp. 122–23.
25. Public Record Office, A.O. 13/129, No. 571 (letter dated 25 March 1783); A.O. 12/99, p. 175, T. 50/8 through T. 50/47; A.O. 13/83, No. 174.

sion his claim for £3,500 for loss of property. The Commission allowed a claim of £2,027, which was later "disallowed for want of satisfactory proof of loss." Hewat continued to seek compensation and in March 1798 sent a packet of testimonies to three former loyalists in Charleston, asking that they place them before the commissioners of American claims whom Hewat thought would "visit the Capital Towns in each State." But the commissioners, who sat only in Philadelphia, dropped his name from their list and never received the testimonies, and by 1802 Hewat still had not heard from his friends in Charleston. He wrote the commissioners in London in 1802 and again in 1808, but he evidently never received compensation.[26]

In 1790 Hewat visited in Edinburgh, but met with unfriendliness and even suspicion: "With Doors barred and Guards planted; with suspicion hinted, and doubts and fears expressed—no freedom or friendly intercourse even exists." Perhaps his loyalist views or his unwillingness to return to his church in Charleston caused this hostility toward him. He desperately needed money, but he was unwilling to humiliate himself by asking favors from "such as I have but too good reason to despise." He secured an advance on his pension through George Chalmers, then chief clerk of the Privy Council in London, and with another small sum, secured as "Provision against starving," he left Edinburgh for London. When the reactivated Scots Church in Charleston selected him to serve with Dr. William Robertson in 1792 to choose their new pastor, Hewat's "absence from Edinburgh," whether from lack of money

26. Memorial of Alexander Hewat, Loyalist Transcripts, 53:584–595; Public Record Office, A.O. 12/47, A.O. 13/129, A.O. 12/109, p. 166. Hewat testified as witness to the memorial of James Brisbane, a planter of Charleston, on 31 January 1785 (Egerton, *Royal Commission*, p. 296), and to the memorial of Robert Rowand on 23 February 1786. Loyalist Transcripts, 54:314; Public Record Office, T. 79/21.

or because of Edinburgh's lack of cordiality, "prevented him from joining in its execution."[27]

He remained in London for the rest of his life, living for a time at No. 36 Bury Street in Westminster and later at No. 8 Great Quebec Street near Whitechapel. He served in the Gospel Mission in London, and in 1803–5 he published two volumes of sermons. He married a Mrs. Barksdale from Charleston, a widow who had come abroad for the health of her two children, both of whom had died before Hewat met her in England. After her death, Hewat wrote a warm letter to her relatives in Charleston, sending pictures of her children.[28] He continued to feel affection for his congregation in Charleston and provided that a sum of £50 be left to the Scots Church at his death.[29]

Alexander Hewat was one of the casualties of the American Revolution. American animosity against those who had not supported the rebellion relegated loyalists to historical oblivion; nor did the British receive them with generosity or pay them honor for their sacrifice. Hewat lived out his life in London without a con-

27. Letter from Alexander Hewat to George Chalmers, National Library of Scotland, Adv. MS. 21.1.12, ff. 19–20 (cited by permission of the Trustees of the National Library of Scotland). Another letter from Hewat to Chalmers of uncertain date seems to have been written from London. National Library of Scotland, Adv. MS. 81.9.8, ff. 13–14. Sprague, *Annals*, 3:252; *The Centennial Celebration of . . . the First Presbyterian Church*, p. 10.

28. Public Record Office, A.O. 13/83, No. 174, T. 79/21; Sprague, *Annals*, 3:252. Letter from R. J. Watson, Hon. Librarian of the Presbyterian Historical Society of England, dated 31 December 1969, states that a careful search in his records reveals no mention of Hewat. Hewat's wife was probably "Eliza, wife of Rev. Dr. Hewat" whose death is recorded in *Gentleman's Magazine* for May 1814. See Percy Scott Flippin, *Dictionary of American Biography*, s.v. "Hewat, Alexander." Letter of Alexander Hewat to George Edwards of Charleston, dated from the Carolina Coffee House, London, 28 September 1820, now in the possession of the Charleston Library Society.

29. Sprague, *Annals*, 3:252. This sum was received by the treasurer of the church on 4 October 1829. There is a portrait of Hewat in *The Centennial Celebration of . . . the First Presbyterian Church*, p. 118. This rare volume was made available by the generosity of the Rev. Dr. Edward G. Lilly of Charleston, S.C.

gregation and without recognition. No record of his death or burial has been found. But if the record of Hewat's last pension payment, made to his executors, may be assumed to date his death, Alexander Hewat died on 3 March 1824 at the age of 85.[30]

30. Public Record Office, T. 50/47. In space for "Quarter 5 April 1824" is written "19.2.5 for 58 days Pension to 3rd March 1824—pd to Exors." There are no further entries.

8.

Robert Proud and *The History of Pennsylvania*

JOSEPH E. ILLICK, III

Between the years 1775 and 1780, there being a great change from the former happy condition of this country, since called, The United States, with a general cessation, at that time, from the former and useful employments among the people, who were then strangely disposed for revolution, rebellion and destruction, under the name and pretence of Liberty, I endeavoured to divert my mind from those popular and disagreeable objects, at times, by such meditations and reflections as took my attention; which, in part, I committed to writing, on various subjects, both in prose and verse, but mostly in the former, during part of my retirement, in that afflictive and trying season, besides the compilation of the History of Pennsylvania since printed.[1]

So wrote Robert Proud in his autobiography—or *Commentariolum De Vita R. Proudi,* as he titled it, certain that Latin lent a dignity which his native tongue could not convey. He was seventy-eight, and the disappointments of his long life were almost over. More than ever, he was out of tune with his times. By the early nineteenth century there was hardly a historian—indeed, hardly an American—who did not see the American Revolution as

---

1. "Autobiography of Robert Proud, the Historian," *Pennsylvania Magazine of History and Biography* 13(1889):434–35 (hereafter cited as *PMHB*). The following narrative of Proud's life is based on this short account and on J. H. Powell's "Robert Proud, Pennsylvania's First Historian," *Pennsylvania History* 13 (1946):85–112, unless otherwise noted. The interpretation is, of course, largely mine.

the culmination of two centuries' experience in the New World. But Proud viewed it as a repudiation of those virtues—peace, order, harmony—which he cherished and of that country which he loved. He refused even to discuss the event in his *History of Pennsylvania,* thus investing the work with his own anachronistic point of view and virtually insuring its commercial failure.

Adversity was Robert Proud's fate. During his mature life the unforeseen obstacles he faced—illness, financial difficulties, personal disappointment—led him to conclude that "the wind always blew in his face."[2] His early days were otherwise: secure, tranquil, and, to all appearances, pleasant. He was born on 10 May 1728 in northern Yorkshire, and he grew up in prosperous circumstances among several brothers and a sister. It was not until his eighteenth year that he summoned sufficient independence to leave home for a school fifty miles away. He was given a good deal of encouragement in his studies by David Hall, a Quaker theologian, and this special attention no doubt offset his loneliness and compensated for the absence of parents and siblings. Classical languages and religion thereby assumed a special meaning for him, and he corresponded with Hall in Latin until the teacher's death.

After four years of instruction Proud might have returned to the bucolic scene of his youth as a country schoolmaster and scholar of minor pretentions. But Hall, having assumed a parental role, encouraged him to apply his talents to the larger world of London. Neither his experience nor his limited formal education had equipped him for life in the big city; he was parochial, diffident, and unbending. Yet Hall supplied him with letters of recommendation to friends which touted Proud's literary virtues.

Apparently these letters were of little value, for the young man initially worked as a bookkeeper. But to his good fortune, a relative

2. "Extracts from the Bucks County Patriot of 1826," *PMHB* 28 (1904): 377. This account also quotes Proud as saying that he was disappointed in love, which probably means he was sorry never to have found a wife.

and fellow Yorkshireman, Dr. John Fothergill, the Quaker physician and philanthropist, had attained prominence in London. At the time of Proud's arrival, Fothergill and a fellow scientist, Peter Collinson, were seeing Benjamin Franklin's papers on electricity through the press.[3] Soon Fothergill was seeing to young Robert's future, guiding him into the study of botany and pharmacy and finding him a position as tutor in the Bevan family, reputable Quaker chemists. Proud's classical training now proved an asset, not only in instructing the young, but also in pursuing his own studies in the well-stocked Bevan library. He judged himself successful: "In this pursuit, for several years, I made such proficiency as to attract considerable notice and respect from many:— having then in view the practice of physic." Traveling in this illustrious circle, Proud could no doubt have become a prominent physician.

But life in London, he explained, "not only exposed me to much variety of company, with great intenseness of thought, application and trial, but also frequently to such society and communication, in some things, as were not always agreeable, but, as I thought, injurious to my mind." Perhaps the contrast between his quiet, ordered past and the demands of his present work, accentuated by the frenetic pace of the city, had led to a nervous breakdown. In any case, he gave up thoughts of practicing medicine in favor of migrating to Pennsylvania.

Dr. Fothergill's own father had made three religious sojourns to America, his brother Samuel visited there from 1754 to 1756 and he himself kept in close touch with Friends across the sea. This influence on Robert was evident as early as 1754, when he first conceived of leaving the "Luxury and Av'rice" of London and going:

3. Collinson to Franklin, 25 April 1750, 27 July 1750, 22 February 1750/1, in Leonard W. Labaree, ed., *The Papers of Benjamin Franklin*, 15 vols. (New Haven, 1959—), 3:476; 4:6, 114–15.

> Beyond the vast *Atlantic* Sea
> To *Pennsylvania's* distant Ground;
> Where Peace & Plenty smile around;
> Where now exists, commenc'd by *Penn,*
> The wisest Government of Men.
> This happy Land appears to be
> The Fairest in the World, to me. . . .

His vision of the Quaker colony, its physical as well as its spiritual features, suggests an acquaintance with the promotional literature issued by William Penn in the seventeenth century. Unknowingly, he had begun research for his history of Pennsylvania.

That the halcyon days of the province had given way to political turbulence in the 1750s deterred Proud not at all, though Fothergill might well have warned him. The Quaker doctor knew of the intense rivalry between the Assembly and the proprietary governor, as well as of Franklin's changing political role. When the governor declared war on the Indians in 1756, decisively repudiating the official policy of pacifism, Fothergill advised Friends to resign from their dominant positions in the lower house. Soon afterward, Franklin went to England to represent Pennsylvania's case to the Crown, and Thomas Penn, the proprietor, was warned: "Dr. Fothergill and Mr. Collinson can introduce him to the Men of most influence at Court and he may underhand give impressions to your prejudice." The Quaker physician attended to Franklin during an illness in 1757, and the Philadelphia printer reciprocated the kindness in a reference to Fothergill as "among the best men I have known, and a great promoter of useful Projects."[4] Proud could not have been unaware of Franklin's

4. Biographical note on John Fothergill, ibid., 4:126n; Isreal Pemberton to Fothergill, 19 May 1755 and 4 April 1757, ibid., 6:52–56; 7:173; Richard Peters to Thomas Penn, 31 January 1757, ibid., 7:111n; Franklin to Fothergill, October 1757, ibid., 7:271; biographical note on Samuel Fothergill, ibid., 7:173n; Fothergill to Isreal Pemberton, 12 June 1758, ibid., 8:100n; quotation from Franklin, *Autobiography*, ibid., 7:317.

presence in London, and he may even have been apprised of the opportunities for success in Philadelphia by a man who had a way of glossing over conflict. That Proud never later mentioned Franklin might be attributed to his distaste for the printer's politics.

Whatever the nature of Franklin's advice, if any, the message of William Smith's *A Brief State of the Province of Pennsylvania* and *A Brief View of the Conduct of Pennsylvania*, issued in London in 1755 and 1756, was clear: a power-hungry and insatiable Assembly had poisoned the political life of the province. But Proud set off for Pennsylvania anyway in November 1758, apparently undaunted by reports of political conflict, military combat, and turmoil within the Society of Friends. His object was to be clear of London; his hope was to find a more settled and pleasant existence in Pennsylvania.

He was disappointed. His personal life was no more settled than the public affairs of the province. During his first twenty years in Philadelphia he moved fourteen times, partly because of his early employment as a tutor. (One of his rare satisfactions during this time appears to have been entering the surnames of his pupils in Latin in his account book.) Isreal Pemberton, so-called "King of the Quakers" to whom Proud brought a letter of recommendation from Fothergill, wrote to a friend: "I am not out of Hopes we shall be able to engage Robert Proud to undertake the Care of the School, tho' he at present chooses only the Care of a few Children, & seems rather calculated for that than a Publick school."[5] Pemberton's evaluation was accurate, but Proud nevertheless accepted the post as master of the Quaker school in Philadelphia. He later wrote that he had decided to teach rather than practice medicine because he had "with Regret, observed a very remarkable Defect, in literary Education & Science, prevalent in the Society of

5. Pemberton to Josiah Thomson, 12 April 1760, Society Collection, Historical Society of Pennsylvania (hereafter HSP).

Friends, in this Country." The education of youth, he thought, was "a Religious Duty and Concern."[6]

It became a cross to bear. To his dismay, he faced young Quakers of "uncultivated, rough ignorant, and demi-savage Deportment and Behaviour." He yearned for but did not receive the respect he thought due a teacher from his community. As a defense against this wilderness barbarism, though his salary never exceeded £250, he regularly bought expensive books from London, some Quaker works but usually Latin classics. He also corresponded with his brother William, perhaps to recapture memories of more carefree days, and suggested that the two of them enter a business venture together in Philadelphia. William, younger than Robert and also warmer and wiser, coaxed his brother to return to England instead.[7]

At this point a third brother unfortunately entered the picture. John Proud, a failure in an entrepreneurial venture in soapmaking, arrived penniless in Pennsylvania, anxious to recoup his losses. Robert, lonely and dissatisfied with teaching, welcomed the opportunity to enter the world of commerce with his brother. He resigned from his school post in 1770, not to return to it for a decade. This period was one of almost uninterrupted business failure which, at one point, brought him to the brink of bankruptcy. John retreated to England after a few years, but Robert remained to speculate innocently and unsuccessfully in land and currency. Finally the certain salary of teaching, even if it meant dealing with uncouth boys, seemed reassuring compared with the instability of his business affairs.

Proud's sense of personal misfortune during the 1770s was accentuated by the Anglo-American conflict. Like most other

6. "Notes on Teaching Quaker Youth," Proud Papers, HSP.
7. Proud's book orders can be found in the letters from Robert Horsfield in the Proud Manuscripts, Library Company of Philadelphia (hereafter LCP), as can his correspondence with William Proud.

Quakers, he displayed the neutrality of pacifism. But he was a Tory at heart. The England of his youth had been tranquil; the America of his middle age was tumultuous. The government at Whitehall wanted order; the provincial pamphleteers cried out for freedom. England was aristocratic, while in America an alliance of grasping merchants, whose financial success Proud envied, and inconsiderable mechanics, whose boisterousness he detested, controlled or were trying to control the government. Proud had no doubts about which side was in the right. To his brother William he wrote during the early years of the war:

After more than two years Interruption of our Correspondence . . . the way is now opened again between us, the King's Troops having taken Possession of this City by Land. . . . On the Commencement of open Rebellion here, I had so great reason to fear, having not only been obnoxious to the Incendiaries and Usurpers, but also particularly pointed out and threatened by them. . . . Contrary to my expectation I have suffered no Abuse, nor ever been molested, which I consider as a Providential and very remarkable Favour.[8]

Nevertheless, the change brought by revolution was very upsetting to Proud's conservative temperament. Even when the British occupied Philadelphia the "Vigilance of the Rebel Party by Means of the Country Militia, supported by Washington's Army has on every Side distressed the Inhabitants of this City to a high Degree." That he suffered "a severe Fit of Sickness" at this time may have stemmed directly from this distress.[9] Proud had a different explanation, however: "I believe I applyed myself last Summer too closely in adjusting some Papers, in part drawing up an Essay toward a History of the first Settlement of the Province an Affair recommended by some Fr'ds, but which now lyes inter-

8. Robert Proud to William Proud, 1 December 1777, *PMHB* 34 (1910): 62–63.
9. Robert Proud to John Proud, October 1778, *PMHB* 34 (1910):70.

rupted."[10] Given his agitated state of mind, the time hardly seemed propitious for Proud to have launched into a history of Pennsylvania. That it would be biased could hardly be doubted. But the two major narratives of the province which preceded Proud's had also reflected the special interests of their respective authors.

Ironically, the first chronicle of Pennsylvania was generated by two associates of John Fothergill. In 1755 Peter Collinson proposed the project of a history to Benjamin Franklin, who acted on the suggestion for political reasons: he wanted an antiproprietary version of the legislative-executive struggle as an antidote to William Smith's tracts and as an aid to his case before the Crown. Collinson introduced him to one Richard Jackson who, supplied with charters, bills, messages, and minutes of both Council and Assembly, wrote a narrative to Franklin's specifications.[11]

An Historical Review of the Constitution and Government of Pennsylvania, from its Origin; So far as regards the several Points of Controversy which have, from Time to Time, arisen between The several Governors of that Province, and Their several Assemblies was published in 1759. Thomas Penn was furious, and with good reason, for his father was portrayed as a benevolent patriarch who succumbed to power, ultimately combining "the Subtlety of the Serpent with the Innocence of the Dove." Thomas and his brothers looked even worse, "disposed to convert free Tenants into abject Vassals." James Logan, secretary of the province, was shown to be the wily and vindictive agent of the proprietor, while David Lloyd, speaker of the Assembly, was the watchful guardian of the people's liberties.

10. Robert Proud to William Proud, October 1778, *PMHB* 29 (1905): 230.
11. The account of the early histories, unless otherwise noted, is drawn from Joseph E. Illick, "The Writing of Colonial Pennsylvania History," *PMHB* 94 (1970):3–9.

Politics in early Pennsylvania proved to be a prefiguration of the scene in the middle of the eighteenth century, the time when Franklin was most active and the period to which most of *An Historical Review* was devoted. At this point in the province's history, there was no doubting the clear division between popular liberty and personal tyranny, the one represented in the Assembly and the other perpetrated by the proprietary. The Crown was depicted as neutral, a role which well suited Franklin's purposes. Although there was a solid basis of fact to *An Historical Review*, Philadelphia's most eminent citizen "did not reject the benefits of partial colouring," according to a sympathetic but candid historian.

As official printer of the Assembly, Franklin had access to state documents. Samuel Smith, a Quaker merchant and provincial officeholder in New Jersey, came into possession of a different sort of material about Pennsylvania. Caleb Pusey, one of the first settlers and an erstwhile member of Council and Assembly, left his papers to the Philadelphia Yearly Meeting. These passed through the hands of David Lloyd and Isaac Norris I, then to James Logan and finally to John Kinsey, speaker of the Assembly and chief justice of the province. Each man added papers of his own; they all came into Smith's hands in 1751.

The work that emerged was in two parts. In the first, Smith focused on Pennsylvania politics from the establishment of the government to 1726, the terminal year of Sir William Keith's administration, and paid little attention to imperial affairs. He carried out his promises to "preserve a Philosophical indifference" and to eschew "the inconvenience of descending minutely into the particulars" for "a general view of the times." The result was rather bland. Except for the unavoidable assertion that the governor and the Assembly were at odds during the administrations of John Evans (1704–1709) and Charles Gookin (1709–1717), Smith muted conflict and judged generously. William Penn was assigned almost saintly status, and even Governor Evans, who

spread a false alarm that the French were sailing up the Delaware
to attack Philadelphia, was characterized as "a man of natural
good sense but had much the rake in his character."

The second part of Smith's history concerned Quakers in New
Jersey and Pennsylvania, men of "reputation and credit" who had
to be neglected in favor of those who "were active in legislation
. . . in the first part." Depicting prominent Friends, describing
the establishment of Meetings, and reproducing letters and testimonies, Smith here displayed less "Philosophical indifference,"
especially toward the schismatic George Keith, whose theological
inconsistencies and constitutional intemperance were thoroughly
documented.

Although neither part of Smith's history was published until
long after his death in 1776, the manuscript which he had hoped
would "at least furnish materials—perhaps otherwise excite to a
more compleat & finished work," came into the hands of Robert
Proud in 1774. Indeed, it was probably Proud's rigorous critique of
Smith's work which delayed its publication.[12] "Having perused
the Manuscript," he wrote, "it appears to me extremely deficient
in certain Particulars." These included "a proper Introduction,"
drawing on William Penn's *A Brief Account of the Rise and Progress of the People Called Quakers* (1694), Penn's *Works* (1726),
and the writings of Quaker theologian Robert Barclay; an account
of the prior settlements on the Delaware and the natural history of
the province, drawn from Penn's promotional literature; "an *Appendix, containing all the Charters, Agreements* & other *Public
Writings*" as well as letters; a map of the province and a plan of
Philadelphia; and matters more diverse than the debates between
governor and Assembly.

12. "R. Proud's observations on S. Smith's history" can be found under
American Authors, Etting Papers, HSP. The sixth and final objection, calling
for the excision of certain material, was clearly heeded when the second part
of Smith's history was printed in Samuel Hazard, ed., *Register of Pennsylvania* . . . , 16 vols. (Philadelphia, 1828–1836), vols. 6–7.

Proud was talking about the history he would and did write. It included the features he mentioned when he criticized Smith, although his coverage of the years from the founding to 1763 (somewhat over half the text) was almost wholly a narrative of domestic and imperial political events. But this portion of his work was more vital than the pallid first part of Smith's history because, like Franklin, Proud was promoting a point of view with political meaning. *An Historical Review* had celebrated Franklin's social ascent by applauding the popular forces that made it possible and by rationalizing the printer's antiproprietary position. *The History of Pennsylvania* traced the decline of the province from its original pristine state in a narrative which recalled Proud's failure to realize his own early promise; the fault was not the Quakers' but that of the society which grew up around them.

Pennsylvania had been founded with the highest goals in mind: "the restoration of those natural and civil rights and privileges" denied in England. It was guided by a man whose views were "the best and most exalted, that could occupy the human mind." William Penn, as proprietor, provided the political restraint that was essential to true liberty. The public affairs of the province became stormy after his departure in 1684, but an excessive turbulence would not have befitted Proud's theme at this point. Smith's Quaker bias had led him to focus on the divisive activities of George Keith in the early 1690s, but Proud purposely avoided the conflict, commenting on Smith's manuscript: "In the Manner it stands there, I think it not only unnecessary, but also improper, to publish; or, to revive a Controversy about a Man, who has been dead now near one hundred years:—I have introduced an Abridgment of it into the Hist. of Pennsa."[13] It may also have been significant that Keith was the first Quaker schoolmaster in Philadelphia.

13. Robert Proud to James Pemberton, 20 December 1784, English Prose Writers, Dreer Collection, HSP.

On Penn's return the affairs of the province returned to their previous calm, and as a token of his benevolence he "presented" the Assembly with a charter of privileges. But after his second departure the lower house fell into "an ill humor." Although Proud always found conflict disagreeable, his increasingly bleak view of life told him it was inevitable. Nor were its effects always bad. In moderate doses party spirit, "the offspring of narrow and selfish views . . . deeply interwoven in human nature," caused men to pay attention to their real interests. During the Gookin and Evans administrations, unfortunately, this spirit ran rampant, a development for which Proud held the Assembly largely responsible.

Gookin's successor, Sir William Keith (1717–26), was "acquainted with the art of gaining the affection of the people"—a quality Proud would not ordinarily have admired, save for the fact that this talent allowed Keith to moderate party passions. In the end, however (and one senses the tone of inevitability), his popular predilections overcame him and he disregarded proprietary instructions. The administration of his successor, Patrick Gordon (1726–36), was distinguished by "moderation and prudence," but with the coming of the war and the consequent demands for defense funds, party passions were revitalized. Here Proud's Quaker sympathies were most apparent. George Thomas (1738–47), the governor who attempted to reconcile imperial demands with provincial pacifism, was "a man of abilities and resolution, but, in some things, did not sufficiently understand the nature and genius of the people, over whom he presided."

Proud did not hold Quakers responsible for the accentuation of partisanship. He rather argued that Pennsylvania's reputation for liberty ("than which nothing is more desirable, [but] when carried beyond a certain point degenerates into licentiousness") lured great numbers to the province, "many of whom were persons of very different principles and manners from those of the gen-

erality of the more early settlers." It was these people and their
descendants who jeopardized liberty "through the formation and
increase of party," who joined the Assembly "to foment the spirit
of opposition against the *old interest* . . . being chiefly *Quakers.*"
Beyond this point Proud would not go in his history. Although his
narrative appeared to end in 1763, the twenty war years preceding
the Peace of Paris received a scant four-page consideration. The
Quaker resignation from the Assembly in 1756 was not mentioned.

Pennsylvania, Proud believed, had been founded on "peace and
tranquillity, . . . primative truth and simplicity," but the "unhappy reverse" of these principles seemed to be "fast approaching." It was part of a Grand Design:

All things have their time; and both kingdoms and empires, as well as
smaller states, and particular persons, must die; *"finis ac ab origine
pendet;"* yet folly often shortens their duration, as wisdom and virtue
prolong their more happy existence: and we may plainly see men
frequently and greedily embrace the former, for the latter, and with
great zeal and confidence often pursue their own misery, under a
strong persuasion of the contrary: for, as the human body, when in its
most plethoric state, and in the greatest appearance of health and
vigour, is often then most in danger, or nearest a sudden change, so
the late and present extraordinary prosperity, the increasing, flourishing
and happy state of this country, at present, above others, may probably
be a prognostic, or sign, of its being in a more critical situation and
danger.

This metaphor may simply have been a reflection of Proud's
medical training, but it was not unlikely that he saw a parallel
between his own ebbing health and the impending decline of
Pennsylvania.

Proud's motive for writing *The History of Pennsylvania* was
clear enough: "My Endeavour is to call the Attention of the
present & future Generations to the virtuous and beneficial Example of their pious *Forefathers & Predecessors.*" But the work
could not be published during the revolution when it was written:

"The general *military* & *hostile* Temper of that Time . . . with the love of *Novelty* & *Change* did not favour the *Design*." Perhaps, however, the social transformation wrought by the political upheaval was an aberration, only to be dispelled by a return to Godly principles: "A true Acct. of Things in former Time may, if rightly applied & used, instruct the present Generation, that the Trust, Rank, Dignity & Station, which, for wise & good Purposes, have been conferred on the *Fathers* of a *People*, by an over-ruling & all-wise *Providence*, have been taken away, or removed, from the *Children*, or Successors, because of the *Unworthiness*, or, *Incapacity*. . . ."[14]

Most historians of this generation were celebrating the revolution. Proud condemned it, though without once mentioning it, by calling for a return to the principles of deferential politics which would have denied it.[15] Like Cotton Mather, who, when his world was collapsing about him, wrote *Magnalia Christi Americana* to remind his contemporaries of the glory that was Puritan Massachusetts, Proud was attempting to restore the past. He enjoyed a success equal to Mather's.

Proud's purpose in publishing *The History of Pennsylvania* conflicted with his earlier motive for writing it. He wanted to make money. He had returned to teaching in the 1780s, when the war was over and the book was essentially finished, but he was nagged by debts from his business ventures. In 1790 he quit the classroom and began preparations for publication. To realize a profit he would have to please the public. Yet it has been said, and correctly, that "no other American historian in the post-Revolu-

14. "Design in Compiling & Publishing the History of Pennsylvania," Proud Papers, HSP. The drafts of the history are also in this collection.
15. Dr. Charles Moore recalled to Proud on 22 February 1796 that he had earlier suggested publication of the manuscript: "no objections then occurred, as to Matter or Stile, that I now recollect, except the Strictures on the late Revolution in America, which thou says, upon the last Revisal, have been totally expunged." Physicians &c., Dreer Collection, HSP.

tionary era compiled a history that was intended for so small an audience."[16] Surely friends of the revolution would not find Proud's work congenial, nor did the author expect them to.

But Proud was taken aback to find that Quakers were not buying the two-volume study either. He had been assured by a fellow Friend on the eve of publication that "a book of this kind must be wished for by every Native of the State"[17]—a statement which, while reflecting the ideological insularity of the Society, suggested its support at least. Proud quickly concluded that he had been denied this support for failing to submit *The History of Pennsylvania* to the collective judgment of the Society before publication. In self-defense he wrote a paper demonstrating that in this case the submission procedure was inappropriate (his was an account of civil rather than ecclesiastical affairs), unwise (the imprimatur of the Society would have offended the general reader), and unnecessary (the manuscript had been read by prominent Friends and was open to the inspection of all during the years between writing and publication). Proud likened his situation to that of William Penn, a man victimized by ingratitude.[18] It was true that he, like Penn, failed to see the internal inconsistency of his position. At the time he was writing, his book could not be both general and Quaker.

Unfortunately, the work had particular appeal for neither audience. Two thousand copies of it were published, and Proud rather than the printer was responsible for its sale. In America it moved very slowly, though such distinguished patriots as John Adams, John Dickinson, and Thomas Jefferson were on the small list of

16. This point is made and documented in John A. Neuenschwander, "Robert Proud: A Chronicle of Scholarly Failure," *PMHB* 92 (1968):501–2, as well as in Powell, "Robert Proud," pp. 108–9.

17. Moore to Proud, cited in note 15.

18. "Robert Proud's Explanation & Reasons for Publishing his History of Pennsylvania in the Manner he has done it, &c.," 1797, Proud Manuscripts, LCP.

subscribers. Proud hoped to broaden the market by distributing copies in England through his brother William. There, he thought, his prejudice against the revolution should boost sales.[19] But such was not the case. William suggested that if more recent events had been included in the history its appeal would have been greater. He also pointed out that "many Friends dislike the Plate of Pen's head, supposing it an unfair likeness [for unknown reasons, Proud chose the least flattering portrait extant] also a want of perspicuous conciseness in Historical parts."[20]

Proud could tolerate none of this criticism. He wrote to his brother John, who also had raised questions about the accuracy of his work: "The History principally contains an impartial Account, or Statement, of real Facts . . . the Truth of which cannot be controverted, for some other Hand here after to improve upon. . . . It is the most authentic, complete & best Acct. of Wm. Penn & of the Prov. of Pennsa. that has ever yet appeared." Only "the late & present prevailing Spirit of Innovation, Novelty & Revolution" could account for "the slow Sale of it."[21] Proud was hardly the only man unable to see he was out of touch with his times and therefore arguing that the times were out of step with him.

He was an anachronism in appearance as well as in thought. A sympathetic biographer noted:

Robert Proud was in person tall—his nose was of the Roman order, and "overhung with most impending brows." I remember having seen him when I was quite a small boy; his appearance was striking, and could not readily be altogether forgotten. I have not been able to recall the expression of his countenance; but I well remember the imposing

19. John A. Neuenschwander draws a distinct line between the superior loyalist histories produced by George Chalmers, Thomas Hutchinson, and Justice William Smith, and the inferior work of Alexander Hewat, Samuel Peters, and Robert Proud, in "Robert Proud," pp. 504–5.

20. William Proud to Robert Proud, 28 July 1800 and 4 September 1801, Proud Manuscripts, LCP.

21. Robert Proud to John Proud, 6 May 1800, Proud Manuscripts, LCP.

effect, which the curled, gray wig, the half-cocked, patriarchal-looking hat, and the long, ivory-headed cane, had on my boyish imagination. I believe Proud was one of the last of the old school—I mean those who adhered faithfully to the dignified dress of our ancestors.[22]

He lingered on to 1813, passing from the American scene just as he entered it, in the midst of a war. He was still an anglophile, having recently penned a poem, "Where my Friend is, there is my country," part of which read:

> But where my nearest Friend I find
> There is *Britannia* to my Mind.

He was more reconciled to death than to American nationalism ("Men die to live, & live to die"); his view of life was ambiguous to the end. He was never quite sure of human nature, of whether the rational faculty could be trusted or not:

> Get learning in thy early Days,
> And ever walk in Virtue's Ways:
> As to the Body, Life we find
> So is true Learning to the Mind.[23]

*   *   *   *

But the human mind is so very prone to Idolatry, that even by endeavouring to avoid one Species thereof, it is often liable to fall into another, or its opposite, &c.[24]

Proud's ambivalence was grounded in experience. Never doubting the wisdom of his own scholarly training, he always suspected the integrity of those whose values were different from his own.

Robert Proud was not a popular historian, and *The History of Pennsylvania* has only once been reprinted. Not until 1829, the year of Andrew Jackson's inauguration, did another narrative of

---

22. Charles West Thomson, "Notices of the Life and Character of Robert Proud," *Memoirs* of the HSP, 14 vols. (Philadelphia, 1826–1895), 1:pt. 2, 405–6.
23. The three quotations in this paragraph are from the Proud Papers, HSP.
24. Robert Proud to James Pemberton, July 1806, Proud Papers, HSP.

the province appear. Although its author, Thomas F. Gordon, followed Proud's lead in matters of fact and organization, his message was totally different: the story and glory of Pennsylvania was the steady growth of democracy. The interpretation was geared to the times, as Proud's was not. Echoes of Gordon are still heard today, while Proud's viewpoint, which has the virtue of contemporary authenticity, was disregarded.

9.

William Smith, Jr. and *The History of Canada*

JOHN M. BUMSTED

The first general history by an English-speaking inhabitant of the territory successively called New France, Quebec, and Lower Canada was William Smith, Jr.'s *History of Canada*. The work was one of the first in English about that part of British North America which eventually formed the Dominion of Canada.[1] Smith's *History*, like most such pioneer efforts, has been more often referred to than read and has been viewed as a historic document rather than as serious scholarship. Such a perception was aided by the author's own apologetic diffidence about his work. The *History*'s frequently noted pro-British emphasis is hardly surprising since the author was the son of one of Lower Canada's leading loyalist officials.[2] Nevertheless, Smith claimed objectivity for his writing and made some genuine attempts to achieve it.[3] Writing before von Ranke had made a virtue of his-

1. For a discussion of early history in English-speaking Canada, see Kenneth N. Windsor, "Historical Writing in Canada to 1920," in Carl F. Klinck, ed., *Literary History of Canada: Canadian Literature in English* (Toronto, 1965), pp. 208–50, especially 208–14. Smith's *History* is dated 1815 on the title page, but it was not sold publicly until 1826.

2. See Windsor's comments in "Historical Writing in Canada," Klinck, ed., *Literary History*, p. 213; Carl F. Klinck, "Literary Activity in the Canada's 1812–1841," in ibid., pp. 127–28; Norah Story, *The Oxford Companion to Canadian History and Literature* (Toronto, 1967), p. 771; and the signed article on Smith by Michel Brunet in *Encyclopedia Canadiana*, IX (Ottawa, 1958):341.

3. William Smith, Jr., *History of Canada*, 2 vols. (Quebec, 1815), preface.

torical objectivity, Smith had great difficulty overcoming the partisanship which characterized the loyalist historical tradition with which he was familiar.[4] That he should make the attempt in the absence of a philosophy of objectivity is explicable only in terms of his own personality.

Despite the ostensible importance of his position ("Clerk of the Parliament and Master in Chancery of the Province of Lower Canada"),William Smith has never been the subject of anything beyond brief encyclopedia entries, perhaps because of the peripheral nature of the man to important developments in his province. Smith was one of Lower Canada's leading plural officeholders and a member of the infamous "Chateau Clique"; yet he was never involved in an important public controversy, surviving even the Rebellions of 1837 with his pension intact. As author of *The History of Canada*, however, Smith is certainly entitled to some biographical attention, if only to demonstrate that no historical work can transcend the personality of its author.

William Smith, Jr. was born in New York in 1769, the son of William and Janet Smith. His grandfather had been an important New York politician, and his father, one of the leading figures in the province, was once deftly characterized by a contemporary: "few men so able—if he could be trusted."[5] Senior had actively opposed the Stamp Act, but by the time of his son's birth he was moving in a direction which would ultimately lead him to support Great Britain in the War for Independence. Throughout most of his son's early childhood, Senior was retired from politics, attempting to avoid taking sides in the revolutionary crisis. In 1778 he

4. The best discussion of loyalist history remains Moses Coit Tyler, *The Literary History of the American Revolution 1763–1783*, II (reprint edition, New York, 1957):383–428.

5. For a full biography of Smith's father, see L. F. S. Upton, *The Loyal Whig: William Smith of New York and Quebec* (Toronto, 1969). The quotation is from a review of Upton's book by G. N. D. Evans in *Journal of American History* 56 (1969):653.

came off the fence and soon afterward was appointed chief justice of British-occupied New York, although he never exercised the authority of that office. When the British evacuated New York late in 1783, young William joined his father in exile in England.

Little is known of the early lives of most biographical subjects, the years before they achieve prominence. In the case of William Smith, Jr., however, more information is available on his life between the ages of fourteen and seventeen than is available for any other period, largely because his father kept a detailed diary of the London exile and regularly wrote to his wife, who remained in New York.[6] "Bringing up William" is a constant theme in both diary and letters, as Senior worked to give his son advantages which he himself had never enjoyed and attempted to mold him into something he was incapable of becoming. Senior always had a strain of indecisiveness in his nature. While the father's indecision did not produce passivity, young William had great difficulty achieving genuine aggressiveness; his father's overprotective paternalism toward an only son did not help at all. William tried to please his father, speaking words his father wanted to hear and doing what his father wanted done. This strategy succeeded so well by 1784 that Senior reported to his wife with obvious pleasure that "I find my mind leaning to a better opinion of his Capacity than I have formerly indulged." But William's statements to his father that "those who had no opinions of their own, could neither have understanding nor honesty" were hardly the signs of an independent spirit.[7] The son was not precocious and the father tried too hard. The story is a familiar one.

By dint of extraordinary parental effort and attention, young

6. The diary has been edited and published by L. F. S. Upton as the *Diary of William Smith*, 2 vols. (Toronto, 1963, 1965). The letters (quoted extensively in Upton's notes) are in the Smith-Sewell Papers at the Public Archives of Canada, Ottawa (hereafter PAC).

7. William Smith to Janet Smith, 20 May 1784, Smith-Sewell Papers, PAC.

William was made into a "gentleman." He also matured into a lightweight personality rarely taken seriously. His "achievements" resulted from impeccable manners and a not-always-adroit use of parental and family connections. Swollen with the importance of his position, Smith never realized what a ludicrous figure he cut and how much others saw through him and smiled at his efforts.

While in England, Senior kept a close watch over his son's manners, morals, and associates. Education was important, and young Will was placed at a prestigious boarding school. He lasted for three months, ultimately returning to his father's lodgings. His father then engaged a private tutor, from whom William could learn languages, especially French, without the "Danger of contracting Low Habits."[8] The young man became fluent in French, an accomplishment which would serve him in good stead in Lower Canada. Senior's diary indicates that he often took William to uplifting and broadening events (the theatre, museums, lectures) and afterward held lengthy and often pontifical discussions of their importance.[9] Letters to William's mother stressed the manners the youth was acquiring: "Will you believe that the ladies of our House have so far polished him, that he made a Pains of having introductory Letters for Ten Parties."[10]

Whether Will had a record of sinful behavior or his father simply feared that weakness would lead him into sin is unclear, but parental concern about temptation was obvious. Senior limited Will's visits to London because of the dangers of "Prostitutes of the Streets," described to Janet Smith as "the vilest and handsomest of your Sex, from 14 to three Score."[11] On the eve of departure for Quebec, Smith observed that his son was "not fond

8. Upton, ed., *Diary*, 1:73; Smith to Janet Smith, n.d., Smith-Sewell Papers, PAC.

9. See, for example, Upton, ed., *Diary*, 1:94, 171, 202, 270, 287.

10. Smith to Janet Smith, 20 May 1784, Smith-Sewell Papers, PAC.

11. Upton, ed., *Diary*, 2:15.

of the Prospect of leaving the Country," but added, "He may perhaps see it again, when his Mind is better fortified ag't the Seductions of Pleasure and Vice."[12] Whatever his feelings in the matter, young Smith left England with his father (recently appointed chief justice of Lower Canada) on 21 August 1786.[13]

What William really thought of his father and of the parental domination exerted well beyond the elder Smith's death in 1793 must remain unknown. Smith mentioned his father favorably in his *History* and in glowing terms in a biographical introduction he wrote for the third volume of Senior's *History of New York*. But what else could a man do whose career, more than thirty years after his father's death, still depended on parental reputation and position? In repudiating his father, Smith would have repudiated himself. An absence of private papers and the conventions of the time screen the modern historian from any resentment Smith may have felt for his father. But it would be entirely consistent with what is known of Smith if he lacked any resentment of the father who dominated his early life and was responsible for whatever position of prominence and security he enjoyed.

In Quebec, Senior continued his son's education. The university, which in 1785 the chief justice had hoped would be "supported by the Royal Munificence," did not materialize because of religious and national divisions in the province, and Senior turned instead to practical training.[14] He frequently sent his son on errands and in 1789 dispatched him to New York to deal with the family's complicated landholdings in the United States.[15] By 1792, young William's apprenticeship was completed; his father, extremely ill and probably aware of impending death, undertook

12. Smith to Janet Smith, 1 October 1785, Smith-Sewell Papers, PAC.
13. Upton, ed., *Diary*, 2:143.
14. Smith to Janet Smith, 1 October 1785, Smith-Sewell Papers, PAC. The bulk of the documentation on the chief justice's efforts to establish a university in Quebec was reprinted by his son in the *History of Canada*, 2:177–210.
15. Smith to Smith, Jr., 8 February 1789, Smith-Sewell Papers, PAC.

to launch him on his own. Although provisions for landgrants in the province limited farmlots to two hundred acres with one thousand additional acres at discretion, Councillor Smith responded to a petition of 23 February 1792 by his son and son-in-law (John Plenderleath) for a township of 108 square miles on the Saint Francis River with the argument that the limitation was unworkable in Lower Canada. The Council of the province agreed, and on 3 May 1792 the younger Smith and Plenderleath were granted Sympson Township Number 5. Twelve hundred acres apiece they kept for themselves; the remainder they sold to bonafide settlers. In the 1792 provincial elections William ran for the assembly but was defeated; it was his only attempt at elective office.[16]

His son's landed patrimony assured, Senior turned to the vexing problem of finding him a position. William, "anxious to be employed," had mentioned to the lieutenant governor "his wish to be Clerk of the Executive and Legislative Council," but he had been put off by His Excellency. So on 2 November 1792 the elder Smith stepped in and wrote Lord Dorchester—the family's patron—about "the possibility that a patronage wanted by the youth of *this* Country may be given to others who ought not to look for it *here*." On 17 December 1792 young William was duly appointed clerk of the Legislative Council by the lieutenant governor.[17] There was, of course, nothing unusual about Senior's using his position and connections to insure that his only son was well begun in life. Senior's father had done the same for him; to have done otherwise in the eighteenth century would have been far more unusual. William Smith, Jr. controlled large amounts of land in Canada and the United States through parental influence and

16. Upton, ed., *Diary*, 2:297–301; Lower Canada Land Papers, 1:142, PAC; *Gazette de Québec*, 24 May 1792.
17. Smith to Lord Dorchester, 2 November 1792, reprinted in Upton, ed., *Diary*, 2:311; *Gazette de Québec*, 20 December 1792; Lower Canada Blue Book, 1821, PAC.

inheritance, and he acquired a series of offices in the same way. He married to increase his comforts and wrote his *History of Canada* partly because his father had written a *History of New York*. For the next forty years, much of what is known about William Smith consists of efforts—usually labored, frequently successful—to acquire new offices and marks of status. In his declining years he concentrated on getting pensions in order to retire in style from the offices he had acquired.

Little is known of William Smith, Jr. from his appointment to public office in 1792 to his trip to England in 1803–4. Having been made clerk of the Legislative Council, Smith now found it necessary to appeal for a salary to accompany the office. The House of Assembly received a petition and fixed the salary at £450 sterling in April 1793. After a long illness, Smith, Sr. died in December 1793. William inherited three-elevenths of his father's estate (which consisted largely of enormous tracts of uninhabited land in New York and Vermont). As the only male heir (the remainder of the estate went to Smith's mother and his three sisters), Smith became chief custodian of the family estate, a role for which his father had attempted to fit him. He remained nominally in charge of the Smith lands until his death, but the bulk of the work was done by his brother-in-law, Jonathan Sewell, attorney general and later (1808–38) chief justice of Lower Canada. The reasons for this are not hard to find. When faced with the need to act, Smith ran into great difficulty, as a whining letter to Sewell from St. John's, Vermont, in 1799 indicated. On his way to New York City on important family business, Smith complained of a sore throat and pains in the breast and head, and regretted coming "on a Journey, to which I seem so unequal." In no case, he said, would he go further than Albany, "as there are acc'ts of the Yellow Fever at New York."[18]

18. Lower Canada Blue Book; Smith Miscellaneous Papers, 2148, PAC; Smith to Jonathan Sewell, 1 September 1799, Smith-Sewell Papers, PAC.

Smith's lack of decisiveness seemed to have only one exception, and that was the business of scrounging for public office. He may not have enjoyed this hustling, but he did engage in it with considerable success. By 1800 he was again looking for some kind of public patronage. A letter to his brother-in-law of 23 February mentioned "strong assurances of support" in Britain from Adam Gordon (a cousin who was a protégé of Henry Dundas) and from what Smith referred to as "his friends." Smith became fairly expert at playing this game of securing interests. Whatever imperial sinecure he sought in 1800 apparently did not materialize. But in 1803 the Legislative Council and House of Assembly of Lower Canada agreed to the appointment of a master in chancery "to carry Messages" between the two bodies, and on 6 April 1803 William Smith was appointed "a Master in Chancery for the Province of Lower Canada."[19] The only hitch was that the office did not carry any remuneration, a drawback which Smith worked busily to remove on his journey to England in 1803–4.

Smith had not been to England since his departure with his father for Quebec in 1786, and he had a variety of reasons to make the journey. In terms both of his immediate goal—a salary as master in chancery—and of his long-range ambitions for future positions, he needed the support of influential people in London. He also enjoyed the prestige of hobnobbing with important people: "It was worth a voyage to England," he wrote in November 1803, "to find one stood so well in the opinion of one's Friends." Then too, William Smith was probably looking for a wife. He was now more than thirty years old, unmarried, and apparently unable to find a suitable mate in Lower Canada. "You know," he commented to Jonathan Sewell, "how very indecisive I am and respecting matrimony, am the more so, as I am not sufficiently informed as to the advantages that are attached." But marriage could have one overriding advantage to a man who believed that "Money is

19. Smith to Jonathan Sewell, 23 February 1800, Smith-Sewell Papers, PAC; Lower Canada Blue Book, 1821.

everything, with it or without it"; as Smith wrote, "unless I marry a Woman of Fortune, I shall be ruined." In addition to the quest for wife, money, and ego-fulfillment, Smith undertook a number of errands for friends and associates in Lower Canada and sought to refresh himself on how things were done in England.[20]

The London journey was extremely successful for Smith. He found his wife in the person of Susanna Webber, a niece of merchant Brook Watson and the daughter of Admiral Charles Webber of Hampshire.[21] Smith may have had Susanna in mind in advance, since she was part of the circle of boyhood acquaintances he had enjoyed in England twenty years earlier. In any case, she had "attractions," as Smith explained in a letter home:

> She is pretty, not handsome, of a very good Family, with £200 a year *now* [the italics are his] & one hundred more, at her Mother's death— of a very amiable disposition, good Temper and good Sense—and what is better than all, will go to Canada, a country in the estimation of the women of this Country, the most barbarous and the most uncomfortable of the World.[22]

As the diary he kept of the trip indicates, he met, dined, and visited with a number of minor British officials and the families of colonial ones. Throughout the visit, he never lost sight of the need for a salary as master in chancery, and he pulled every string available to him.

The most important person whose assistance Smith solicited was Edward Augustus, Duke of Kent (a younger son of George III), who had been in Lower Canada from 1791–93 and had been acquainted with Smith's parents. Their personal meeting in November 1803 was most gratifying. The duke, Smith wrote, "re-

20. L. F. S. Upton, "The London Diary of William Smith, 1803–1804," *Canadian Historical Review* 47 (1966):146–55; Smith to Jonathan Sewell, 7 November 1803, 9 March 1804, Smith-Sewell Papers, PAC.

21. William Doyle to Jonathan Sewell, 13 April 1804, Smith-Sewell Papers, PAC.

22. Ibid., Smith to Sewell, 9 March 1804.

ceived me with the utmost attention—he took me by the hand and said he was happy to see me—He immediately inquired after my Mother's Health." This inquiry was important; although Edward chose as a rule not "to meddle" in colonial affairs because of the royal family's jealousy of interference, he could be persuaded to serve the Smith family, as he explained to Smith, "from the respect and regard I entertain for your worthy mother, whose politeness and attention, during my residence at Quebec, I shall ever gratefully remember." Smith succeeded in cadging from the duke a letter to be handed to the under secretary of state for the Colonial Department introducing "Mr. William Smith son of the late Chief Justice of Canada whom I am anxious to introduce to your good offices and to recommend warmly to your attention." With this evidence of royal patronage, Smith confidently petitioned the colonial secretary for "such salary as your Lordship shall conceive honorable to Government and an adequate Support to the Office." He was granted £81 sterling per annum, for which he thanked the duke. In reply, the duke noted that he "esteems himself happy in having been able to render Mr. Smith the little service which is mentioned in his letter, and is most amply recompenced for any trouble it has given him by a knowledge that he has been the means of adding to Mr. Smith's comfort."[23]

When he returned to Quebec in July 1804, Smith could feel quite satisfied with his English sojourn. He brought with him a wife, additional income, and important names to drop in Lower Canada, as well as the patronage of the royal family. For ten years, this appears to have satisfied his ambitions. Minor sinecures and

23. Smith to Sewell, 7 November 1803; Edward, Duke of Kent, to William Smith, 18 December 1803; Edward, Duke of Kent, to Mr. Sullivan, under secretary of state for the colonial department, 26 December 1803; "To the Right Hon'ble Lord Hobart, London 4 January 1804 the Memorial and Representation of William Smith of Quebec"; Edward, Duke of Kent, to Smith (extract), 23 July 1804, Smith Papers, New York Public Library (hereafter NYPL).

offices came his way in this period. In 1810 he was appointed
justice of the peace for the District of Quebec, and in 1812 was
promoted to major in the Third Battalion, Militia, Quebec.[24] But
in 1812, Smith began to mount another office-seeking campaign,
this time to gain appointment to the Executive Council of Lower
Canada. A letter to the governor in 1813 noted: "In consequence
of my desire to be appointed one of the Executive Council of this
Province I applied last summer, to his Royal Highness the Duke of
Kent, to point out the course best calculated to effect the object in
question—in the answer, your Excellency will see, what His Royal
Highness has suggested."[25]

Unlike his other offices, which required merely execution of
duties specified by others, the position of executive councillor at
least implied independent judgment and decision-making abilities,
since the Council was the executive arm of the provincial government. Smith's friends and relatives dragged their feet on the
matter, and he wrote a flurry of letters pressing for action. Success
was a long time in coming, but Smith persevered and was rewarded on 1 November 1822 with an appointment *in mandamus*
by the prince regent as a member of the Council. He was chosen
Council chairman, a position from which he could not debate and
seldom had to vote. A few days after becoming a councillor, Smith
was appointed a "Commissioner for the Management of the Jesuit
Estates." The Jesuit Estates were a terribly complicated and
involved bone of contention in Lower Canada for over one
hundred years, but apparently the commissioners were never a part
of the controversy.[26]

24. *Gazette de Québec*, 25 January 1810, 19 March 1812.
25. William Smith to "His Excellency," 24 January 1813, Civil and
Provincial Secretary, Lower Canada, "S" Series, 1760–1840, Volume 127,
40690, PAC.
26. Smith to Sewell, 1 July 1814, Smith-Sewell Papers; Lower Canada
Blue Book, 1821; *Gazette de Québec*, 21 November 1822; Roy C. Dalton,
*The Jesuits' Estates Question 1760–1888: A Study of the Background for the
Agitation of 1889* (Toronto, 1968), p. 4.

For a period of over ten years after 1822, William Smith vanished back into political anonymity, despite his collection of some of the most impressive-sounding offices in Lower Canada. Although an *anglais*, a loyalist (or at least the son of one), and a plural officeholder, Smith was never attacked by the *Canadien* party in Lower Canada. His bilingualism perhaps helps explain this. When Smith found the serenity of his political existence disturbed in 1835, it was, fittingly enough, a result of his plural officeholding, and the attack was mounted by the governor.

Concerned over continual mutterings from the *Canadien* popular party about the *anglais* oligarchy called the "Chateau Clique," the Colonial Office in 1835 sent Lord Gosford, as governor and high commissioner, with instructions to investigate the complaints and conciliate the factions. Gosford was directed "to Inquire into all cases which occur in Lower Canada of Persons holding more than one office"; if one office were being held at His Majesty's pleasure incompatible with another, he was to ask for a resignation, giving the holder the option of which office he would retain. When he undertook the inquiry, Gosford wrote Smith, he was struck that "some Members of the Executive Council hold other offices of inferior station, and such as are scarcely consistent with the dignity which ought to attach to the Executive Council, for which reason as well as for others which have been made the subjects of frequent dissension," he decided that Smith's offices of executive councillor and clerk to the Legislative Council were incompatible. Gosford must have known that Smith's offices were not really a bone of contention and that the status of the offices was not what the government had meant by compatibility, but Smith was a sitting duck as a plural officeholder. Gosford's offensive put Smith in a difficult position, for his office of executive councillor was high in prestige but without remuneration, while his office of clerk was low in prestige but extremely well-paid. Smith opted for his comfort rather than his status. He offered to resign his seat on the Executive Council, an offer the governor rejected because he needed an adequate number of councillors to form a court of appeals as required by the Constitutional Act of 1791.[27]

The governor's refusal to accept his resignation gave Smith a chance to minimize his losses. The result was a remarkable letter to Sir Charles Gray, the colonial secretary, offering to resign the clerkship in return for a "retiring pension charged upon the hereditary revenues of Lower Canada," and requesting the "honor of Knighthood" as recompense for being forced to resign from the Executive Council. Gray's response noted that "43 years service would seem to be one of the soundest foundations, on which any one could rest his pretensions" for a pension. Moreover, it would not "be deemed unreasonable on your part to suggest that the mark of approbation should be conferred upon you, if you have to resign the office of Executive Counsellor," and that "the station and services of your father as Chief Justice would no doubt contribute much to facilitate the attainment of the latter object." Gray also made it clear that he refused to permit the neat finesse that Smith was attempting—getting a knighthood as reward for giving up an office that he would not have to surrender if he retired with a pension from the other office. "It would," Gray warned plainly, "probably be fatal to both applications to urge them separately by different or indirect courses."[28] Since it would have been fatal to the applications to have them considered together, Smith apparently dropped the project.

Because of political unrest in the province, Smith was not permitted to retire from the Executive Council until October of

27. For background of the Gosford Commission, see Helen Taft Manning, *The Revolt of French Canada 1800–1835* (London, 1962), and Mason Wade, *The French Canadians 1760–1967*, rev. ed., 2 vols. (Toronto, 1968), 1:153 ff.; Gosford to Smith, 22 October 1835, 26 October 1835, Smith Papers, NYPL.
28. Sir Charles Gray to Smith, 2 April 1836, Smith Papers, NYPL.

1837.[29] The reorganization of the Canadas which followed the Rebellions of 1837 severely affected Smith's remaining offices, since Upper and Lower Canada were reunited and all officeholders found themselves starting from the beginning. Smith was granted half his salary as a retirement pension but thought himself "entitled to the other half, on the common principle, that when an office is taken away a just compensation is due to the officer, so compelled to retire." He apparently got no further with this quest than with efforts to provide for his son (who had been assistant clerk to the legislative council) by having him continued in his father's offices.[30]

Having only minimal political power in Lower Canada, Smith discovered that despite "48 years in the Public Service" he had no influence in the newly-unified province of Canada. The times had changed, new men had risen, and new political constitutions had been created. There was no end of influence-peddling and patronage in the new province, but the kind of government left over from the eighteenth century, which made possible the career of William Smith, Jr., was no more. Smith's declining years before his death in 1847 were spent quietly in retirement in his house on Saint Lewis Street in Quebec. Virtually his only move into the wider world during the 1840s was a typical one. Fearful of the trouble the family was having with its tenants in the United States—there were complaints of rack-renting and lawsuits disputing Smith ownership of lands—Smith in 1843 separated his interests in the estate from the rest of the family, since in case of legal difficulty "he might find it difficult and expensive to satisfy all parties that he has acted for their best interests in relation to the

29. Notation in Smith's hand on Gosford's letter of 22 October 1835. Smith commented that the delay evidently showed that "he did not think the offices incompatable."

30. Smith to unknown recipient, 15 September 1840, Canada Secretary of State's Papers, S448, PAC; Canada Blue Book, 1841.

lands." On 17 December 1847, aged seventy-eight years and ten months, William Smith died, "deeply regretted by numerous relations and friends, and by society in general."[31]

Smith's *History*: Its Appearance

Smith's ventures into the realm of historical writing were in general as ineffectual as his political career, though equally fascinating. The Smith Papers contain only scattered references to the *History of Canada*, but the complete publication history of the work can be reconstructed from papers preserved by its printer, John Neilson. Because the publication details of most early histories of North America have been lost, the material on the publication of Smith's *History of Canada* makes the work significant beyond its textual value, particularly since it did not appear for eleven years after the publication date on its title page. Smith's problems with his printer—undoubtedly exacerbated by his indecisive personality and complicated by Neilson's close connection with the *Canadien* popular party in the province which Smith did not wish to alienate—illustrate the sorts of difficulties which could face the historian in early North America and which certainly confronted an *anglais* historian in Lower Canada.

William Smith, Sr. had written and published a history of New York in 1757, at the age of 29.[32] Not surprisingly, his son began to project a history of Canada at approximately the same age. Early in 1800, Smith wrote to his brother-in-law about obtaining papers from the "Semanary" for historical research and, characteristically, asked Sewell to "cull out, such as you think useful."[33] An octavo

31. J. Dexter to Reverend Henry Sewell, 9 January 1843, Smith-Sewell Papers, PAC; *The Morning Chronicle* [Québec City], 20 December 1847.
32. Upton, *The Loyal Whig*, pp. 37–39.
33. Smith to Jonathan Sewell, 13 February 1800, Smith-Sewell Papers, PAC.

volume of 344 pages was apparently completed by 1805—probably a version of what eventually became Volume I of the published *History*—since John Neilson at the time provided an estimate of the cost of printing 600 copies of such a volume.[34] Nothing more was heard of Smith's project until 1809, when Neilson again furnished printing estimates for 600 copies, this time for an octavo volume of 304 pages.[35]

Despite the two estimates for printing what evidently was a completed work, Smith did nothing about publication for some years. However, in 1814, he stirred himself to consider making the work available in print, although it apparently had been circulating in manuscript form for some time, probably so that Smith could gain assurances from others of its value and accuracy before making it public. In the midst of the war against the United States, Smith wrote to Sewell: "You enquire whether my History of Canada would sell at this time: it appears to be a favorable Moment for such a book—what would a London Printer charge to print 370 pages. . . . Pray let me know as I could put a Volume in hand immediately, as a friend of mine has one in London."[36]

The notion of printing in London came to nothing, and in 1815 Smith was again dealing with John Neilson, who by this time was

34. "Estimate Mr. Smith's History," 9 March 1805, John Neilson Papers, PAC. Neilson (1776–1848) was a Scotsman who emigrated to Lower Canada in 1790, became editor and publisher of the Québec *Gazette* in 1796 and, like most eighteenth-century printers, combined bookselling, general printing, and the production of a newspaper in his business. Of radical Whig proclivities, Neilson was one of a long line of Scotsmen in Lower Canada who supported the French Canadians (or *Canadiens*) over the *anglais* establishment. Although he did not enter politics actively until 1818, his newspaper tended to be antigovernment in tone from its inception. In the 1820s and 1830s Neilson worked closely with the French Canadian leader Louis Joseph Papineau, but broke with him before the abortive Rebellion of 1837. There is no substantial modern study of Neilson.

35. "Copy of an Estimate furnished to the Hon. Wm. Smith on Nov'r 1809," Neilson Papers, PAC.

36. Smith to Sewell, 8 October 1814, Smith-Sewell Papers, PAC.

an active ally of the popular party. By August of that year Smith was reading proof for the work and still worrying about what he had written. He evidently had asked for Neilson's comments, since the printer wrote him:

I have looked at the parts regarding the Montreal Seminary, Joncaire, & the New (Law?) on Tythes. The latter is the most objectionable as it is brought into the history before the period at which the discussion occurred. This may be construed as an intention of attacking the rights claimed & long enjoyed by the Bishop. Besides you give only one side of the question, & you pronounce positively against the Bishop.

Despite these criticisms, Neilson attempted to reassure Smith that "for my part I have no objection to publish the work as it stands. Even the part above mentioned is valuable, and, in my opinion can do no harm." Understandably concerned by Smith's procrastinations with a considerable investment now made in printing, Neilson asked not only for his printing charges and sales commissions, but that the author "allow me interest from the present time" on the bill.[37] Smith seized on the proposed financial arrangements as an excuse to delay making the work available for sale. He refused to permit the *History* to be sold so long as Neilson insisted on charging interest, since "allowing commission and the interest upon it (the debt), I think would be too much."[38] But his real concern was probably with public reaction from the French to the work, since one of his chief political assets was his acceptability to all parties in the province, and since he was still attempting to gain appointment to the Council.[39] An objection by Neilson "to the anachronism about Lavigne's case" was sufficient to lead Smith to conclude, "it may be proper to delay the

37. Neilson to Smith, 26 August 1815, Neilson Papers, PAC.
38. Smith to Neilson, n.d. [26 August 1815], Neilson Papers, PAC.
39. At this time Smith was also projecting plans for what eventually became the Literary and Historical Society of Quebec.

second volume until my return in the Spring."[40] The impasse, ostensibly on the question of interest, apparently postponed publication of the work in 1815, despite the appearance of that date on its title page.

Nothing more is known regarding the fate of the *History* until August 1817, when Neilson wrote Smith, "The 600 volumes of the History of Canada are ready to be delivered and have been long waiting the orders Mr. Smith may please to give respecting them." Neilson subsequently requested advertising copy for the work and, receiving no reply, indicated to the author that he was apprehensive that you have . . . changed your mind." The printer threatened to go to court. Smith's reply is worth quoting *in extenso*, since it is extremely revealing both of his personality and of the reasons for the delay:

I called on you, but found you had gone to the country. I wished much to have had another conversation with you, before an ultimate decision was taken, as to the publication of the History: I have since I had the pleasure to see you seriously and deliberately considered the question, and have come to the determination to suspend, *for this Winter,* the publication under the impression, that many errors may be corrected, the Amendment you suggested made—and a large collection of Papers added by way of an Appendix to the Second Volume. I am determined of your kindness to me, that your interests shall not suffer, and I am ready to satisfy you, for that I am in your debt. I know you are of a contrary opinion as to the publication, but such logic & reason have been advanced, that I am resolved *not* to publish the work until the beginning of the ensuing spring.

Subsequent negotiation got Smith to agree to authorize Neilson "to publish both vol's at the price I should fix if I could leave out Lavigne's case."[41] But as might be expected, this did not really

40. Smith to Neilson, n.d. [26 August 1815], Neilson Papers, PAC.
41. Neilson to Smith, 7 August 1817, 26 September 1817; Smith to Neilson, 27 September 1817; Note on letter Neilson to Smith, 26 September 1817, Neilson Papers, PAC.

settle the matter and nothing further happened for a number of years.

In 1822 Neilson was still trying to collect his money, complaining that printing "the work was very troublesome and expensive on acc't of the alterations while printing." After a decade of threats, Neilson finally turned the business over to his partner, who wrote suitably .veiled threats of impending legal action in 1824. After what apparently were long and arduous negotiations, the business details were cleared up, all the alterations were made (or the urgency for making them seemed more remote), and Smith decided to publish. Not surprisingly, he could not really face taking the final step himself and sent his wife to Neilson to inform the printer that her husband had finally decided "upon the publication of the History of Canada and was pleased to say that she would authorize us to proceed to . . . sale . . . after submitting an advertisement for her approval." Neilson refused to play the game, and insisted "it seems to us that it would be improper and unwarrantable on our part to offer the Book for Sale without a direct and positive order from its author to that effect." The printer had little doubt "that the sale thereof would be . . . extensive," particularly if the price were kept low.[42]

The requested order to publish apparently was forthcoming, and on 12 May 1826—eleven years after the work had been printed—the following advertisement appeared in Quebec City:

Now first published, and for sale by Neilson & Cowan, No. 3 Mountain Street, in two volumes Royal 8vo in b'ds, price 16/—The "History of Canada from its first discovery to the Year 1791"
By William Smith Esquire: clerk of the Parliament and Master in Chancery of the Province of Lower Canada.

"Ne quid falsi dicere audiat ne quid viri non audiat"

42. Neilson to Smith, 23 December 1822; W. Cowan to Smith, 17 July 1824, 9 September, 1824; Neilson to Smith, 12 May 1826, Neilson Papers, PAC.

This work, which in addition to its historical narration contains a mass of valuable documents no where else to be met with, was printed in 1815 but from unavoidable circumstances remained unpublished till the present time.[43]

In the first year of its availability, the *History of Canada* sold 68 copies; in the following three years, eight more. On 9 January 1830, Neilson and Cowan delivered to Smith the remaining 208 bound copies of the first printing run, which Smith apparently distributed to friends and attempted to sell in dribbles and drabs over the remaining years of his life. The author was apparently not discouraged by the low sales. In any event, in 1829 Smith with some pride brought out a new edition of his father's *History of New York*, and was gratified to see his *History of Canada* displayed for sale in bookstores along with the historical work of William Smith, Sr.[44]

Smith's *History*: An Evaluation

Smith produced an acceptable first volume, particularly for the period before 1690. By comparison with excursions into "history" by other Canadians of his era, which took the form of reprinted documents or dry narrations of events in the form of "annals," Smith's first volume was singularly impressive. It was a full-blown synthetic effort, despite its author's deprecation of it as "Narrative" not deserving of "the name of a History."[45] Not for nearly a generation would any other British North American produce a

43. The original draft of the advertisement is in the Neilson Papers. One interesting editional alteration was that the words "of facts" were scratched out following the words "its historical narration."
44. "Account Sales of the History of Canada," 18 July 1827; Smith to Neilson, 4 February 1830; Memo in Neilson's hand, 9 January 1830; Smith to unknown recipient, November 1832, Neilson Papers, PAC.
45. Smith, *History of Canada*, "Preface," p. ii.

work which matched Smith's *History* as extended and analytical narrative.[46]

Smith succeeded in making a good deal of sense out of his sources. A modern scholar might complain about the limited number of sources employed, but while his research was not exhaustive, Smith was thoroughly familiar with the colony records, the Jesuit Relations, and the best of the contemporary French historians, especially Charlevoix and la Potherie.[47] Since New France in the eighteenth century was badly covered by contemporary French writers, Smith had some justification for relying as heavily as he did on British works, such as that of his father on New York. He himself considered that his major contribution was in extending Charlevoix's *History* to 1763.

For the most part, Smith's judgments and coverage were little different from those of his predecessors and of several subsequent generations of historians of New France. In terms of modern scholarship, he overemphasized Cartier and underemphasized Champlain, lionized Frontenac and was extremely hard on Bigot. But these were general patterns in French Canadian historiography until very recently. His stress on military campaigns and

46. Windsor, "Historical Writing in Canada," in Klinck, ed., *Literary History*, pp. 208–15. The first major work by a French Canadian historian, F. X. Garneau's *Histoire du Canada, depuis 1749 découverte jusqu'à nos jours*, began to appear in 1845; see James S. Pritchard, "Some Aspects of the thought of F. X. Garneau," *Canadian Historical Review* 51 (1970) : 276–91.

47. The Jesuit Relations have been edited and translated by Reuben Gold Thwaite, *The Jesuit Relations and Allied Documents*, 73 vols. (Cleveland, 1896–1901); see also de Baqueville de la Potherie, *Histoire de l'Amerique Septentrionale*, 4 vols. (Paris, 1722). The best bibliography of the pool of contemporary published French sources from which Smith might have drawn is John G. Shea, ed., *History and General Description of New France by Pierre F. X. de Charlevoix*, 6 vols. (Chicago, 1866–1872), 1:67–96. Most of Smith's post-1745 French material came from an anonymous journal subsequently identified as by Sieur de Louis-Léonard Aumasson Courville, published by the Literary and Historical Society of Quebec (which Smith helped found) as *Memoires sur le Canada depuis 1749 jusqu'à 1760* (Montreal, 1838). Courville was a civil servant in Quebec and violently anti-Bigot.

general lack of analysis of institutional structures, as well as his tendency to read post-Conquest institutions back into the French period, were all failings of generations of historians of French Canada, both *anglais* and *français*.[48] In his treatment of the Indians, which relied on Charlevoix but eliminated the Jesuit's heavy overtones of "le bon sauvage," he was in tune with modern assessments.

The many merits of Smith's *History*, especially in the first volume, have unfortunately been obscured by his inability to achieve in tone and point of view the impartiality and absence of prejudice which he himself sought. The failure was minor in his occasional overblown celebrations of the glory of the British constitution and the gratitude which all Quebeckers should feel for the Conquest; much of this rhetoric was part of the public sentiment of the time, voiced by English and French Canadians alike.[49] But the collapse of a balanced point of view was much more critical. The early chapters of the *History* were studiedly neutral, although Smith could not resist commenting on the absence of proper commemoration of General James Wolfe while discussing an earlier British conquest of Quebec (page 23), and footnotes occasionally digressed into post-1763 bias (the note on pages 30–31, for example). For the most part, his history of French Canada before 1690 could have been written by anyone familiar with the sources. Occasionally, as in his discussion of the European-Amerindian conflict (pages 48–50), Smith achieved some genuine insight into the larger dynamics of the seventeenth cen-

48. The best discussion of more recent interpretations of French Canada remains John C. Rule's "The Old Regime in America: A Review of Recent Interpretations of France in America," *William and Mary Quarterly*, 3rd Series, 19 (1962):575–600. For a recent defense of Bigot; see Jean Bosher, "Government and Private Interests in New France," *Canadian Public Administration* 10 (1967):244–57.

49. The best coverage of Smith's era in Lower Canada in English is Wade, *The French Canadians*, 1:93–220, and Manning, *The Revolt of French Canada*.

tury. But when warfare between New France and the British colonies erupted, Smith began to be torn from his perspective by his loyalties. He succeeded in maintaining some balance in the narrative up to 1759, but at that point he gave up all pretense to impartiality and told the story entirely through British eyes.

As if conscious of his gradual and eventually total loss of impartiality, Smith came increasingly to drop his own narrative and to tell the story through contemporary documents. By the time he reached Volume II, which dealt with the province under British rule, he did little more than abstract public papers and reproduce documents *in extenso*. To some extent, he may have run out of energy and found it easier simply to become a compiler—a familiar historical tradition in British North America. But given his personality and the background of the writing and publication of the *History*, it seems clear that he was doing more than exhibiting lethargy; he was also protecting himself against charges of undue partiality. After all, how could anyone argue with the records?

He was undoubtedly unaware that his selection of documentation marked him as much as or perhaps more than his own words.[50] The documents were for the most part obviously British, and when they were not (as in the case of the controversy over education) they involved aspects of the history of the province in which his father had played a dominant role. Perhaps the greatest value the study of Smith's *History of Canada* offers to the present is the reminder that not even the submergence of the voice of the historian in enormous gobs of citations and quotations "from the record" can stifle his own upbringing, background, and personality. Indeed, such a strategy may prove as revealing of the historian as any other he might adopt.

50. Most of Smith's documents, printed in his *History* for the first time, have been frequently reprinted by other historians.

The Contributors

JOHN M. BUMSTEAD, was educated at Tufts College and Brown University. He has taught at Tufts and McMaster University, and is presently at Simon Fraser University. A specialist in New England and Canadian history, he has published numerous articles on ecclesiastical politics and institutions. His latest work is *Henry Alline and The Beginnings of Evangelical Pietism in Canada* (Toronto, 1971).

MICHAEL D. CLARK, was educated at Yale University and the University of North Carolina at Chapel Hill. He is a specialist in American intellectual history at Louisiana State University in New Orleans, and has published articles on Jonathan Boucher, Josiah Royce, Brooks Adams, George Bancroft, and John Fiske.

LAWRENCE HENRY GIPSON, dean of colonial American historians, was educated at the University of Idaho, Oxford University where he was a Rhodes Scholar, and Yale University. He has taught at the College of Idaho, Wabash College, and Lehigh University, where he is presently research professor emeritus. His series on *The British Empire Before the American Revolution* (15 vols., 1936–70) has won him the Loubat Prize, the Bancroft Prize, and the Pulitzer Prize.

JOSEPH E. ILLICK, III, was educated at Princeton University and the University of Pennsylvania. He has taught at Kalamazoo College, Lafayette College, and is presently at San Francisco State College. He has published *William Penn the Politician*

(Ithaca, 1965), *America & England, 1558–1776* (New York, 1970).

GERALDINE M. MERONEY, was educated at Rice University, Vanderbilt University, Trinity College, Dublin, and the University of Oregon. She has taught at Willamette University, Earlham College, and Georgia State University and is presently at Agnes Scott College. She is a specialist in the colonial history of South Carolina and Georgia, and is preparing a study of Lieutenant Governor William Bull.

JOHN A. SCHUTZ, a native Californian, received his advanced degrees from the University of California at Los Angeles. He has taught at the California Institute of Technology, Whittier College, and is presently at the University of Southern California. He is the author of biographies of Thomas Pownall and William Shirley, and has edited *Peter Oliver's Origin and Progress of the American Rebellion* and *Spur of Fame: The Dialogues of John Adams and Benjamin Rush.*

ROBERT J. TAYLOR, was educated at the University of Michigan, Pennsylvania State University, and Brown University. He has taught at Iowa State College, Marrietta College, and is now at Tufts University. He has served as a Fulbright Lecturer at Tokyo University and National Taiwan University, and as visiting editor of publications at the Institute of Early American History and Culture. His publications include *Western Massachusetts in the Revolution* (Providence, R. I., 1954), *Massachusetts: Colony to Commonwealth* (Chapel Hill, 1961), and he has edited several volumes of the *Susquehannah Company Papers* (Ithaca, 1968–69).

71 72 73 74   12 11 10 9 8 7 6 5 4 3 2 1

Revised January, 1970

harper ✦ torchbooks

American Studies: General

HENRY ADAMS Degradation of the Democratic Dogma. ‡ *Introduction by Charles Hirschfeld.*　TB/1450

LOUIS D. BRANDEIS: Other People's Money, *and How the Bankers Use It. Ed. with Intro, by Richard M. Abrams*　TB/3081

HENRY STEELE COMMAGER, Ed.: The Struggle for Racial Equality　TB/1300

CARL N. DEGLER: Out of Our Past: *The Forces that Shaped Modern America*　CN/2

CARL N. DEGLER, Ed.: Pivotal Interpretations of American History
Vol. I TB/1240;　Vol. II TB/1241

A. S. EISENSTADT, Ed.: The Craft of American History: *Selected Essays*
Vol. I TB/1255;　Vol. II TB/1256

LAWRENCE H. FUCHS, Ed.: American Ethnic Politics　TB/1368

MARCUS LEE HANSEN: The Atlantic Migration: 1607-1860. *Edited by Arthur M. Schlesinger. Introduction by Oscar Handlin*　TB/1052

MARCUS LEE HANSEN: The Immigrant in American History. *Edited with a Foreword by Arthur M. Schlesinger*　TB/1120

ROBERT L. HEILBRONER: The Limits of American Capitalism　TB/1305·

JOHN HIGHAM, Ed.: The Reconstruction of American History　TB/1068

ROBERT H. JACKSON: The Supreme Court in the American System of Government　TB/1106

JOHN F. KENNEDY: A Nation of Immigrants. *Illus. Revised and Enlarged. Introduction by Robert F. Kennedy*　TB/1118

LEONARD W. LEVY, Ed.: American Constitutional Law: *Historical Essays*　TB/1285

LEONARD W. LEVY, Ed.: Judicial Review and the Supreme Court　TB/1296

LEONARD W. LEVY: The Law of the Commonwealth and Chief Justice Shaw: *The Evolution of American Law, 1830-1860*　TB/1309

GORDON K. LEWIS: Puerto Rico: *Freedom and Power in the Caribbean. Abridged edition*　TB/1371

GUNNAR MYRDAL: An American Dilemma: *The Negro Problem and Modern Democracy. Introduction by the Author.*
Vol. I TB/1443;　Vol. II TB/1444

GILBERT OSOFSKY, Ed.: The Burden of Race: *A Documentary History of Negro-White Relations in America*　TB/1405

ARNOLD ROSE: The Negro in America: *The Condensed Version of Gunnar Myrdal's* An American Dilemma. *Second Edition* TB/3048

JOHN E. SMITH: Themes in American Philosophy: *Purpose, Experience and Community*　TB/1466

WILLIAM R. TAYLOR: Cavalier and Yankee: *The Old South and American National Character*　TB/1474

American Studies: Colonial

BERNARD BAILYN: The New England Merchants in the Seventeenth Century　TB/1149

ROBERT E. BROWN: Middle-Class Democracy and Revolution in Massachusetts, 1691-1780. *New Introduction by Author*　TB/1413

JOSEPH CHARLES: The Origins of the American Party System　TB/1049

WESLEY FRANK CRAVEN: The Colonies in Transition: 1660-1712†　TB/3084

CHARLES GIBSON: Spain in America †　TB/3077

CHARLES GIBSON, Ed.: The Spanish Tradition in America +　HR/1351

LAWRENCE HENRY GIPSON: The Coming of the Revolution: 1763-1775. † *Illus.*　TB/3007

JACK P. GREENE, Ed.: Great Britain and the American Colonies: 1606-1763. + *Introduction by the Author*　HR/1477

AUBREY C. LAND, Ed.: Bases of the Plantation Society +　HR/1429

PERRY MILLER: Errand Into the Wilderness　TB/1139

PERRY MILLER & T. H. JOHNSON, Ed.: The Puritans: *A Sourcebook of Their Writings*
Vol. I TB/1093;　Vol. II TB/1094

EDMUND S. MORGAN: The Puritan Family: *Religion and Domestic Relations in Seventeenth Century New England*　TB/1227

WALLACE NOTESTEIN: The English People on the Eve of Colonization: 1603-1630. † *Illus.*　TB/3006

LOUIS B. WRIGHT: The Cultural Life of the American Colonies: 1607-1763. † *Illus.*　TB/3005

YVES F. ZOLTVANY, Ed.: The French Tradition in America +　HR/1425

American Studies: The Revolution to 1860

JOHN R. ALDEN: The American Revolution: 1775-1783. † *Illus.*　TB/3011

---

† The New American Nation Series, edited by Henry Steele Commager and Richard B. Morris.
‡ American Perspectives series, edited by Bernard Wishy and William E. Leuchtenburg.
a History of Europe series, edited by J. H. Plumb.
§ The Library of Religion and Culture, edited by Benjamin Nelson.
‖ Researches in the Social, Cultural, and Behavioral Sciences, edited by Benjamin Nelson.
Σ Harper Modern Science Series, edited by James A. Newman.
° Not for sale in Canada.
+ Documentary History of the United States series, edited by Richard B. Morris.
# Documentary History of Western Civilization series, edited by Eugene C. Black and Leonard W. Levy.
Λ The Economic History of the United States series, edited by Henry David et al.
¶ European Perspectives series, edited by Eugene C. Black.
** Contemporary Essays series, edited by Leonard W. Levy.
* The Stratum Series, edited by John Hale.

RAY A. BILLINGTON: The Far Western Frontier: 1830-1860. † *Illus.*   TB/3012
STUART BRUCHEY: The Roots of American Economic Growth, 1607-1861: *An Essay in Social Causation. New Introduction by the Author.*
TB/1350
WHITNEY R. CROSS: The Burned-Over District: *The Social and Intellectual History of Enthusiastic Religion in Western New York, 1800-1850*   TB/1242
NOBLE E. CUNNINGHAM, JR., Ed.: The Early Republic, 1789-1828 +   HR/1394
GEORGE DANGERFIELD: The Awakening of American Nationalism, 1815-1828. † *Illus.*   TB/3061
CLEMENT EATON: The Freedom-of-Thought Struggle in the Old South. *Revised and Enlarged. Illus.*   TB/1150
CLEMENT EATON: The Growth of Southern Civilization, 1790-1860. † *Illus.*   TB/3040
ROBERT H. FERRELL, Ed.: Foundations of American Diplomacy, 1775-1872 +   HR/1393
LOUIS FILLER: The Crusade against Slavery: 1830-1860. † *Illus.*   TB/3029
DAVID H. FISCHER: The Revolution of American Conservatism: *The Federalist Party in the Era of Jeffersonian Democracy*   TB/1449
WILLIM W. FREEHLING: Prelude to Civil War: *The Nullification Controversy in South Carolina, 1816-1836*   TB/1359
PAUL W. GATES: The Farmer's Age: *Agriculture, 1815-1860* △   TB/1398
THOMAS JEFFERSON: Notes on the State of Virginia. ‡ *Edited by Thomas P. Abernethy*
TB/3052
FORREST MCDONALD, Ed.: Confederation and Constitution, 1781-1789 +   HR/1396
BERNARD MAYO: Myths and Men: *Patrick Henry, George Washington, Thomas Jefferson*
TB/1108
JOHN C. MILLER: Alexander Hamilton and the Growth of the New Nation   TB/3057
JOHN C. MILLER: The Federalist Era: 1789-1801. † *Illus.*   TB/3027
RICHARD B. MORRIS, Ed.: Alexander Hamilton and the Founding of the Nation. *New Introduction by the Editor*   TB/1448
RICHARD B. MORRIS: The American Revolution Reconsidered   TB/1363
CURTIS P. NETTELS: The Emergence of a National Economy, 1775-1815 △   TB/1438
DOUGLASS C. NORTH & ROBERT PAUL THOMAS, Eds.: *The Growth of the American Economy to 1860* +   HR/1352
R. B. NYE: The Cultural Life of the New Nation: 1776-1830. † *Illus.*   TB/3026
GILBERT OSOFSKY, Ed.: Puttin' On Ole Massa: *The Slave Narratives of Henry Bibb, William Wells Brown, and Solomon Northup* ‡
TB/1432
JAMES PARTON: The Presidency of Andrew Jackson. *From Volume III of the* Life of Andrew Jackson. *Ed. with Intro. by Robert V. Remini*   TB/3080
FRANCIS S. PHILBRICK: The Rise of the West, 1754-1830. † *Illus.*   TB/3067
MARSHALL SMELSER: The Democratic Republic, 1801-1815 +   TB/1406
JACK M. SOSIN, Ed.: The Opening of the West +   HR/1424
GEORGE ROGERS TAYLOR: The Transportation Revolution, 1815-1860 △   TB/1347
A. F. TYLER: Freedom's Ferment: *Phases of American Social History from the Revolution to the Outbreak of the Civil War. Illus.*
TB/1074
GLYNDON G. VAN DEUSEN: The Jacksonian Era: 1828-1848. † *Illus.*   TB/3028

LOUIS B. WRIGHT: Culture on the Moving Frontier   TB/1053

American Studies: The Civil War to 1900

W. R. BROCK: An American Crisis: *Congress and Reconstruction, 1865-67* ° TB/1283
T. C. COCHRAN & WILLIAM MILLER: The Age of Enterprise: *A Social History of Industrial America*   TB/1054
W. A. DUNNING: Reconstruction, Political and Economic: 1865-1877   TB/1073
HAROLD U. FAULKNER: Politics, Reform and Expansion: 1890-1900. † *Illus.* TB/3020
GEORGE M. FREDRICKSON: The Inner Civil War: *Northern Intellectuals and the Crisis of the Union*   TB/1358
JOHN A. GARRATY: The New Commonwealth, 1877-1890 +   TB/1410
JOHN A. GARRATY, Ed.: The Transformation of American Society, 1870-1890 + HR/1395
HELEN HUNT JACKSON: A Century of Dishonor: *The Early Crusade for Indian Reform.* † *Edited by Andrew F. Rolle*   TB/3063
WILLIAM G. MCLOUGHLIN, Ed.: The American Evangelicals, 1800-1900: An Anthology ‡
TB/1382
ARNOLD M. PAUL: Conservative Crisis and the Rule of Law: *Attitudes of Bar and Bench, 1887-1895. New Introduction by Author*
TB/1415
JAMES S. PIKE: The Prostrate State: *South Carolina under Negro Government.* ‡ *Intro. by Robert F. Durden*   TB/3085
WHITELAW REID: After the War: *A Tour of the Southern States, 1865-1866.* ‡ *Edited by C. Vann Woodward*   TB/3066
FRED A. SHANNON: The Farmer's Last Frontier: *Agriculture, 1860-1897*   TB/1348
VERNON LANE WHARTON: The Negro in Mississippi, 1865-1890   TB/1178

American Studies: The Twentieth Century

RICHARD M. ABRAMS, Ed.: The Issues of the Populist and Progressive Eras, 1892-1912 +
HR/1428
RAY STANNARD BAKER: Following the Color Line: *American Negro Citizenship in Progressive Era.* ‡ *Edited by Dewey W. Grantham, Jr. Illus.*   TB/3053
RANDOLPH S. BOURNE: War and the Intellectuals: *Collected Essays, 1915-1919.* ‡ *Edited by Carl Resek*   TB/3043
A. RUSSELL BUCHANAN: The United States and World War II. † *Illus.*
Vol. I TB/3044; Vol. II TB/3045
THOMAS C. COCHRAN: The American Business System: *A Historical Perspective, 1900-1955*
TB/1080
FOSTER RHEA DULLES: America's Rise to World Power: 1898-1954. † *Illus.*   TB/3021
JEAN-BAPTISTE DUROSELLE: From Wilson to Roosevelt: *Foreign Policy of the United States, 1913-1945. Trans. by Nancy Lyman Roelker*   TB/1370
HAROLD U. FAULKNER: The Decline of Laissez Faire, 1897-1917   TB/1397
JOHN D. HICKS: Republican Ascendancy: 1921-1933. † *Illus.*   TB/3041
WILLIAM E. LEUCHTENBURG: Franklin D. Roosevelt and the New Deal: 1932-1940. † *Illus.*
TB/3025
WILLIAM E. LEUCHTENBURG, Ed.: The New Deal: *A Documentary History* +   HR/1354
ARTHUR S. LINK: Woodrow Wilson and the Progressive Era: 1910-1917. † *Illus.* TB/3023

2

BROADUS MITCHELL: Depression Decade: *From New Era through New Deal, 1929-1941* ∧
TB/1439
GEORGE E. MOWRY: The Era of Theodore Roosevelt and the Birth of Modern America: 1900-1912. † *Illus.* TB/3022
WILLIAM PRESTON, JR.: Aliens and Dissenters: *Federal Suppression of Radicals, 1903-1933*
TB/1287
WALTER RAUSCHENBUSCH: Christianity and the Social Crisis. ‡ *Edited by Robert D. Cross*
TB/3059
GEORGE SOULE: Prosperity Decade: *From War to Depression, 1917-1929* ∧ TB/1349
GEORGE B. TINDALL, Ed.: A Populist Reader: *Selections from the Works of American Populist Leaders* TB/3069
TWELVE SOUTHERNERS: I'll Take My Stand: *The South and the Agrarian Tradition. Intro. by Louis D. Rubin, Jr.; Biographical Essays by Virginia Rock* TB/1072

Art, Art History, Aesthetics

CREIGHTON GILBERT, Ed.: Renaissance Art **
Illus. TB/1465
EMILE MALE: The Gothic Image: *Religious Art in France of the Thirteenth Century.* § *190 illus.* TB/344
MILLARD MEISS: Painting in Florence and Siena After the Black Death: *The Arts, Religion and Society in the Mid-Fourteenth Century. 169 illus.* TB/1148
ERWIN PANOFSKY: Renaissance and Renascences in Western Art. *Illus.* TB/1447
ERWIN PANOFSKY: Studies in Iconology: *Humanistic Themes in the Art of the Renaissance. 180 illus.* TB/1077
OTTO VON SIMSON: The Gothic Cathedral: *Origins of Gothic Architecture and the Medieval Concept of Order. 58 illus.* TB/2018
HEINRICH ZIMMER: Myths and Symbols in Indian Art and Civilization. *70 illus.* TB/2005

Asian Studies

WOLFGANG FRANKE: China and the West: *The Cultural Encounter, 13th to 20th Centuries. Trans. by R. A. Wilson* TB/1326
L. CARRINGTON GOODRICH: A Short History of the Chinese People. *Illus.* TB/3015
DAN N. JACOBS, Ed.: The New Communist Manifesto and Related Documents. TB/1078
DAN N. JACOBS & HANS H. BAERWALD, Eds.: Chinese Communism: *Selected Documents*
TB/3031
BENJAMIN I. SCHWARTZ: Chinese Communism and the Rise of Mao TB/1308
BENJAMIN I. SCHWARTZ: In Search of Wealth and Power: *Yen Fu and the West* TB/1422

Economics & Economic History

C. E. BLACK: The Dynamics of Modernization: *A Study in Comparative History* TB/1321
STUART BRUCHEY: The Roots of American Economic Growth, 1607-1861: *An Essay in Social Causation. New Introduction by the Author.*
TB/1350
GILBERT BURCK & EDITORS OF *Fortune:* The Computer Age: *And its Potential for Management* TB/1179
SHEPARD B. CLOUGH, THOMAS MOODIE & CAROL MOODIE, Eds.: Economic History of Europe: *Twentieth Century* # HR/1388
THOMAS C. COCHRAN: The American Business System: *A Historical Perspective, 1900-1955*
TB/1080

ROBERT A. DAHL & CHARLES E. LINDBLOM: Politics, Economics, and Welfare: *Planning and Politico-Economic Systems Resolved into Basic Social Processes* TB/3037
PETER F. DRUCKER: The New Society: *The Anatomy of Industrial Order* TB/1082
HAROLD U. FAULKNER: The Decline of Laissez Faire, 1897-1917 ∧ TB/1397
PAUL W. GATES: The Farmer's Age: *Agriculture, 1815-1860* ∧ TB/1398
WILLIAM GREENLEAF, Ed.: American Economic Development Since 1860 + HR/1353
ROBERT L. HEILBRONER: The Future as History: *The Historic Currents of Our Time and the Direction in Which They Are Taking America*
TB/1386
ROBERT L. HEILBRONER: The Great Ascent: *The Struggle for Economic Development in Our Time* TB/3030
DAVID S. LANDES: Bankers and Pashas: *International Finance and Economic Imperialism in Egypt. New Preface by the Author* TB/1412
ROBERT LATOUCHE: The Birth of Western Economy: *Economic Aspects of the Dark Ages*
TB/1290
W. ARTHUR LEWIS: The Principles of Economic Planning. *New Introduction by the Author*°
TB/1436
WILLIAM MILLER, Ed.: Men in Business: *Essays on the Historical Role of the Entrepreneur*
TB/1081
GUNNAR MYRDAL: An International Economy. *New Introduction by the Author* TB/1445
HERBERT A. SIMON: The Shape of Automation: *For Men and Management* TB/1245
RICHARD S. WECKSTEIN, Ed.: Expansion of World Trade and the Growth of National Economies ** TB/1373

Historiography and History of Ideas

J. BRONOWSKI & BRUCE MAZLISH: The Western Intellectual Tradition: *From Leonardo to Hegel* TB/3001
WILHELM DILTHEY: Pattern and Meaning in History: *Thoughts on History and Society.*° *Edited with an Intro. by H. P. Rickman*
TB/1075
J. H. HEXTER: More's Utopia: *The Biography of an Idea. Epilogue by the Author* TB/1195
H. STUART HUGHES: History as Art and as Science: *Twin Vistas on the Past* TB/1207
ARTHUR O. LOVEJOY: The Great Chain of Being: *A Study of the History of an Idea* TB/1009
RICHARD H. POPKIN: The History of Scepticism from Erasmus to Descartes. *Revised Edition*
TB/1391
MASSIMO SALVADORI, Ed.: Modern Socialism #
HR/1374
BRUNO SNELL: The Discovery of the Mind: *The Greek Origins of European Thought* TB/1018
W. WARREN WAGER, ed.: European Intellectual History Since Darwin and Marx TB/1297

History: General

HANS KOHN: The Age of Nationalism: *The First Era of Global History* TB/1380
BERNARD LEWIS: The Arabs in History TB/1029
BERNARD LEWIS: The Middle East and the West ° TB/1274

History: Ancient

A. ANDREWS: The Greek Tyrants TB/1103

4

R. H. TAWNEY: The Agrarian Problem in the Sixteenth Century. *Intro. by Lawrence Stone*
TB/1315

H. R. TREVOR-ROPER: The European Witch-craze of the Sixteenth and Seventeenth Centuries and Other Essays ° TB/1416

VESPASIANO: Rennaissance Princes, Popes, and *XVth Century: The Vespasiano Memoirs. Introduction by Myron P. Gilmore. Illus.*
TB/1111

History: Modern European

RENE ALBRECHT-CARRIE, Ed.: The Concert of Europe # HR/1341

MAX BELOFF: The Age of Absolutism, 1660-1815
TB/1062

OTTO VON BISMARCK: *Reflections and Reminiscences. Ed. with Intro. by Theodore S. Hamerow* ¶ TB/1357

EUGENE C. BLACK, Ed.: British Politics in the Nineteenth Century # HR/1427

D. W. BROGAN: The Development of Modern France ° Vol. I: *From the Fall of the Empire to the Dreyfus Affair* TB/1184
Vol. II: *The Shadow of War, World War I, Between the Two Wars* TB/1185

ALAN BULLOCK: Hitler, A Study in Tyranny. ° *Revised Edition. Iuus.* TB/1123

GORDON A. CRAIG: From Bismarck to Adenauer: *Aspects of German Statecraft. Revised Edition* TB/1171

LESTER G. CROCKER, Ed.: The Age of Enlightenment # HR/1423

JACQUES DROZ: Europe between Revolutions, 1815-1848. ° *a Trans. by Robert Baldick*
TB/1346

JOHANN GOTTLIEB FICHTE: Addresses to the German Nation. *Ed. with Intro. by George A. Kelly* ¶ TB/1366

ROBERT & ELBORG FORSTER, Eds.: European Society in the Eighteenth Century # HR/1404

C. C. GILLISPIE: Genesis and Geology: *The Decades before Darwin* § TB/51

ALBERT GOODWIN: The French Revolution
TB/1064

JOHN B. HALSTED, Ed.: Romanticism # HR/1387

STANLEY HOFFMANN et al.: In Search of France: *The Economy, Society and Political System In the Twentieth Century* TB/1219

H. STUART HUGHES: The Obstructed Path: *French Social Thought in the Years of Desperation* TB/1451

JOHAN HUIZINGA: Dutch Civilisation in the 17th Century and Other Essays TB/1453

WALTER LAQUEUR & GEORGE L. MOSSE, Eds.: Education and Social Structure in the 20th Century. ° *Volume 6 of the* Journal of Contemporary History TB/1339

WALTER LAQUEUR & GEORGE L. MOSSE, Ed.: International Fascism, 1920-1945. ° *Volume 1 of the* Journal of Contemporary History
TB/1276

WALTER LAQUEUR & GEORGE L. MOSSE, Eds.: Literature and Politics in the 20th Century. ° *Volume 5 of the* Journal of Contemporary History. TB/1328

WALTER LAQUEUR & GEORGE L. MOSSE, Eds.: The New History: *Trends in Historical Research and Writing Since World War II.* ° *Volume 4 of the* Journal of Contemporary History
TB/1327

WALTER LAQUEUR & GEORGE L. MOSSE, Eds.: 1914: *The Coming of the First World War.* ° *Volume3 of the* Journal of Contemporary History TB/1306

JOHN MCMANNERS: European History, 1789-1914: *Men, Machines and Freedom* TB/1419

PAUL MANTOUX: The Industrial Revolution in the Eighteenth Century: *An Outline of the Beginnings of the Modern Factory System in England* TB/1079

KINGSLEY MARTIN: French Liberal Thought in the Eighteenth Century: *A Study of Political Ideas from Bayle to Condorcet* TB/1114

NAPOLEON III: Napoleonic Ideas: *Des Idées Napoléoniennes, par le Prince Napoléon-Louis Bonaparte. Ed. by Brison D. Gooch* ¶
TB/1336

FRANZ NEUMANN: Behemoth: *The Structure and Practice of National Socialism, 1933-1944*
TB/1289

DAVID OGG: Europe of the Ancien Régime, 1715-1783 ° *a* TB/1271

GEORGE RUDE: Revolutionary Europe, 1783-1815 ° *a* TB/1272

MASSIMO SALVADORI, Ed.: Modern Socialism #
TB/1374

DENIS MACK SMITH, Ed.: The Making of Italy, 1796-1870 # HR/1356

ALBERT SOREL: Europe Under the Old Regime, *Translated by Francis H. Herrick* TB/1121

ROLAND N. STROMBERG, Ed.: Realsim, Naturalism, and Symbolism: *Modes of Thought and Expression in Europe, 1848-1914* # HR/1355

A. J. P. TAYLOR: From Napoleon to Lenin: *Historical Essays* ° TB/1268

A. J. P. TAYLOR: The Habsburg Monarchy, 1809-1918: *A History of the Austrian Empire and Austria-Hungary* ° TB/1187

J. M. THOMPSON: European History, 1494-1789
TB/1431

DAVID THOMSON, Ed.: France: Empire and Republic, 1850-1940 # HR/1387

H. R. TREVOR-ROPER: Historical Essays TB/1269

W. WARREN WAGAR, Ed.: Science, Faith, and MAN: *European Thought Since 1914* #
HR/1362

MACK WALKER, Ed.: Metternich's Europe, 1813-1848 # HR/1361

ELIZABETH WISKEMANN: Europe of the Dictators, 1919-1945 ° *a* TB/1273

JOHN B. WOLF: France: 1814-1919: *The Rise of a Liberal-Democratic Society* TB/3019

Literature & Literary Criticism

JACQUES BARZUN: The House of Intellect
TB/1051

W. J. BATE: From Classic to Romantic: *Premises of Taste in Eighteenth Century England*
TB/1036

VAN WYCK BROOKS: Van Wyck Brooks: *The Early Years: A Selection from his Works, 1908-1921 Ed. with Intro. by Claire Sprague*
TB/3082

RICHMOND LATTIMORE, Translator: The Odyssey of Homer TB/1389

ROBERT PREYER, Ed.: Victorian Literature **
TB/1302

BASIL WILEY: Nineteenth Century Studies: *Coleridge to Matthew Arnold* ° TB/1261

RAYMOND WILLIAMS: Culture and Society, 1780-1950 ° TB/1252

Philosophy

HENRI BERGSON: Time and Free Will: *An Essay on the Immediate Data of Consciousness* °
TB/1021

LUDWIG BINSWANGER: Being-in-the-World: *Selected Papers. Trans. with Intro. by Jacob Needleman* TB/1365

H. J. BLACKHAM: Six Existentialist Thinkers: *Kierkegaard, Nietzsche, Jaspers, Marcel, Heidegger, Sartre* ° TB/1002

MARTIN BUBER: Eclipse of God: *Studies in the Relation Between Religion and Philosophy* TB/12

MARTIN BUBER: Hasidism and Modern Man. *Edited and Translated by Maurice Friedman* TB/839

MARTIN BUBER: The Knowledge of Man. *Edited with an Introduction by Maurice Friedman. Translated by Maurice Friedman and Ronald Gregor Smith* TB/135

MARTIN BUBER: Moses. *The Revelation and the Covenant* TB/837

MARTIN BUBER: The Origin and Meaning of Hasidism. *Edited· and Translated by Maurice Friedman* TB/835

MARTIN BUBER: The Prophetic Faith TB/73

MARTIN BUBER: Two Types of Faith: *Interpenetration of Judaism and Christianity* ° TB/75

MALCOLM L. DIAMOND: Martin Buber: *Jewish Existentialist* TB/840

M. S. ENSLIN: Christian Beginnings TB/5

M. S. ENSLIN: The Literature of the Christian Movement TB/6

HENRI FRANKFORT: Ancient Egyptian Religion: *An Interpretation* TB/77

MAURICE S. FRIEDMAN: Martin Buber: *The Life of Dialogue* TB/64

ABRAHAM HESCHEL: The Earth Is the Lord's & The Sabbath. *Two Essays* TB/828

ABRAHAM HESCHEL: God in Search of Man: *A Philosophy of Judaism* TB/807

ABRAHAM HESCHEL: Man Is not Alone: *A Philosophy of Religion* TB/838

ABRAHAM HESCHEL: The Prophets: *An Introduction* TB/1421

T. J. MEEK: Hebrew Origins TB/69

JAMES MUILENBURG: The Way of Israel: *Biblical Faith and Ethics* TB/133

H. H. ROWLEY: The Growth of the Old Testament TB/107

D. WINTON THOMAS, Ed.: Documents from Old Testament Times TB/85

Religion: Early Christianity Through Reformation

ANSELM OF CANTERBURY: Truth, Freedom, and Evil: *Three Philosophical Dialogues. Edited and Translated by Jasper Hopkins and Herbert Richardson* TB/317

MARSHALL W. BALDWIN, Ed.: Christianity through the 13th Century # HR/1468

ADOLF DEISSMAN: Paul: *A Study in Social and Religious History* TB/15

EDGAR J. GOODSPEED: A Life of Jesus TB/1

ROBERT M. GRANT: Gnosticism and Early Christianity TB/136

WILLIAM HALLER: The Rise of Puritanism TB/22

ARTHUR DARBY NOCK: St. Paul ° TR/104

GORDON RUPP: Luther's Progress to the Diet of Worms ° TB/120

Religion: The Protestant Tradition

KARL BARTH: Church Dogmatics: *A Selection. Intro. by H. Gollwitzer. Ed. by G. W. Bromiley* TB/95

KARL BARTH: Dogmatics in Outline TB/56

KARL BARTH: The Word of God and the Word of Man TB/13

WHITNEY R. CROSS: The Burned-Over District: *The Social and Intellectual History of Enthusiastic Religion in Western New York, 1800-1850* TB/1242

WILLIAM R. HUTCHISON, Ed.: American Protestant Thought: *The Liberal Era* ‡ TB/1385

SOREN KIERKEGAARD: The Journals of Kierkegaard. ° *Edited with an Intro. by Alexander Dru* TB/52

SOREN KIERKEGAARD: The Point of View for My Work as an Author: *A Report to History.* § *Preface by Benjamin Nelson* TB/88

SOREN KIERKEGAARD: The Present Age. § *Translated and edited by Alexander Dru. Introduction by Walter Kaufmann* TB/94

SOREN KIERKEGAARD: Purity of Heart. *Trans. by Douglas Steere* TB/4

SOREN KIERKEGAARD: Repetition: *An Essay in Experimental Psychology* § TB/117

SOREN KIERKEGAARD: Works of Love: *Some Christian Reflections in the Form of Discourses* TB/122

WOLFHART PANNENBERG, et al.: History and Hermeneutic. *Volume 4 of* Journal for Theology and the Church, *edited by Robert W. Funk and Gerhard Ebeling* TB/254

F. SCHLEIERMACHER: The Christian Faith. *Introduction by Richard R. Niebuhr.*
Vol. I TB/108;   Vol. II TB/109

F. SCHLEIERMACHER: On Religion: *Speeches to Its Cultured Despisers. Intro. by Rudolf Otto* TB/36

PAUL TILLICH: Dynamics of Faith TB/42

PAUL TILLICH: Morality and Beyond TB/142

Religion: The Roman & Eastern Christian Traditions

A. ROBERT CAPONIGRI, Ed.: Modern Catholic Thinkers II: *The Church and the Political Order* TB/307

G. P. FEDOTOV: The Russian Religious Mind: *Kievan Christianity, the tenth to the thirteenth Centuries* TB/370

GABRIEL MARCEL: Being and Having: *An Existential Diary. Introduction by James Collins* TB/310

GABRIEL MARCEL: Homo Viator: *Introduction to a Metaphysic of Hope* TB/397

Religion: Oriental Religions

TOR ANDRAE: Mohammed: *The Man and His Faith* § TB/62

EDWARD CONZE: Buddhism: *Its Essence and Development.* ° *Foreword by Arthur Waley* TB/58

EDWARD CONZE: Buddhist Meditation TB/1442

EDWARD CONZE et al, Editors: Buddhist Texts through the Ages TB/113

ANANDA COOMARASWAMY: Buddha and the Gospel of Buddhism TB/119

H. G. CREEL: Confucius and the Chinese Way TB/63

FRANKLIN EDGERTON, Trans. & Ed.: The Bhagavad Gita TB/115

SWAMI NIKHILANANDA, Trans. & Ed.: The Upanishads TB/114

Religion: Philosophy, Culture, and Society

NICOLAS BERDYAEV: The Destiny of Man TB/61

RUDOLF BULTMANN: History and Eschatology: *The Presence of Eternity* ° TB/91

RUDOLF BULTMANN AND FIVE CRITICS: Kerygma and Myth: *A Theological Debate* TB/80

RUDOLF BULTMANN and KARL KUNDSIN: Form search. *Trans. by F. C. Grant* TB/96

LUDWIG FEUERBACH: The Essence of Christianity. § *Introduction by Karl Barth. Foreword by H. Richard Niebuhr* TB/11

KYLE HASELDEN: The Racial Problem in Christian Perspective TB/116